LA CUCINA ITALIANA

LA CUCINA ITALIANA

THE ENCYCLOPEDIA OF
Italian Cooking

By the Editors of La Cucina Italiana

RIZZOLI
NEW YORK

Introduction

Italy achieves a uniquely high degree of gastronomic excellence because of the variety and vitality of its regional and local culinary traditions, the impact of various external cultural influences over the years, and the richness and quality of the food grown there. All of these things combine to form a truly one-of-a-kind culinary heritage. Italian cooking, with its wide array of ingredients, its incredible smells, tastes, and creative hallmarks, is appreciated and loved around the world, yet remains strongly rooted in its native land.

La Cucina Italiana magazine was founded in 1929 and has been published regularly ever since. The magazine highlights and shares Italian culinary arts with easy-to-follow instructions and a professional tone, never talking down to readers. The recipes published in the magazine are dreamed up and created by chefs and then tested by a staff that adjusts look and taste, cooking techniques, and final results for home cooks. That magazine and this book share the same philosophy: respecting a culinary tradition that has strong and deep roots, but also takes a somewhat adventuresome approach and isn't afraid to mix old and new.

This encyclopedia is a sort of cooking school on paper, intended for those who are new to cooking and need to get food on the table every day, those who want to try something more challenging for a special lunch or dinner, and even experts who want to perfect their cooking skills. Committed home cooks who want to learn new techniques, the secrets that chefs use in their own kitchens, and the tricks to making dishes come out well every time will also find much that is useful in these pages.

The chapters in this book are broken down by ingredients and richly illustrated throughout. You will find step-by-step photos of preparation techniques, key information on ingredient types, as well as information on how to shop for and store food, cooking methods, and the best way to prepare and present a wide variety of food items. There are hundreds of recipes for traditional Italian dishes here, as well as some that highlight a specific ingredient in a more updated fashion. These recipes, destined to become new classics in their own right, reflect the way many Italians cook in their homes today, with respect for tradition, but a curiosity about new flavors and combinations as well.

This book also contains useful information about the best utensils and tools to use to handle these ingredients; detailed information about ingredient varieties, as well as historical background and nutritional information; and entire sections dedicated to the tricks of the trade and secrets for perfecting a dish and achieving perfect results that are pleasing to both the eye and the palate every time.

In short, this is a book that makes cooking wonderful Italian food accessible to everyone, so that all can enjoy the flavors, and sometimes the contradictions, that make it so beloved. Here you will find dishes that are both simple and refined, subdued and yet bursting with flavor. And you will be able to cook each and every one of them successfully. With this book in hand, you can ensure that every dish, from antipasto to dessert, serves as an opportunity to exercise your creativity and, most importantly, to eat well.

Guide to using the book

This illustrated encyclopedia consists of 21 chapters dedicated to various types of ingredients and dishes. You can work your way through it and try recipes that catch your eye, consult the index for dishes using an ingredient that you have on hand, or skip around and read only a certain type of section. No matter how you like to learn and to cook, you will find it a rich resource. The chapters are broken down as follows:

Each chapter begins with an introduction about the ingredient or type of dish to be covered and provides some general history and background.

THE INGREDIENT GUIDE sections—marked in gray—cover varieties of vegetables, types of grains, cuts of meat, and so forth. These provide in-depth discussion of taste, smell, and texture and also offer advice on purchasing and storing ingredients and recommend the best preparations for them.

The sections marked in yellow present **ESSENTIAL METHODS** and each one provides instructions for a basic technique using the ingredient that is the chapter's focus. Because these are meant to impart instructions for techniques that are used throughout—and that more experienced cooks will utilize as a jumping-off point for their own creative experimentation—these instructions are in the form of text, often with step-by-step numbered photographs.

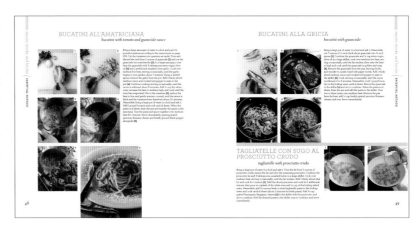

The beige-marked **FEATURE RECIPE** sections are in traditional recipe format. These are either classic Italian recipes or modern takes on the dishes, but they all focus on the ingredients being covered. Many of the Feature Recipes are also accompanied by photographs showing recipe steps. These recipes always highlight the subject of the chapter in which they appear.

The dark blue–gray **FROM THE EXPERTS** sections include step-by-step photographs and provide tips and tricks for achieving good results. These reflect the wisdom accumulated by professional chefs and practiced home cooks over the years.

Boxes titled **THE RIGHT TOOL** provide advice about equipment that will make your cooking experience both more convenient and more pleasurable. Italian cooking doesn't require a lot of fancy gadgets, but a good set of pots and a few specialty items may make your job easier. See Sources on page 454 if you would like to purchase any of these items.

Additional boxes provide shortcuts and other useful information. These may also list some simple ways to use a specific ingredient or a variation for a recipe on the same page.

$\mathscr{B}$READ IS EATEN ALMOST EVERYWHERE IN THE WORLD AND HAS been at least since the days of ancient Egypt. Italy shares this history of bread, but identifying one single "Italian" bread would be impossible—no two regions in Italy serve the same kind, and sometimes cities only a few kilometers apart serve wildly different types, each with its own specific preparation, shape, and cooking method. As a result, there are a good 250 different kinds of "basic" yeast-risen bread in Italy, from the dark, seeded rye bread of Alto Adige to Sardinia's thin disks of crackerlike pane carasau. Since it would be impossible to be comprehensive here, rather than a compendium of all of Italy's regional specialties, you'll find a couple of recipes for rolls that aren't too time-consuming or complicated— the kinds of breads baked at home in Italy today. If trying these recipes sparks your interest in exploring Italian bread further, there are many excellent books dedicated to the subject, such as Carol Field's *The Italian Baker,* as well as others dedicated to baking the best bread possible in a home kitchen, such as Maggie Glezer's *Artisan Baking*.

Of course, with all that bread around and with the waste not, want not attitude of Italian cooks, there are numerous Italian dishes that incorporate leftover bread—we've included some of those, too.

And then there are flatbreads. Until not too long ago, Italians did not commonly have ovens in their homes. They brought their bread to a communal oven once a week to bake it, and at home they made flatbreads on their stovetops. As a result, the country has a rich repertoire of flatbreads, most of which are ideal to serve with cheeses and cold cuts.

Italy's most famous flatbread—pizza—is baked in an oven, preferably a wood-burning oven, and is a favorite around the world. Pizza has traveled far from its roots in the Campania region of Italy. In its original form, it is a paean to its ancestral home, exalting local products: fresh fior di latte mozzarella melted temptingly over San Marzano tomatoes on a classic pizza Margherita. Over time, of course, pizza has evolved. Not only is it available in far-flung locations these days, but even the purist pizzerias of Naples and the surrounding area (certified by the very serious Associazione Verace Pizza Napoletana) may offer toppings such as *ortolana* (vegetables), *capricciosa* (the word literally means "fanciful"—or "capricious"—and usually includes a combination of prosciutto cotto, artichokes, mushrooms, and olives), and *quattro stagioni* ("four seasons," with each of the four quadrants hosting a single topping).

BREADS & FLATBREADS

Natural, tasty, simple bread has sustained man for ages. It also has deep symbolism in many cultures, playing pivotal roles in both classical mythology and in the story of Christianity itself.

Bread, pizza, and focaccia are amazing foods, no doubt about it. With just a few humble ingredients—yeast, flour, salt, and water—you create a dough that is so much more than the sum of its parts. It's true that you can use a stand mixer fitted with the dough hook or a food processor fitted with the dough blade to knead dough, but you really should give kneading by hand a try—it's relaxing, it's not difficult, and as you gain more practice, you'll find that you get a feel for a proper dough and know when it needs a little more water or a touch more flour. That just can't be achieved when a machine is doing the work.

Kneading Dough by Hand

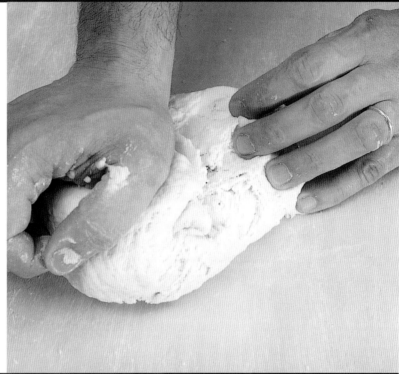

To create a dough, start by placing your dry ingredients—flour and salt—in a bowl. Dissolve the yeast in a small amount of warm water. You don't want the water to be hot—that would kill the yeast. It should be just bathwater warm, 100 to 110 degrees F, so that if you stick a finger into it, you don't want to yank it out. Instructions here and elsewhere will tell you to set aside the yeast and water mixture until it gets foamy. (If the yeast does not become foamy, it is no longer active. Discard it and start over with new yeast. Storing your yeast in the refrigerator or freezer will help to ensure that it remains active.) When the liquid is foamy, pour it—probably along with some additional water—into the dry ingredients and stir them together in the bowl. This should create a shaggy dough.

Transfer the dough to a lightly floured work surface. Take care not to be heavy-handed when flouring the work surface; using too much flour will result in a heavy, dry dough and finished product. At this point, the dough is probably still fairly wet and the ingredients aren't well incorporated. You can start kneading by just pulling it up into the air and then pushing it back down. Again, resist the urge to add too much flour. If you find the dough unmanageable, use a bench scraper to manipulate it. Keep working at it, and you'll find that the ingredients start to meld. When the dough forms a ball, knead it by pushing it away from you with the heel of your hand, then folding it in half back toward you. Give the dough a quarter turn and repeat. A properly kneaded dough, which you will achieve in 5 to 10 minutes with most recipes, will feel smooth and elastic, even springy. If you cut into it, you won't see any swirls of flour; the ingredients will be completely combined and integrated.

Panini con erbe aromatiche
herb bread rolls

POOLISH

1 cup unbleached all-purpose flour

½ teaspoon active dry yeast

DOUGH

3½ cups unbleached all-purpose flour

2 tablespoons extra-virgin olive oil

1 teaspoon fine sea salt

1 teaspoon finely chopped mixed herbs, such as oregano, rosemary, and thyme

1. To make the poolish, in a bowl, stir together the flour, yeast, and ½ cup tepid water (100 to 110 degrees F). Let stand at room temperature at least 10 hours.

2. For the dough, in a large bowl, combine the poolish, flour, oil, and salt with an additional ¾ cup plus 1½ tablespoons warm water; mix to form a shaggy dough. Turn the dough out onto a clean surface and knead until smooth and elastic, about 5 minutes.

3. Stretch and pat the dough into a 10-inch square and sprinkle it with the herbs. Knead for 1 minute to incorporate the herbs. Form the dough into a ball, transfer it to a large bowl, and cover it with a clean, damp dish towel. Set the dough in a draft-free place to rise until doubled in bulk, about 1 hour.

4. Spread a clean, dry dish towel on a work surface. Dust the work surface and dish towel with flour. Divide the dough into 12 equal pieces and roll each into a ball. Arrange the balls of dough, not touching, on the work surface and cover them with a clean, damp dish towel. Let rest 10 minutes. Leaving the other dough balls under the dish towel, place one ball on the work surface and stretch it into a 2-by-8-inch rectangle. With a short side of the rectangle facing you, fold the bottom edge to the center, then fold the top edge to the center. Press firmly with your fingertips to seal the seams, then fold in half, folding bottom edge over top. Pinch together all the seams, then gently roll the dough to create a 5-inch-long loaf.

5. With the edge of your hand, press firmly in the center of the loaf to create a deep indentation. Transfer the loaf to the floured dish towel. Repeat with the remaining pieces of dough. Sprinkle flour over the indentations, then cover the loaves with a clean, dry dish towel. Let them rise in a draft-free place for 25 minutes.

6. Heat the oven to 450 degrees F with a rack in the middle. Line two baking sheets with parchment paper. Arrange the loaves on the baking sheets. Bake one batch at a time until deep golden, about 20 minutes. Let the rolls cool on a wire rack for at least 10 minutes before serving.

MAKES 12 ROLLS COOKING TIME: 40 MINUTES PLUS PRE-FERMENT AND RISING

USING LEFTOVER BREAD

panzanella, bruschetta, and passatelli

One great way to use up leftover bread is to make an appetizer (or a hearty snack) of bruschetta. The simplest form of bruschetta is grilled or toasted bread rubbed with a peeled clove of garlic, drizzled with high-quality olive oil, and seasoned with salt and pepper. If you find yourself with leftover slices of bread, try one or all of the following:

PANZANELLA

Bread baked in a wood-burning oven is best for this salad. If your bread is rock-hard, rehydrate it first by sprinkling it with water until you can crumble it with your hands. Chop tomatoes, then toss them with a little salt and pepper, extra-virgin olive oil, torn basil leaves, and thinly sliced red onion. Combine the bread pieces and the tomatoes with their juices and toss. Let sit at room temperature for 30 minutes to 1 hour so that the bread soaks up the tomato juices. Drizzle on a little more oil if the mixture seems dry, and serve.

BRUSCHETTA AL POMODORO (TOMATO BRUSCHETTA)

Chop tomatoes that are as ripe as possible. Drizzle them with olive oil, season with salt, toss, and set aside. When the mixture is very juicy, toast or grill the bread slices, rub them with a peeled garlic clove, and spoon the tomato mixture and juices over the top. Tear a few small basil leaves and scatter them over the tomato.

BRUSCHETTA ALLA MELANZANA (EGGPLANT BRUSCHETTA)

Cook or grill a whole eggplant. Slice the eggplant in half and scrape out the flesh; discard the skin. In a food processor fitted with the metal blade, process the eggplant flesh with a few tablespoons extra-virgin olive oil. Season to taste with salt and pepper. Grill or toast bread and top it with eggplant puree, diced tomato, thin slices of ricotta salata cheese, and a few basil leaves.

BRUSCHETTA ALLA CIPOLLA (ONION BRUSCHETTA)

Cook thinly sliced shallots in a few tablespoons extra-virgin olive oil over medium heat, stirring frequently, until golden and crisp, 8 to 10 minutes. Grill or toast the bread. Top each slice with some thinly sliced salami of your choice, drizzle with a little honey, and sprinkle on the fried shallots.

**BRUSCHETTA ALLE SARDINE
(SARDINE BRUSCHETTA)**

Combine lime juice with some extra-virgin olive oil. Place butterflied fresh sardines in a single layer in a small non-reactive dish. Pour the lime juice–olive oil mixture over the fish (enough just to cover). Cover and marinate, in the refrigerator, for 1 hour. Remove the fish from the marinade and season with salt. Top slices of grilled or toasted bread with the fish and some quartered cherry tomatoes; grate on a little lime zest, if desired, and serve.

**BRUSCHETTA AL RADICCHIO
(RADICCHIO BRUSCHETTA)**

Cut radicchio into ribbons and sauté them in extra-virgin olive oil until soft, about 5 minutes. Season with salt and pepper. Top slices of toasted bread (whole wheat is especially good) with some of the radicchio and small pieces of soft cheese, such as goat cheese.

PASSATELLI

In Italy, passatelli pasta is made using a dedicated tool, but a potato ricer with large holes works well. Use a food processor fitted with the metal blade to process leftover bread into bread crumbs. Combine the crumbs with grated Parmigiano Reggiano cheese (using about twice as much cheese as bread crumbs), egg, freshly grated nutmeg, a pinch of salt, and a little grated lemon zest. The mixture should hold together if you squeeze it in your fist. Add a bit of water if it's dry. Bring a pot of broth (see page 56) to a boil. Place the dough in a potato ricer with ¼-inch holes and press it through the ricer into the pot. It should form noodles. Use a paring knife to cut the noodles every 2 inches or so. Cook until the passatelli float to the surface, about 2 minutes. Serve with broth.

Tortino rustico

savory tart

About 6 tablespoons extra-virgin olive oil

About ½ loaf bread

1 medium zucchini

1 red bell pepper

4 ounces green beans, trimmed and blanched

10 large eggs

Fine sea salt to taste

Freshly ground black pepper to taste

2 tablespoons minced parsley

¼ cup ricotta cheese

¼ cup plus 2 tablespoons grated aged cheese, such as Parmigiano Reggiano

1. Preheat the oven to 400 degrees F. Oil a 10-inch springform pan with 1 tablespoon of the olive oil. Line it with parchment paper and set aside. Cut the bread into slices about ½ inch thick. Generously brush the bread slices on both sides, using about 3 tablespoons of the olive oil, then use them to line the bottom and sides of the pan, trimming them as needed to fit without overlapping. Bake this crust for 10 minutes.

2. Meanwhile, julienne the zucchini. Stem and seed the pepper and cut it into julienne. Cut the green beans in half. Briefly sauté the zucchini and pepper in the remaining 2 tablespoons oil until just softened. Add the green beans and sauté for 1 additional minute, then remove the pan from the heat.

3. In a large bowl, beat the eggs with salt, pepper, and parsley. Stir in the ricotta and ¼ cup of the grated cheese.

4. Remove the bread from the oven and turn the heat down to 350 degrees F. Pour the egg mixture over the bread crust and set the pan aside for 20 minutes or so to allow the mixture to soak into the bread. Sprinkle the vegetables on top and sprinkle on the remaining 2 tablespoons grated cheese.

5. Return the pan to the oven and bake until the filling is set, about 20 minutes. Remove the ring and allow the tart to cool to room temperature before cutting it into wedges and serving it with a small salad.

SERVES 6   COOKING TIME: 45 MINUTES

PIADINA ROMAGNOLA

piadina flatbread from romagna

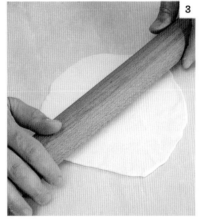

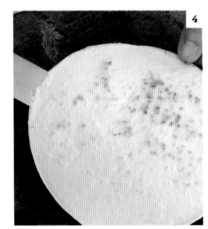

To make piadina, sift 3 cups unbleached all-purpose flour, 1 teaspoon salt, and 1 teaspoon baking powder into a bowl, then add ½ cup melted lard [1]. Add enough hot (not boiling) water to make a firm dough [2]. Transfer the dough to the work surface and knead until smooth, 10 minutes.

Cut the dough into 10 pieces, roll the pieces into balls, cover them with a clean dish towel, and let rest for 30 minutes. On a lightly floured work surface, roll each dough ball into a very thin disk about 1/10 inch thick [3].

Heat a soapstone or other griddle or a cast-iron skillet on the stove. Put in a disk of dough and cook it for 10 seconds without moving it. Turn it and cook the other side for 10 seconds. Using a fork, poke the flatbread, rotating it frequently in the same direction and turning it over once more, until it is golden and speckled with brown spots, about 3 minutes total [4]. Serve the flatbread with all types of sliced meats, aged cheeses, and flavorful soft cheeses, such as squacquerone [5].

PANINI RIPIENI ARROTOLATI
fresh tomato rolls

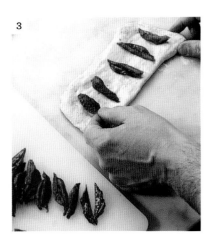

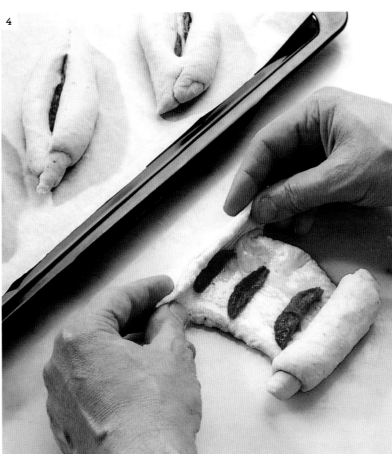

Preheat the oven to 250 degrees F. Bring a large saucepan of water to a boil and peel 8 tomatoes, following the instructions on page 205. Quarter the tomatoes lengthwise, and seed them **[1]**. Set the tomato pieces on a pan lined with parchment paper and sprinkle them with ½ teaspoon fine sea salt. Roast them in the preheated oven until they are somewhat but not completely dried, about 2 hours.

Meanwhile, prepare the dough. In a large bowl, stir together ⅓ cup warm water (100 to 110 degrees F.), 2¼ teaspoons (1 envelope) active dry yeast, and a pinch of sugar. Let stand until foamy.

To the yeast mixture, add 4 cups unbleached all-purpose flour, ⅔ cup warm water, ⅓ cup extra-virgin olive oil, and 1 tablespoon fine sea salt **[2]**. Mix to form a shaggy dough, then turn it out onto a lightly floured work surface and knead until it is smooth and elastic, about 10 minutes. Lightly oil a large bowl (a bowl much larger than the dough) and place the dough in it. Turn to coat the dough with oil, cover it tightly with plastic wrap, and let rise until doubled in bulk, about 2 hours.

Line a baking sheet with parchment paper. Turn the dough out onto a lightly floured surface. Cut it into 6 equal pieces, then roll each piece into a rectangle about 8½ by 3½ inches. Brush each piece with oil, then arrange the tomatoes on top **[3]**. Roll the short ends of each rectangle toward the center, stopping just before they touch. Pinch the open ends of the rolls together to seal in the tomatoes **[4]**. Arrange the rolls on the prepared baking sheet and let them rise in a draft-free place at warm room temperature for 45 minutes.

Preheat the oven to 375 degrees F, then bake, turning the pan once halfway through, until the rolls are golden brown, about 25 minutes.

REGIONAL FLATBREADS

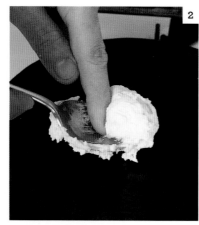

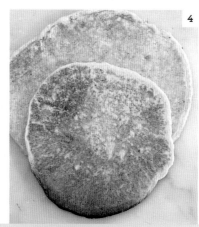

CIACCI

In a bowl, combine 1¼ cups all-purpose flour, about ½ cup sheep's milk ricotta, ½ cup milk, 1¾ teaspoons baking powder, and a pinch of salt [1]. Heat a flat-surface waffle iron. Brush both surfaces lightly with lard or extra-virgin olive oil and drop 1 table-spoon of the mixture onto the iron. The mixture will be fairly thick [2]. Close the waffle iron and cook on one side for 1½ minutes, then flip the flat-bread and cook on the other side for an additional 1½ minutes [3]. Remove the flatbread and keep it warm while you cook the remaining batter [4]. Ciacci are a specialty from the Emilia region, where they are served with cured meats. If you don't have a waffle iron, thin the batter slightly with additional milk and cook like pancakes on a griddle or in a cast-iron skillet.

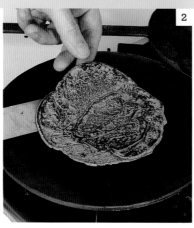

NECCI

Combine 4 cups chestnut flour with a pinch of salt and enough water to make a smooth batter the consistency of sour cream or a little thinner [1]. Heat a cast-iron griddle on the stove. Grease it with a piece of pork rind or a small amount of extra-virgin olive oil, and pour spoon-fuls of the batter onto the hot surface. Cook the necci (they will spread out to a little less than ¼ inch thick) until they set on the bottom and are golden, then flip them and cook until the other sides are golden [2]. Serve this Tuscan spe-cialty warm with ricotta and sausages or small cubes of pancetta [3].

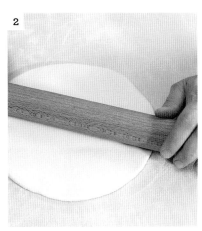

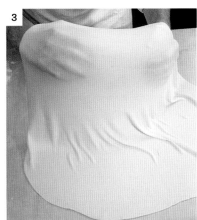

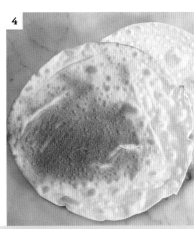

SIMPLIFIED PANE CARASAU (SARDINIAN FLATBREAD)

Combine 2 cups unbleached all-purpose flour, 2 cups semolina flour, salt, and 1 cup water **[1]**. Knead energetically on a work surface until the dough is smooth and elastic and the ingredients are well distributed. Form the dough into a ball, set it in a large bowl, cover it tightly with plastic wrap, and set it aside to rest for about 30 minutes. Then, roll out the dough in a circle using a rolling pin **[2]**. Using your hands, stretch the disk until it is as thin as possible. (But do keep in mind the size of your oven.) **[3]** Thoroughly preheat a soapstone griddle or a pizza stone in an oven set to 450 degrees F, then cook the flatbread for 1½ minutes on one side and 2 minutes on the other side. Brush it with oil and salt lightly **[4]**.

TIGELLE

Combine 4 cups unbleached all-purpose flour with ¼ cup lard, 2¼ teaspoons (1 envelope) active dry yeast dissolved in ¾ cup water, and a pinch of salt. Knead until smooth, about 10 minutes. Place the dough in a large bowl, cover it tightly with plastic wrap, and let rest for 30 minutes. Roll the dough to about ⅛ inch thickness, or a little thinner. Use a cookie cutter to punch out disks about 4 inches in diameter **[1]**. Cook for 8 minutes, turning once, in a cast-iron pan lightly coated with fatback or extra-virgin olive oil. Tigelle are traditionally served with cunza, a spread of cured lardo with garlic and rosemary, that is found in the Apennine mountains in the Emilia region. **[2]**

Tigelle farcite
stuffed tigelle

DOUGH

2¼ teaspoons (1 envelope) active dry yeast

2¾ cups pizza flour (or a combination of bread flour and unbleached all-purpose flour)

1½ cups cornmeal

Fine sea salt to taste

3 tablespoons lard

¼ cup milk, scalded and cooled

FILLING AND ACCOMPANIMENTS

1 medium carrot, cut into small dice

1 scallion, cut into small dice

¼ cup extra-virgin olive oil

4 stalks asparagus, cut into small dice

1 medium zucchini, cut into small dice

Fine sea salt to taste

¼ cup heavy cream

1 tablespoon minced herbs, such as sage, rosemary, and parsley

1 pound stracchino cheese

¼ cup basil leaves

Freshly ground pepper to taste

12 slices (about 8 ounces) prosciutto cotto

1. In a medium bowl, dissolve the yeast in ¾ cup warm water (100 to 110 degrees F) and set aside until foamy, about 15 minutes. Stir in 2 cups of the pizza flour. Cover the bowl and set aside to rise for 1 hour.

2. Sift the remaining ¾ cup pizza flour into a clean large bowl. Stir in the cornmeal and a pinch of salt, then stir in the lard, yeast mixture, and milk. Cover the bowl and set it aside in a warm place to rise for an additional 40 minutes.

3. Divide the dough into 24 equal portions. Shape each into a ball and set it on a lightly floured tray or baking sheet; cover with a damp dish towel and allow them to rise for 1 hour.

4. To make the filling, place the carrot and scallion in a pot. Add water to cover and 2 tablespoons of the olive oil. Cover and cook over medium heat for 8 minutes. Most of the water should evaporate during this time. Add the asparagus and zucchini, a pinch of salt, the cream, and the minced herbs. Cover and cook for an additional 5 minutes, then remove from the heat.

5. While the filling cooks, puree the stracchino with the basil and the remaining 2 tablespoons oil. Season to taste with salt and pepper and set aside.

6. When the dough has risen, press each of the balls into a disk. Brush the tops with water. Divide the cooked vegetable mixture evenly on top of 12 of the disks. Place the other 12 disks over the filling, brushed side down, and press the edges together gently to seal.

7. If you are lucky enough to own a special tigelle pan (it looks like a very shallow muffin tin), brush it with a small amount of extra-virgin olive oil and heat it over medium heat. If not, use a well-seasoned cast-iron pan (your tigelle won't be perfectly round, but they'll still taste great). Place the tigelle in the indentations or directly in the cast-iron pan and cook until golden, about 6 minutes, turning once. Serve topped with the basil-flavored stracchino and the prosciutto.

SERVES 12   COOKING TIME: 1 HOUR

Pizza margherita

pizza margherita

DOUGH

¼ teaspoon active dry yeast

4 cups unbleached 00 flour (see note) or unbleached all-purpose flour

2 teaspoons fine sea salt

2 tablespoons extra-virgin olive oil

TOPPING

1 (28-ounce) can whole San Marzano tomatoes, with juices, passed through a food mill

12 ounces mozzarella di bufala or fior di latte mozzarella cheese (see note), cut into ¼-inch slices

4 large or 8 small basil leaves, torn into pieces

Extra-virgin olive oil

Medium coarse sea salt

1. To make the dough, sprinkle the yeast over 1¼ cups warm water (100 to 110 degrees F); let stand until the yeast is creamy, 5 to 10 minutes. In a large bowl, whisk together the flour and salt; form them into a mound with a well in the center. Pour the yeast mixture and oil into the well; stir until the dough just comes together. Turn out the dough onto a lightly floured work surface and knead vigorously for 10 minutes. Cover with a damp dish towel and let rest for 10 minutes, then knead vigorously for 10 minutes more.

2. Lightly oil a large bowl. Form the dough into a ball, transfer it to the bowl, and turn it to lightly coat with oil. Cover the bowl tightly with plastic wrap and refrigerate overnight. Punch down the dough with your fist (the dough will be stiff), then fold the edges under to form the dough back into a ball, turn the dough to coat it with oil, re-cover the bowl with plastic wrap, and refrigerate for at least 4 hours or up to 24 hours.

3. Divide the dough into 4 pieces, shape them into balls, and place them on a lightly floured work surface with a few inches between them. Loosely cover them with a damp dish towel and let rise at warm room temperature until doubled, about 2 hours; the time will vary depending on the room temperature and the freshness of the yeast. If skin forms on the dough during this time, lightly spray the surface with water.

4. While the dough is rising, position a rack in the lower third of the oven. Place a pizza stone on the rack. At least 45 minutes before baking the pizza, heat the oven to maximum temperature (500 to 550 degrees F).

5. To assemble the pizza, on a lightly floured work surface, press 1 dough ball with your fingers to begin to shape it into a disk. Use your fist and hands to gently stretch the dough to a 10-inch round. Transfer the round to a lightly floured peel or an upside-down baking sheet; gently shake the peel to make sure the dough does not stick. Working fairly quickly, spread about ⅓ cup sauce over the dough, leaving about a ½-inch border. Arrange a quarter of the cheese pieces on top of sauce. Tear 1 or 2 basil leaves into small pieces and arrange them on top. Drizzle very lightly with oil and sprinkle with salt. Slide the pizza onto the hot stone and bake until the cheese is melted and bubbling in spots and the edge of the dough is crisp and golden, about 7 minutes. Using the peel and a large spatula or pair of tongs, transfer the pizza to a plate and serve. Repeat with the remaining ingredients.

NOTE: *Fine 00 flour produces a pliable, easy-to-work-with pizza dough and a tender yet sturdy crust with a crisp, not too dry edge. Fior di latte mozzarella has a firmer texture than mozzarella di bufala, which falls apart when cut, though both cheeses are creamy when melted. You can find 00 flour, San Marzano tomatoes, mozzarella di bufala, and fior di latte mozzarella at Italian markets, specialty stores, and online. See Sources on page 454 for mail-order options.*

SERVES 4   COOKING TIME: ABOUT 1 HOUR ACTIVE PREPARATION, BUT BEGIN DOUGH AT LEAST 2 DAYS AHEAD OF SERVING TO ALLOW FOR THE SLOW RISE

FROM THE EXPERTS

The associazione verace pizza napoletana, the arbiter of all things appropriate when it comes to pizza, has sanctioned only two types: pizza Margherita (page 17), with the colors of the Italian flag, and pizza marinara, with tomatoes, garlic, and oregano. But your imagination is the only limit to the other toppings that you can put on pizza and focaccia.

Toppings for Pizza and Focaccia

Next time you're feeling creative, try any of the following:

- pesto topped with julienned zucchini

- canned tuna packed in olive oil, drained, and thinly sliced onion

- tomato puree, olives, and ricotta salata cheese

- sautéed strips of porcini mushroom and shavings of Parmigiano Reggiano cheese

- stracchino cheese and cooked spinach, squeezed dry and chopped

- tomato puree, thinly sliced garlic, capers, and chile pepper

- quattro stagioni ("four seasons"): a Margherita with olives, mushrooms, artichoke hearts, and prosciutto cotto arranged separately (each on a quarter wedge of the pizza)

- olive oil, rosemary, and coarse salt

- mozzarella, arugula, and prosciutto cotto

Just don't overload your pizza, especially with cheese. Not only is that in contrast to the Italian pizza ethic, but it will make the pizza soggy, and the pizza may tear when you try to take it out of the oven.

When is a pizza not a pizza? When it's a calzone. To make a calzone, prepare the dough for pizza Margherita (page 17) and, rather than topping the entire surface of the dough, top only half. Fold the dough over the topping to form a semicircle and seal the edges, pinching with your fingers. Brush the top of the calzone with additional olive oil and place it on a parchment-lined baking sheet. Repeat with the remaining dough and bake as directed on page 17.

FOCACCIA, PIZZETTE, E CHIOCCIOLE

focaccia, small pizzas, and focaccia rolls

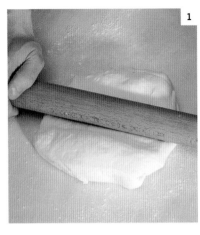

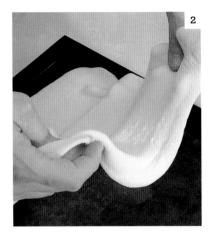

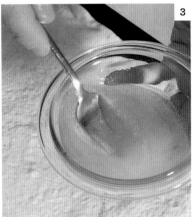

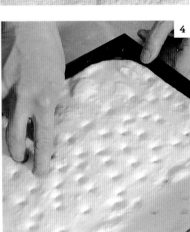

FOCACCIA

Make a dough of 4 cups unbleached all-purpose flour, 1 tablespoon salt, 1 teaspoon active dry yeast, 1 cup warm water (100 to 110 degrees F), and 2 tablespoons extra-virgin olive oil following the instructions on page 17. Knead the dough, place it in an oiled bowl, and it let rise until doubled, about 1 hour. Transfer the dough to a lightly floured surface and use a rolling pin to shape it into a rectangle [1]. Oil an 11-by-17-inch rimmed baking sheet. Transfer the rectangle to the center of the pan [2]. Use your fingers to push it out to the edges of the pan, making it slightly uneven in thickness. If it keeps springing back as you press it into shape, let it rest for 5 minutes and try again. Whisk together 2 tablespoons extra-virgin olive oil, 2 tablespoons water, and ½ teaspoon sea salt and drizzle it over the surface of the dough [3]. Use a brush to cover the surface of the dough completely. Dimple the dough all over with your fingers [4]. Allow the dough to rise for 45 minutes, then bake the focaccia at 475 degrees F until golden, about 18 minutes.

The right tools

PIZZA STONE AND PIZZA PEEL

Pizza is a simple food, but there are a few tools that will make it easier for you to create at home. One is a pizza stone. This is a flat piece of earthenware that you place in your oven, on a rack. Be sure the pizza stone is in place when you start preheating the oven—you want it to be very hot when you put the pizza on it. (Leave the stone in place as the oven cools down, too. If it cools too quickly, it may crack.) Pizza stones aren't expensive, but an even less expensive alternative—and one you may want to seek out if your oven is an unusual size or shape—is to place several unglazed tiles on a rack. (Double-check that the tiles are lead free.) Pizza baked directly on a stone is superior to pizza baked on a metal pan, because moisture gets trapped between the pizza and the pan and partially steams the crust.

A pizza peel is a long-handled wooden paddle used to move pizza (and bread) in and out of the oven. When preparing to bake the pizza, always flour the peel lightly to be sure the dough will slide off it easily. (Alternatively, you can place a piece of parchment on top of the peel and rest the pizza on top of it. Slide the parchment right into the oven along with the pizza.) Give the peel a very gentle shake before you put the pizza into the oven to be sure that the dough is moving freely. If you don't have a peel, you can use an upside-down baking sheet.

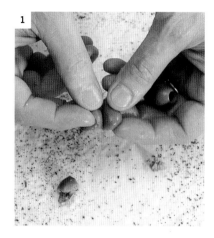

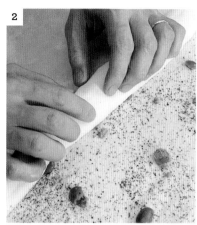

CHIOCCIOLE

Roll out a batch of risen focaccia dough (page opposite) and distribute herbs, chopped pitted olives, spices, and anything else you like on top [1]. Roll up the dough jelly-roll style from one long side [2]. Pinch the seam to seal. Cut the jelly roll into slices ½ inch thick. Lightly oil a round baking pan and set the rolls in it, spiral side up. Leave a little space between them [3]. Allow the chiocciole to rise until the rolls are puffy and touching each other, about 45 minutes [4]. Bake them at 400 degrees F until golden, 10 to 15 minutes.

PIZZETTE

To make small pizzas, make the pizza Margherita dough on page 17. In step 3, cut the dough into smaller balls of equal size—10 to 16, depending on the size you want your pizzette [1]. Arrange the dough balls on a lightly floured tray or sheet pan. Cover them with a damp dish towel and let them rise at room temperature until doubled [2]. Once you've stretched out the risen dough into disks, place the disks on parchment-lined baking sheets, top them with anything you like (including sliced meats, mozzarella, and vegetables), and bake as indicated, placing the baking sheets on a pizza stone, if possible. The pizzette will be ready in 4 to 5 minutes, depending on their size [3].

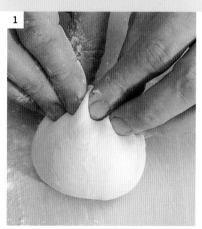

Focaccia mediterranea

stuffed focaccia

DOUGH

2¼ cups bread flour

⅛ teaspoon sugar

½ teaspoon fine sea salt

2¼ teaspoons (1 envelope) active dry yeast

FILLING AND TOPPING

1 yellow bell pepper

1 small onion, minced

¼ cup extra-virgin olive oil

4 cups roughly chopped escarole

3 tablespoons finely chopped flat-leaf parsley

¼ teaspoon fine sea salt

7 ounces provolone cheese, cut into ½-inch cubes

1 large tomato, cut into ½-inch slices

1 teaspoon dried oregano

1. To make the dough, in a large bowl, whisk together the flour, sugar, and salt. Dissolve the yeast in ¾ cup warm water (100 to 110 degrees F). Add the liquid to the dry ingredients and stir until you have a shaggy dough, then transfer to a lightly floured work surface and knead until the dough is smooth and compact, about 8 minutes. Return the dough to the bowl, cover it with a clean, damp dish towel, and set it in a warm place to rise until doubled, about 40 minutes.

2. While the dough is rising, prepare the filling. Roast the bell pepper (see page 200 for instructions) and set it aside. Sauté the onion in 3 tablespoons of the oil until softened, about 4 minutes. Stir in the escarole and parsley and cook, covered, until the escarole is tender, about 3 minutes. Remove from the heat and stir in ⅛ teaspoon of the salt. Set the mixture aside.

3. Generously oil a 10-inch square baking pan. Place two-thirds of the dough on a lightly floured work surface and roll it out to an 11-inch square. Transfer the dough to the pan and press it against the bottom and sides. There should be enough dough to cover the sides of the pan. If it does not, gently push the dough farther up the sides of the pan.

4. Skin the roasted pepper and stem and seed it. Cut it into 1-inch strips.

5. Spread the escarole mixture evenly over the dough in the pan. Scatter the provolone evenly over the escarole. Roll the remaining dough into a 10-inch square for the top crust. Place it on top to cover the filling and pinch together to seal.

6. Whisk together the remaining 1 tablespoon olive oil, 1½ teaspoons water, and the remaining ⅛ teaspoon salt. Brush the top crust with this mixture. Place the tomato slices and pepper strips in a single layer on the surface. Sprinkle the oregano over all. Cover with a damp dish towel and let rise for 1 hour. Partway through the rising, preheat the oven to 450 degrees F.

7. Bake the focaccia until the crust is golden brown, about 30 minutes, rotating the pan halfway through. Using a spatula, loosen the focaccia from the pan and transfer it to a wire rack to cool. Cut it into pieces and serve while it is still slightly warm or at room temperature.

SERVES 8 COOKING TIME: 1 HOUR 10 MINUTES

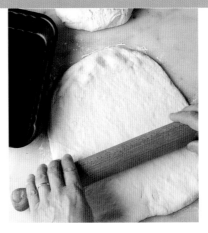

*S*AUCES ARE ANCIENT. The Latin word *salsu* was first used to indicate any item used to flavor a savory dish. The first sauce was probably the *garum* of the ancient Romans—a very salty fermented fish paste. The Middle Ages favored a different concoction of wine, honey, and vinegar. Those ingredients also went into sauces during the Renaissance era, when they were thickened with bread crumbs and often given a heavy dose of the spices that were then finding their way into what would later become Italy.

Because pasta—a kind of culinary blank canvas—is eaten almost everywhere in Italy, the country has developed a rich repertoire of sauces of every imaginable type. Like nearly everything in Italy, sauces are broken down along regional lines. Liguria has sauces rich with herbs, like its world-famous pesto with basil, garlic, pine nuts, cheese, and extra-virgin olive oil. Liguria's lesser-known sauces include a delicious walnut sauce. Throughout the North, wild mushrooms are widely used. In Valle d'Aosta and Trentino–Alto Adige, game such as venison often comes into play. Lombardy loves its sausages, while Tuscany and Umbria offer sauces made with boar and squab. Emilia-Romagna is the source of perhaps the world's most famous sauce, Bolognese ragù, a tomato and meat sauce made tender with the inclusion of milk. Lazio relies on guanciale for both carbonara and amatriciana, and in the South, the full gamut of vegetables is used—broccoli rabe, peppers, eggplant, broccoli, zucchini, artichokes, and so on. Naples is the birthplace of tomato sauce, which has come to represent Italian cooking all over the world. And, of course, as Italy is surrounded by water, it is also a source of wonderful fish sauces, with anchovies used everywhere from the Veneto to Sicily, and shellfish made into both white and red sauces. Indeed, Sicily is the source of an astounding variety of dishes, many of them with an Arab influence, like pasta con le sarde, which combines sardines with pine nuts, wild fennel, saffron, and raisins. These seemingly disparate ingredients play in perfect harmony. In the end, that's the job of a sauce—to tie it all together.

Though the terms *stock* and *broth* are often conflated in modern cooking, they are actually different: Stock is made using only bones, while broth is made by boiling meat or poultry. You can collect the occasional bone or shrimp shell and store it in a resealable plastic bag in your freezer with an eye to making stock. In Italy, the meat used for broth, having been boiled until tender, is often served as a second course, accompanied by a simple green sauce such as the ones on page 65 or drizzled with a little oil and seasoned with salt and pepper.

SAUCES, STOCKS, & BROTHS

Sauces either act as components in a dish or accompany simply prepared meat, fish, and other items to add a flavor boost. Homemade stocks and broths are relatively easy to make and add a depth of flavor to dishes that can't be achieved with the store-bought variety.

SALSA DI SAN MARZANO E ORTAGGI AROMATICI

san marzano tomato sauce **with aromatics**

Dice 2 medium onions, 3 large carrots, and 3 stalks celery
[1]. In a large pot, sauté the vegetables in ⅓ cup extra-
virgin olive oil. Salt to taste. After 3 to 4 minutes, add 6
pounds roughly chopped fresh San Marzano tomatoes, 1
bay leaf, and a pinch of coarse salt [2]. Bring to a boil, then
reduce to a simmer and cook, covered, until the tomatoes
have broken down, about 40 minutes. Remove and discard
the bay leaf and adjust the salt and pepper to taste. Cook,
uncovered, for an additional 20 minutes [3]. When the
sauce is completely cooked, pass it through a food mill
with medium-sized holes [4]. It can be used immediately
or vacuum-packed in glass jars for long-term storage.

SPAGHETTI CON POMODORI AL FORNO
spaghetti with roasted tomato sauce

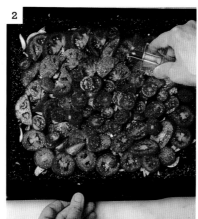

Preheat the oven to 400 degrees F. Lightly oil a baking sheet or jelly-roll pan. Bring a large pot of water to a boil and salt it. Slice 2 to 3 pounds of tomatoes (a combination of various types works nicely) [1]. Spread about ⅓ cup chopped onion and the chopped leaves of a bunch of flat-leaf parsley onto the prepared baking sheet in a single layer; season with ¼ teaspoon salt. Scatter the tomato pieces in a single layer over the onion mixture. Season with dried oregano and salt, then drizzle with about 2 tablespoons extra-virgin olive oil [2]. Bake until the tomatoes are tender, 10 to 15 minutes. Meanwhile, cook 1 pound spaghetti in salted boiling water until al dente (see page 72). Drain the pasta, transfer it to the baking sheet, and toss it gently with the tomato mixture and about ¼ cup torn basil leaves [3]. Adjust seasoning to taste. Divide the pasta among 4 to 6 plates, garnish with fresh basil leaves and a drizzle of extra-virgin olive oil, and serve immediately [4].

PACCHERI CON CILIEGINI ALLA MARINARA

paccheri with cherry tomato marinara sauce

Bring a large pot of water to a boil and salt it. When it boils, add 1 pound paccheri or other short pasta such as penne. Meanwhile, in a pan, heat 2 tablespoons extra-virgin olive oil with a minced garlic clove and some slices of fresh chile pepper. When the oil begins to sizzle, add 1 to 2 tablespoons minced flat-leaf parsley **[1]** and 1 pound halved cherry tomatoes. After a minute or two, add about ¼ cup of the pasta cooking water **[2]**. When the pasta is cooked al dente, drain it and add it to the pan. Toss over medium heat until the pasta is fully cooked, about 2 minutes.

FUSILLI COL BUCO AL RAGÙ NAPOLETANO
fusilli col buco with neapolitan ragù

Thinly slice 2 medium onions. Mince 1 carrot, 1 stalk celery, and 1 clove garlic **[1]**. In a wide, heavy pot with a lid, combine the onions, 4 ounces chopped pancetta, and 2 tablespoons lard or extra-virgin olive oil. Cook over medium heat, stirring occasionally, until the onions begin to soften, 8 to 10 minutes. Add the carrot, celery, and garlic; continue to cook for 3 to 4 additional minutes **[2]**. Add a 1½-pound boneless chuck roast and cook 5 minutes per side **[3]**, then add 1 cup dry white wine **[4]**, increase the heat to high, and cook until most of the wine has evaporated, 5 to 7 minutes. Dilute ⅓ cup tomato paste in 2 cups water and add to the pot **[5]**. Reduce the heat to the barest simmer, cover, and cook for 2 hours. Add 2 tablespoons extra-virgin olive oil and ½ teaspoon salt; if the sauce appears dry, add a little water. Continue to simmer gently, covered, for 2 additional hours. When the ragù is finished, bring a large pot of water to a boil and salt it. Add 1 pound fusilli col buco or other long pasta and cook until al dente. Meanwhile, remove the meat from the pot and set it aside. When the pasta is ready, drain it and add it to the pot with the sauce; toss to combine. Adjust the seasoning, if necessary, and serve the pasta immediately **[6]**. Serve the meat as a second course.

29

RAGÙ DI MAIALE

pork ragù

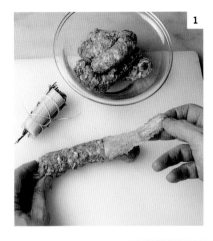

Cut 1 stalk celery in half crosswise, place 1 sprig each of rosemary and sage between the celery pieces, and tie the bundle together with kitchen twine. Remove and discard the casings from 1 pound pork sausage **[1]**. In a wide, heavy pot, heat ¼ cup extra-virgin olive oil over medium heat. Add the herb bundle and 1 garlic clove with the peel still on. Add the sausage meat and cook, breaking it up into bits, until it loses its raw pink color, about 3 minutes more **[2]**. Add the contents of a 14-ounce can or jar of tomato puree, 2 teaspoons tomato paste, and 1½ cups water; stir to combine well **[3]**. Bring the sauce to a very gentle simmer and cook, uncovered, stirring occasionally, for 1½ hours. Season with salt to taste. Remove and discard the celery and herb bundle and the garlic clove.

SUGO CON BRACIOLETTE

sauce with beef rolls

Pound 6 slices of beef until they are thin. On top of each, arrange some parsley, grated Grana Padano cheese, and thin shavings of pecorino Romano cheese. Mince 1 clove garlic and sprinkle it over the beef slices [1]. Salt to taste. Roll up the braciolette and use toothpicks to hold them closed. In a pan large enough to hold the braciolette in a single layer, heat ¼ cup extra-virgin olive oil and sauté 1 small onion, diced, for 5 minutes, stirring occasionally. Add the braciolette [2] and cook until browned on all sides. Add the contents of a 28-ounce can of crushed tomatoes. Add enough water to cover the braciolette and simmer for 1 hour [3]. Bring a large pot of water to a boil, salt it, and cook 1 pound orecchiette until al dente. Top the orecchiette with the sauce [4] and serve the meat as a second course.

Malloredus con salsiccia

malloredus with sausage

MALLOREDUS (see note)

1¼ cups semolina flour

¾ cup unbleached all-purpose flour

SAUCE

3 tablespoons extra-virgin olive oil

1 medium onion, roughly chopped

1 pound sausage, casings removed and discarded

1 cup dry white wine

Pinch saffron, crumbled and dissolved in ¼ cup water

1 (28-ounce) can whole peeled tomatoes with juices, preferably San Marzano

Fine sea salt

½ cup freshly grated pecorino Romano cheese, plus more for serving

1. To make the malloredus, in a large bowl whisk together semolina and all-purpose flours; form the flour into a mound and make a well in the center. Add 1 cup warm water (100 to 110 F). Using your hand or a fork, combine the flour and water.

2. Transfer the shaggy dough to a lightly floured work surface and knead until it is smooth, about 10 minutes. Wrap the dough in plastic and set it aside for 30 minutes.

3. Meanwhile, start the sauce. In a large saucepan, heat the oil over medium-high heat; add the onion and cook, stirring frequently, until softened, 3 to 4 minutes. Add the sausage, breaking it up with a fork as you transfer it to the pot. Add the wine and the saffron mixture. Bring the liquid to a brisk simmer and cook, stirring occasionally, for 2 minutes.

4. Turn the heat down slightly and add the tomatoes to the pot; cook at a low simmer, breaking up the tomatoes. Salt to taste (keep in mind that the sausage is already seasoned). Gently simmer the sauce until it is thickened and flavorful, about 1 hour.

5. Break off a piece of pasta dough about the size of an egg; rewrap the remaining dough in plastic. Roll the dough into a ⅓-inch cylinder and cut it into pieces ⅓ inch long.

6. Roll each piece along a gnocchi board (or down the back of a fork) to mark it with ridges and put it on a floured baking sheet. Repeat with the remaining dough.

7. Bring a large pot of water to a boil and salt it. Add the malloredus and cook for 3 to 4 minutes after the water returns to a boil. Drain the pasta and transfer it to a large serving bowl, then immediately toss with the sauce and the cheese, and serve.

NOTE: *Malloredus, sometimes called gnocchetti sardi, or small Sardinian gnocchi, are little ridged dumplings with a delicious consistency. Traditionally, the ridges are made by rolling each dumpling along a grooved wooden paddle. You can find this kind of paddle, usually labeled as a "gnocchi board," at gourmet shops (see Sources on page 454), or use the back of a fork as for potato gnocchi (see page 86), though your ridges won't be as deep. You can also purchase packaged malloredus in some Italian specialty stores—use a 1-pound package to replace the freshly made version in the recipe above. This sauce also pairs well with farfalle or potato gnocchi.*

SERVES 4 TO 6 ⌒ COOKING TIME: 1 HOUR 30 MINUTES

 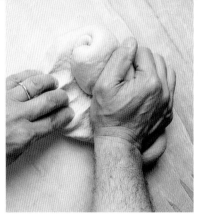 

RAGÙ BOLOGNESE CLASSICO
classic bolognese ragù

There are many variations on Bologna's famed sauce, but there is one thing that all versions share: a true ragù must simmer on very low heat for a long time. It is that slow evaporation of liquid that creates the signature rich flavor. Ragù is traditionally paired with fresh tagliatelle, but it's equally delicious with short dried pasta. It is also a key component in lasagne alla Bolognese (page 36).

Mince 2 ounces pancetta **[1]**. Separately, mince 1 small carrot, 1 small onion, and 1 stalk celery for soffritto (page 260). In a large saucepan or pot, cook the pancetta for 5 minutes. Add the vegetable mixture and cook for an additional 8 minutes **[2]**. Add about 1 pound ground beef. Cook, stirring with a wooden spoon, for 10 minutes **[3]**. Add ½ cup dry white wine **[4]**; bring to a boil. As soon as the wine has evaporated, add 2 tablespoons tomato paste dissolved in 1½ cups water or beef stock (page 55) **[5]**.

Cover and cook the ragù at the barest simmer. Measure out ¾ cup whole milk. Every 10 minutes or so, stir and add a small amount of this milk; by the end of the cooking time, you should have added it all to the sauce [6]. Cook until the meat is very tender and the sauce is very thick, about 2 hours. Season to taste with salt and pepper. To serve, toss 1½ to 1¾ cups ragù with each pound of pasta. Serve immediately with freshly grated Parmigiano Reggiano cheese on the side [7].

Lasagne alla bolognese
bolognese lasagne

BÉCHAMEL

5 tablespoons unsalted butter

½ cup unbleached all-purpose flour

2½ cups whole milk

Fine sea salt to taste

Pinch ground nutmeg

SPINACH NOODLES

1 small bunch spinach

Fine sea salt to taste

1½ cups OO flour (see note, page 17)
or unbleached all-purpose flour,
plus more if needed

1 large egg

1 tablespoon extra-virgin olive oil

ASSEMBLY

About 2 cups ragù Bolognese
(see page 34)

⅔ cup freshly grated Parmigiano
Reggiano cheese

1. To make the béchamel, in a medium saucepan, melt 4 tablespoons of the butter over medium heat. Stir in the flour with a wooden spoon and cook, stirring constantly, until you have a light golden roux (see page 57). Whisk in the milk in a thin stream and continue to cook, stirring constantly, until the mixture thickens, about 5 minutes. Season with the salt and nutmeg. Remove the béchamel from the heat, add the remaining 1 tablespoon butter, and stir to combine. The béchamel can be set aside while the pasta is made. Let it cool and cover the surface with plastic wrap.

2. To make the pasta, trim and discard the stems from the spinach and rinse the leaves in several changes of cold water. Do not dry. Place the damp spinach leaves in a medium saucepan with a pinch of salt and cook, covered, over medium heat until tender, 3 to 5 minutes. Drain and cool, then squeeze out the excess liquid and mince the spinach as finely as you can.

3. On a clean work surface, mound the flour and form a well in the center. Add the egg, olive oil, a pinch of salt, and the spinach to the well. Using a fork, gently break up the yolk and slowly incorporate flour from the inside rim of the well. Continue until the liquid is absorbed. When the dough gets too stiff to work with a fork, knead by hand until it is no longer sticky, adding additional flour in 1-tablespoon increments as necessary. Wrap the dough in plastic and let it rest at room temperature for 30 minutes.

4. Cut the pasta dough in half. Either roll out each piece with a rolling pin (see page 80) or use a pasta machine to roll the dough to a scant ¹⁄₁₆ inch thick. Cut the sheets of pasta into noodles about 7 inches square (or the width of the pasta roller if rolling by machine). Lay the noodles on a lightly floured baking sheet in a single layer until you are ready to use them. If they don't fit in a single layer, place floured pieces of parchment or waxed paper between the layers.

5. To assemble and bake the lasagne, preheat the oven to 400 degrees F. Bring a large pot of water to a boil and salt it; prepare a large bowl of ice water and have it ready. Add the noodles, a few at a time, to the boiling water. Cook for about 15 seconds, then remove them with a slotted spoon and transfer them to the ice water. Drain the cooked noodles well and pat them dry with a lint-free kitchen towel.

6. Spread about 2 tablespoons of the ragù on the bottom of an 11-by-7-by-2-inch baking dish or similar-size gratin dish. Top the ragù with a layer of noodles, overlapping the noodles slightly and letting some excess hang over the sides of the dish. Cover with about a fifth of the ragù, a fifth of the béchamel, and a fifth of the grated cheese. Top with another layer of pasta, trimming the noodles to fit inside the dish with no overhang. Top the noodles with layers of ragù, béchamel, and cheese, using the same amounts as before. Repeat this process twice more for a total of four layers.

7. Fold any overhanging pasta onto the top of the dish. Top with the remaining ragù, béchamel, and cheese, and bake in the preheated oven until brown and bubbly, about 20 minutes. Let rest for 5 to 10 minutes before serving.

SERVES 4 TO 6 · COOKING TIME: 3 HOURS

SPAGHETTI ALLE VONGOLE

spaghetti with clam sauce

Bring a large pot of water to a boil and salt it. Soak 3 pounds Manila clams, cockles, or small littleneck clams in salt water, discarding and refreshing the water every 30 minutes, until they no longer give up any sand. Quarter 1 pint cherry tomatoes. Mince ⅓ cup flat-leaf parsley leaves and 1 clove garlic [1]. In a large pan, combine ¼ cup extra-virgin olive oil, sliced fresh red chile pepper to taste, the garlic, and the parsley. When the oil begins to sizzle, add the cleaned clams [2], stir once, then cover and cook until the shells open, 3 to 4 minutes. Discard any unopened clams. Add the tomatoes to the clams, along with 4 or 5 basil leaves. Cook 1 pound spaghetti, then drain and transfer the pasta to the pan with the clams, tossing to combine [3]. Divide the pasta among the serving plates and top with a little fresh minced parsley [4].

LINGUINE CON ARAGOSTA

linguine with lobster sauce

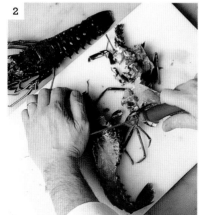

Peel 1⅓ pounds San Marzano or other plum tomatoes, following the directions on page 205 **[1]**. Cut 2 lobsters, about 1½ pounds each, in half lengthwise. Chop each half into pieces **[2]**. In a large pan, heat 3 tablespoons extra-virgin olive oil and add the lobster. Toss the lobster pieces in the oil, then cover the pan and cook over low heat for 6 minutes **[3]**. Add some minced parsley and salt and pepper to taste and cook for an additional 7 minutes. Chop the peeled tomatoes and add them to the pan, along with about ¾ cup water **[4]**. Cover and cook for an additional 10 minutes. In the meantime, cook 1 pound linguine in boiling salted water. Drain the pasta, add it to the pan with the lobster, toss it over medium heat for a minute or so, and serve.

SUGO AL TONNO SOTT'OLIO

tuna sauce

Cook 2 medium onions, minced, and 1 garlic clove with the peel left on in 3 tablespoons extra-virgin olive oil until the onions are just transparent. Add ½ cup dry white wine and simmer, covered, for 10 minutes. Add the minced leaves from a few sprigs of flat-leaf parsley; 1 teaspoon salted capers, soaked and rinsed; and 2 rinsed anchovy fillets **[1]**. Cook for 1 minute, then add 5 ounces high-quality Italian tuna belly packed in oil (sold in jars and labeled ventresca di tonno), drained and flaked with a fork. Add ⅓ cup tomato paste diluted in ⅓ cup water **[2]**, plus another 1½ cups water. Cover and simmer for 30 minutes, then uncover and cook until the sauce thickens, about 15 minutes more. Serve with spaghetti.

39

Pasta cu li sardi

pasta with sardines

Fronds from 1 to 2 bulbs fennel, including the thin stalks

1 pound fresh sardines

2 medium onions, sliced

¼ cup extra-virgin olive oil

⅛ teaspoon crumbled saffron soaked in 1 tablespoon water

1 pound spaghetti or bucatini

1½ tablespoons golden raisins, soaked to soften

2 tablespoons pine nuts

2 anchovy fillets in salt, rinsed

Fine sea salt to taste

Freshly ground black pepper to taste

1 tablespoon finely chopped flat-leaf parsley

1. Bring a large pot of water to a boil, salt it, and boil the fennel fronds for 10 minutes, then remove them with a slotted spoon and drain. Leave the water in the pot.

2. In the meantime, scale the sardines, taking care not to nick the skin. Cut off the heads and fins with kitchen shears. Under cold running water, slit them open down the belly and gut them with your thumb. Remove and discard the bones (they should lift away from the flesh easily). After running your thumb over the sardines to check for any remaining small bones, cut off and discard the tails.

3. In a large pan, combine the onions and ¾ cup water. Cook for 5 minutes and let the liquid evaporate, then add the olive oil and the saffron mixture.

4. Return the fennel-cooking water to a boil, add the spaghetti, cook to al dente (see page 72), and drain.

5. Meanwhile, mince the fennel fronds and drain the raisins. Coarsely chop the raisins and add them to the pan with the onions, along with the fennel fronds, pine nuts, and anchovies. Season with salt and pepper. Cook over medium heat until combined, 2 to 3 minutes.

6. Add the sardines to the pan and cook for an additional 5 minutes. Taste and adjust seasoning. Add the al dente spaghetti to the pan and toss over medium heat for 1 minute. Serve immediately topped with the minced parsley.

SERVES 4 TO 6 ⟋⟍ COOKING TIME: 40 MINUTES

ORECCHIETTE ALLE CIME DI RAPA

orecchiette with broccoli rabe

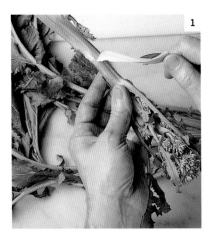

Bring a large pot of water to a boil and salt it; bring a smaller pot of unsalted water to a boil. Trim 1¼ pounds broccoli rabe. Pull the leaves off the stalks and set them aside. Trim away and discard any stringy portions on the outside of the thinner stems and cut the stems in half lengthwise. Peel the thick central stalks and cut them into quarters lengthwise [1]. Cut any larger pieces into strips about 4 inches long. Cook the stalks and leaves in the unsalted boiling water for 10 minutes [2]. Drain the cooked greens and chop them roughly. In a skillet, sauté 3 ounces guanciale in ¼ cup extra-virgin olive oil until the meat begins to crisp, about 4 minutes. Add the broccoli rabe and continue cooking, stirring occasionally, for 3 minutes [3]. Meanwhile, add 1 pound orecchiette pasta to the boiling salted water and cook until al dente. Transfer the broccoli rabe mixture to a serving bowl large enough to toss the pasta in. Return the skillet to medium heat and add 2 tablespoons extra-virgin olive oil and ½ cup coarse plain bread crumbs. Cook, stirring constantly, until the bread crumbs are golden, about 5 minutes. Reserving ½ cup of the pasta cooking liquid, drain the pasta and add it to the bowl with the broccoli rabe. Add the bread crumbs [4] and drizzle in about ¼ cup of the pasta cooking liquid. Toss to combine. Moisten with additional pasta cooking liquid, if desired. Serve immediately, sprinkled with grated ricotta salata cheese.

SPAGHETTI CON CIPOLLA E VERNACCIA

spaghetti with onions and vernaccia

In a large skillet over high heat, combine 4 cups thinly sliced onions and 3 cups Vernaccia wine [1]; cook until the wine evaporates, about 15 minutes. Reduce the heat to low and braise, stirring occasionally, until the onions are meltingly tender, about 30 minutes. If the pan looks dry, add a little more wine. When the onions are cooked, add ¼ cup minced flat-leaf parsley, 6 tablespoons extra-virgin olive oil, and fine sea salt and freshly ground black pepper to taste [2]; stir to combine. Meanwhile, bring a large pot of water to a boil and salt it. Cook 1 pound spaghetti until al dente (see page 72). Drain the pasta and transfer it to the skillet with the onions. Toss over medium heat for 1 minute and serve.

LASAGNETTE RICCE CON BROCCOLO ROMANESCO

lasagnette ricce with romanesco broccoli

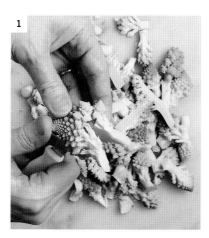

Bring a large pot of unsalted water to a boil. Cut 2 pounds Romanesco broccoli into florets; cut any large florets into halves or quarters **[1]**. Add the broccoli to the pot and cook for 5 minutes after the water returns to a boil **[2]**. Remove the broccoli with a slotted spoon and set it aside, reserving the cooking water. Meanwhile, rinse 4 anchovy fillets, mince the leaves of 1 sprig flat-leaf parsley, and peel 1 clove garlic **[3]**. In a large skillet over medium-high heat, sauté the anchovies in ¼ cup extra-virgin olive oil, with the whole garlic clove and chile pepper to taste, until the anchovy fillets dissolve, about 1 minute **[4]**. Add the contents of a 14-ounce can peeled tomatoes. As soon as the sauce starts to simmer, add the broccoli **[5]**. Cover the skillet and cook for 20 minutes **[6]**. About halfway through the cooking time, bring the broccoli cooking water back to a boil, salt it, and cook 1 pound lasagnette ricce or other pasta in it. When the sauce is ready, sprinkle on the parsley and add the drained pasta. Toss over medium heat for a minute or two to combine, then serve immediately with additional minced parsley, if desired.

FARFALLE CON RAGÙ VEGETARIANO
farfalle with vegetable ragù

ake this sauce anytime from late spring to late summer, when eggplants, peppers, tomatoes, and zucchini are at their peak. Of course, if you freeze summer vegetables (see page 196), you can enjoy it all year long.

Dice 1 medium zucchini, ½ seeded red bell pepper, ½ seeded yellow bell pepper, and 1 celery stalk; slice 2 scallions **[1]**. Peel ½ pound eggplant in strips, so that some of the skin remains, then cut it into dice. Place the diced eggplant in a colander set over a bowl and sprinkle it with 1 teaspoon salt **[2]**. Place a plate on top of the eggplant, set a large can or other heavy object on top, and let the eggplant drain under this weight, at room temperature, for 1 hour. Squeeze out the excess moisture and discard the liquid. Bring a large pot of water to a boil and salt it. Add 1 cup shelled fresh fava beans (from about 1 pound beans in pods) and cook for 2 minutes; immediately transfer the beans, using a slotted spoon, to a bowl of ice water to stop the cooking process; reserve the pot of cooking water. Drain the beans; gently peel and discard the skins **[3]**. Return the cooking water to a boil. Make an X at the base of each of 2 small tomatoes and immerse them in the water for 30 seconds. Using a slotted spoon, transfer the tomatoes to a colander to drain (again reserving the pot of water), then peel, seed, and finely chop them. Sauté the celery and scallions in a pot with 3 tablespoons extra-virgin olive oil for 2 minutes. Add the zucchini and bell peppers and cook for 8 additional minutes. Add the fava beans, ¾ cup shelled fresh or frozen peas (no need to thaw if they're frozen), and the eggplant and cook for 6 additional minutes **[4]**. Add ¼ cup heavy cream and gently simmer for 1 minute **[5]**. Stir in the chopped tomatoes, ¼ teaspoon fine sea salt, and a generous pinch freshly ground black pepper and cook for 1 minute longer. Meanwhile, return the pot of water to a boil and cook 1 pound farfalle pasta until al dente. Drain the pasta and transfer it to a large serving bowl; add the ragù and toss to combine. Serve immediately **[6]**.

FUSILLI CON SUGO ROSSO CON CARCIOFI

fusilli with artichokes in tomato sauce

Trim 4 baby artichokes, leaving a little of the stem. Slice them thinly the long way and place them in a bowl of cold water with the juice of ½ lemon. In a large pot, sauté 2 ounces minced pancetta in ¼ cup extra-virgin olive oil for 2 minutes. Add 1 minced medium onion and cook for an additional 2 minutes, then drain the artichokes and add them [1]. Cook for 5 minutes, then add the contents of a 14-ounce can peeled tomatoes, pureed smooth, and 2 cups water [2]. Cook, uncovered, until the sauce thickens, about 30 minutes. When the sauce is nearly ready, bring a large pot of water to a boil, salt it, and cook 1 pound fusilli until al dente. Drain the pasta, add it to the pot with the sauce, toss to combine, and serve.

LASAGNETTE CON TOCCO DI PORCINI

lasagnette with porcini mushrooms

Mince 1 tablespoon fresh rosemary leaves. Separately, mince about ⅓ cup flat-leaf parsley and 1 clove garlic [1]. In a large pot with a tightly fitting lid, combine the herbs with 3 tablespoons unsalted butter and 2 tablespoons extra-virgin olive oil; heat over medium-high heat, stirring occasionally, until the butter foams. Add the contents of a 28-ounce can whole peeled tomatoes, roughly chopped, with ½ cup of their juices [2]. Bring the sauce to a simmer and cook briefly, then stir in ¾ pound fresh porcini mushrooms, sliced. Season to taste with salt. Reduce the heat to low and gently simmer, covered, until the mushrooms are tender, about 30 minutes [3]. Meanwhile, bring a large pot of water to a boil and salt it. When the sauce is very close to done, cook 1 pound lasagnette (or other wide, long pasta) in the boiling water until al dente, then drain and transfer it to a large bowl. Add the sauce and toss to combine well. Serve immediately [4].

Tagliolini alla carbonara

7 ounces pancetta or bacon, diced

3 large egg yolks

Fine sea salt to taste

Freshly ground black pepper to taste

1 cup freshly grated pecorino Romano cheese, plus more for serving

¾ cup freshly grated Grana Padano or Parmigiano Reggiano cheese

3 tablespoons extra-virgin olive oil

1 pound tagliolini or spaghetti

1. Bring a large pot of water to a boil and salt it. Dice the pancetta.

2. In a medium bowl, whisk together the egg yolks, salt, and a generous amount of pepper with the grated cheeses.

3. Whisk ¼ cup water into the egg yolk mixture until perfectly smooth.

4. In a nonstick skillet, combine the pancetta and oil; cook over medium heat, stirring frequently, until the meat is browned and crisp, about 15 minutes. About halfway through the pancetta cooking time, add the pasta to the boiling water and cook until al dente. (Ideally, the pancetta and pasta will be ready at about the same time.) Reserving about ½ cup pasta cooking liquid, drain the pasta and return it to the pot. Add the pancetta and its rendered fat; toss to combine.

5. Immediately add the egg yolk mixture to the pasta and stir to combine. Moisten with a little of the reserved pasta cooking liquid, if needed. Serve immediately, passing pecorino and pepper alongside.

SERVESES 4 TO 6　　COOKING TIME: 30 MINUTES

BUCATINI ALL'AMATRICIANA
bucatini with tomato and guanciale sauce

Bring a large saucepan of water to a boil and peel 1½ pounds tomatoes according to the instructions on page 205. Cut the tomatoes into quarters; set aside. Trim and discard the rind from 5 ounces of guanciale [1] and cut the guanciale into matchsticks [2]. In a large saucepan, combine the guanciale with 3 tablespoons extra-virgin olive oil [3] and 1 peeled and smashed clove garlic. Cook over medium-low heat, stirring occasionally, until the garlic begins to turn golden, about 7 minutes. Using a slotted spoon, remove the garlic from the pot. Add 1 thinly sliced medium onion and crushed red pepper to taste to the pot [4]. Continue cooking, stirring occasionally, until the onion is softened, about 6 minutes. Add ¼ cup dry white wine, increase the heat to medium-high, and cook until the wine has evaporated. Stir in the tomatoes [5], reduce the heat to low, and gently simmer, covered, until the sauce is thick and the tomatoes have dissolved, about 50 minutes. Meanwhile, bring a large pot of water to a boil and salt it. Add 1 pound bucatini and cook until al dente. When the pasta is al dente, drain the pot and transfer the pasta to the saucepan. Toss the pasta and sauce together over medium heat for 1 minute. Serve immediately, passing grated pecorino Romano cheese and freshly ground black pepper alongside [6].

BUCATINI ALLA GRICIA

bucatini with guanciale

Bring a large pot of water to a boil and salt it. Meanwhile, cut 7 ounces of ⅛-inch-thick slices guanciale into ¾-inch pieces [1]. Combine the guanciale and ¼ cup extra-virgin olive oil in a large skillet; cook over medium-low heat, stirring occasionally, until the fat renders, then raise the heat to high and cook until the guanciale is golden and crisp [2]. Remove the guanciale from the pan, leaving the fat, and transfer to a plate lined with paper towels. Add 1 thinly sliced medium onion and crushed red pepper to taste to the skillet [3]. Cook, stirring occasionally, until the onion is softened, 2 to 3 minutes. Meanwhile, cook 1 pound bucatini in the boiling water until al dente. Return the guanciale to the skillet [4] and stir to combine. When the pasta is al dente, drain the pot and add the pasta to the skillet. Toss two or three times over medium heat. Remove the pan from the heat, add ½ cup freshly grated pecorino Romano cheese, and toss. Serve immediately.

TAGLIATELLE CON SUGO AL PROSCIUTTO CRUDO

tagliatelle with prosciutto crudo

Bring a large pot of water to a boil and salt it. Trim the fat from 5 ounces of prosciutto crudo; mince the fat and dice the remaining prosciutto. Combine the prosciutto fat and 3 tablespoons unsalted butter in a large skillet. Cook over medium heat, stirring occasionally, until the fat renders. Add 1 thinly sliced shallot and cook for 1 minute [1]. Add the diced prosciutto and cook for 1 additional minute, then pour in a splash of dry white wine and ½ cup of the boiling salted water. Meanwhile, add 14 ounces fresh or dried tagliatelle pasta to the boiling water and cook until al dente (about 3 minutes for fresh pasta). Add ¾ cup grated Parmigiano Reggiano cheese [2] to the skillet with the prosciutto and stir to combine. Add the drained pasta to the skillet, toss to combine, and serve immediately.

49

PANSOTTI CON SALSA DI NOCI

pansotti with walnut sauce

This uncooked walnut sauce is a specialty of Liguria, as are pansotti, triangular ravioli filled with foraged greens such as borage and stinging nettle. A filling made with ricotta and spinach (see page 101) is a fine substitute. You can also serve this sauce over store-bought vegetable ravioli or even dried pasta. The sauce usually uses prescinseua, a creamy cheese that is rarely found outside Liguria; a combination of ricotta and yogurt can be used in its place.

Shell walnuts until you have ¾ cup [1]. Bring a medium saucepan filled with water to a boil and blanch half of the nuts for 7 minutes. Meanwhile, cut day-old rustic bread into ½-inch cubes [2]. Place the bread in a bowl, cover it with tepid tap water, and let stand for 5 minutes; drain and squeeze out the excess water. Drain the blanched nuts and let them cool slightly. Using the tip of a paring knife, gently remove the skins [3]. In a large mortar, combine all the nuts, the moistened bread, salt, and freshly ground black pepper to taste. Grind with a pestle until combined [4]. Add 1 thinly sliced clove garlic and grind until the mixture is smooth [5]. Very slowly drizzle in ⅓ cup extra-virgin olive oil, grinding continuously to incorporate [6].

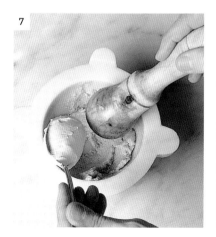

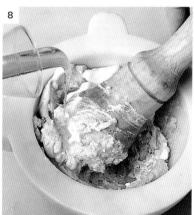

Stir in ½ cup fresh ricotta and then add ¼ cup nonfat Greek yogurt [7]; stir until the sauce is combined [8]. Bring a large pot of water to a boil and salt it. Boil the pansotti or other ravioli until tender. Using a slotted spoon or skimmer, transfer the pansotti to a colander to drain as they are finished, then transfer them to a large serving bowl; reserve the pasta cooking liquid. Once all the pansotti are cooked, thin the sauce with a little pasta cooking liquid and pour it over the pasta; gently toss to combine. Serve immediately [9].

The right tool

MORTAR AND PESTLE

When ingredients are ground in a mortar with a pestle their structure changes. As you grind them together, the texture becomes increasingly fine, and their flavors combine and evolve. Crushing ingredients in a mortar with a pestle releases essential oils without heating them up the way pulsing them in a food processor does, so the taste remains strong. When you use a mortar and pestle, you also avoid incorporating air, so the resulting paste has good body and does not become liquid. A food processor is wonderful for many things, but when it comes to creating pesto, it cannot compete with this ancient tool.

51

PESTO ALLA GENOVESE

genovese pesto

Rinse 2 cups basil leaves and gently pat them dry with paper towels **[1]**. Place them in a large mortar. If your mortar isn't big enough to hold all the leaves at once, add them in batches. Grind them to a paste with a pestle **[2]**. Add ¼ cup toasted, cooled pine nuts, 1 sliced garlic clove, and a pinch of coarse sea salt, and grind to a paste **[3]**. Add 6 tablespoons freshly grated Parmigiano Reggiano cheese and 2 tablespoons freshly grated pecorino Romano cheese and grind to combine **[4]**. Add ½ cup extra-virgin olive oil in a thin stream, grinding constantly **[5]**. To dress pasta, dilute the pesto with a tablespoon or two of pasta cooking water and toss it with hot pasta **[6]**.

Authentic pesto

The original Genovese pesto is made with a special local variety of basil that has small oval leaves. The best substitute is the freshest basil you can buy. In a simple uncooked sauce, there's no hiding lesser-quality ingredients, so be sure to spring for the best-quality olive oil and cheese that you can—it's even better if you can find Ligurian olive oil, which is particularly sweet. Pesto is traditionally made in a mortar with a pestle carved from the wood of an olive tree. It marries beautifully with trofie (see page 85) or trenette, and even potato gnocchi like those on page 86.

LINGUINE CON PESTO DI ACCIUGHE
linguine with anchovy pesto

Bring a large pot of water to a boil and salt it. Soak 2 tablespoons raisins in warm water until soft. Rinse and drain 4 salt-packed anchovy fillets. Place the anchovies in a mortar with 1 clove coarsely chopped garlic and ½ cup flat-leaf parsley leaves. Using a rotary movement, grind the mixture with the pestle against the wall of the mortar until combined [1]. Drain the raisins and add them to the mortar, along with 5 to 6 capers (rinsed and drained if salted) and 2 tablespoons pine nuts; grind the ingredients to combine [2]. Drizzle in 3 tablespoons extra-virgin olive oil, grinding and mixing to incorporate as you go, until the pesto is smooth [3]. Cook 1 pound linguine (or other long pasta) in the boiling water until al dente, then drain, reserving the cooking liquid. Thin the pesto with a little of the pasta cooking liquid and toss it with the cooked pasta. Serve immediately [4].

53

INGREDIENTS FOR STOCK AND BROTH

HERBS AND VEGETABLES

Aromatics such as carrots, celery, and onions, and mixed herbs, black peppercorns, and juniper berries all work well in stock. Use yellow onions for meat, poultry, and vegetable stocks, but substitute leeks or shallots for fish stock, as they marry better with the more delicate flavor. No need to cut your vegetables carefully when making stock—rough chunks will work fine, since you'll be straining them out at the end anyway. For broth, cut them into bite-sized pieces.

MEAT AND POULTRY

Ask your butcher for bones for stock—he or she may even give them to you for free. Use beef, not pork or lamb. Chicken wings and backs also work well. Trim away any obvious lumps of fat and rinse the bones before you begin. For broth, use a whole chicken, cut up (or left whole if it will fit in your pot that way) and rinsed, or a long-cooking cut of beef, such as brisket.

FISH

The best choices for fish stock are the bones from white fish such as fluke, sole, and sea bass. Avoid the bones of fattier fish, such as salmon. Fish heads are good for stock as well, and shrimp shells will boost the flavor.

MAKING STOCK

CLEAR STOCK

For a clear meat or poultry stock, use veal, chicken, or beef bones or a combination of the three. First boil the bones alone with abundant water for 1 minute. You will see fat and other impurities rise to the surface. Drain the bones of their boiling liquid, rinse them, and rinse out the pot. Briefly sauté carrot, onion, and celery in the pot in a small amount of oil, and then add the bones, bay leaf, thyme, parsley, and water to cover. Bring the water to a boil, reduce the heat to maintain a simmer, and cook, uncovered, for about 4 hours. Filter through a fine sieve or a cheesecloth-lined colander placed over a bowl. Discard the solids.

BROWN STOCK

To make a richer brown stock, first roast the poultry or meat bones in a pan at 475 degrees F for about 30 minutes, until they are nicely browned. Drain off the fat. In a large pot, briefly sauté carrot, onion, and celery in a small amount of oil, and then add the bones, bay leaf, rosemary, sage, thyme, and a couple of whole garlic cloves (no need to peel them), and water to cover. You can also add red wine, 1 or 2 dried porcini mushrooms, and a small amount of tomato paste or tomato puree. Bring the liquid to a boil, reduce the heat to maintain a simmer, and cook, uncovered, for about 4 hours.

FISH STOCK

Rinse the bones and scraps carefully to be sure you remove any blood or other impurities. Then, in a pot, combine the bones and scraps, carrot, leek (yellow onion is too overpowering for fish stock), celery, parsley, thyme, and water to cover. Bring the water to a boil, turn down the heat to maintain a simmer, and cook for 30 minutes.

VEGETABLE STOCK

Brown a generous amount of roughly chopped vegetables in oil in a stock pot. Add parsley, peppercorns, and any other flavorings you like. Add cold water to cover, bring to a boil, turn down to a simmer, and cook until the vegetables are soft and have given up all of their flavor, at least 45 minutes.

STORING STOCK AND BROTH

Stock and broth will keep for 4 to 5 days in the refrigerator and almost indefinitely in the freezer. If you plan to freeze it, boil the liquid to reduce it first. That way it will take up much less space. You can add water to adjust the strength when you defrost and use it.

MAKING BROTH

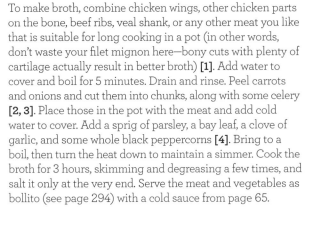

To make broth, combine chicken wings, other chicken parts on the bone, beef ribs, veal shank, or any other meat you like that is suitable for long cooking in a pot (in other words, don't waste your filet mignon here—bony cuts with plenty of cartilage actually result in better broth) [1]. Add water to cover and boil for 5 minutes. Drain and rinse. Peel carrots and onions and cut them into chunks, along with some celery [2, 3]. Place those in the pot with the meat and add cold water to cover. Add a sprig of parsley, a bay leaf, a clove of garlic, and some whole black peppercorns [4]. Bring to a boil, then turn the heat down to maintain a simmer. Cook the broth for 3 hours, skimming and degreasing a few times, and salt it only at the very end. Serve the meat and vegetables as bollito (see page 294) with a cold sauce from page 65.

SKIMMING AND DEGREASING STOCK AND BROTH

As your stock or broth boils, you will see foam rising to the top, especially at the beginning of cooking. Simply skim this off, using a strainer, and discard it [1]. When the stock or broth has finished cooking, pour it through a fine-mesh strainer such as a chinoise [2]. For stock, discard the solids; for broth, set them aside. There will be a large amount of fat at the top of your stock or broth. If you chill the resulting liquid, the fat will solidify into a raft at the top, and you can carefully lift it off and discard it. If you don't have time for that, use a ladle and try to skim off the visible fat. You can also blot the fat off with a paper towel—just lay the towel very gently on the surface.

56

ROUX and BÉCHAMEL

*R*oux is a cooked paste of equal amounts of butter and flour used as a thickener. By starting with a roux, you'll end up with a smooth sauce—such as béchamel—that is free of the lumps that might form if you were simply to add flour to the pot.

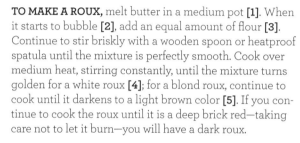

TO MAKE A ROUX, melt butter in a medium pot **[1]**. When it starts to bubble **[2]**, add an equal amount of flour **[3]**. Continue to stir briskly with a wooden spoon or heatproof spatula until the mixture is perfectly smooth. Cook over medium heat, stirring constantly, until the mixture turns golden for a white roux **[4]**; for a blond roux, continue to cook until it darkens to a light brown color **[5]**. If you continue to cook the roux until it is a deep brick red—taking care not to let it burn—you will have a dark roux.

TO MAKE BÉCHAMEL, make a blond roux, then gradually drizzle milk into it and continue to cook, stirring constantly, until it reaches the desired thickness.

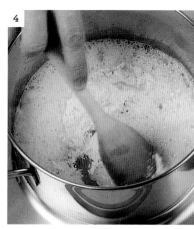

Vellutata di pesce con canestrelli

fish velouté with scallops

5 tablespoons butter

¼ cup unbleached all-purpose flour

4 cups fish stock (see page 55)

8 scallops (see note)

1 cup dry vermouth

Fine sea salt

Fresh chives

1. Prepare a blond roux (see page 57) with 4 tablespoons of the butter and the flour. Add the fish stock in a thin stream, whisking constantly. Bring the mixture to a boil, reduce the heat to maintain a simmer, and cook for 10 minutes, stirring occasionally.

2. Meanwhile, in a separate small pan, melt the remaining 1 tablespoon butter and quickly sauté the scallops in it until just cooked through and still creamy in the center, 1 to 2 minutes per side. Add the vermouth and cook until it evaporates. Salt the scallops to taste and remove them from the heat.

3. Divide the soup and scallops among 4 soup plates.

4. Snip chives directly onto the soup and serve immediately.

SERVES 4 AS A FIRST COURSE ⟶ COOKING TIME: 30 MINUTES

NOTE: *Canestrelli are sweet, pink scallops, about 2 inches in diameter. You're unlikely to find them in the United States, but if you do, they will still be in their shells and will need to be shucked raw before proceeding with the recipe. You can substitute either sea scallops or true bay scallops, which are sold without their shells. Simply strip away the small tendons, which you can peel off easily with your fingers, and proceed. (Do not give in to the temptation to buy diminutive calico scallops, which are rubbery and unpleasant.) Buy scallops from only a reputable fish market and be sure to specify that you want dry or unsoaked scallops. Unfortunately, many scallops today are soaked in phosphates after they are shucked, which means that when you cook them, they will give off large amounts of water and will taste like nothing.*

FILETTI IN SALSA ROSSINI

fillets in rossini sauce

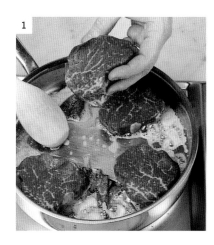

Brown 4 beef fillets in 2 tablespoons butter with minced shallot and sage leaves, 2 minutes per side [1]. Remove the beef from the pan and cook 4 slices of foie gras, 30 seconds per side [2]. Remove the foie gras (place it right on top of the fillets) and add some additional diced foie gras to the pan. Cook until melted, then deglaze the pan with ½ cup dry Marsala and ½ cup brown stock (page 55) [3]. Meanwhile, work together 1 tablespoon softened butter with 1 tablespoon all-purpose flour until thoroughly combined. Cook the sauce in the pan until it is reduced, then stir in the flour paste and whisk as it melts. Return the fillets and foie gras slices to the pan and cook for an additional 3 minutes, basting them with the sauce [4]. Shave thin slices of truffle over the top before serving.

POLLO ALLA CACCIATORA

chicken cacciatore

In a pot large enough to hold the chicken in a single layer, brown 4 chicken legs and thighs with their skin in a small amount of extra-virgin olive oil. Remove the chicken and add 1 julienned carrot, ½ stalk julienned celery, and 1 sliced onion; cook until browned. Add 10 sliced button mushrooms [1]. Then add about ⅓ cup canned chopped tomatoes and their juices, ½ cup white wine, and 1 cup brown stock (page 55). Return the chicken to the pot. Bring the sauce to a boil, turn the heat down to maintain a simmer, and stew, covered, for 50 minutes [2].

59

Coniglio alla cacciatora
rabbit cacciatore

5 tablespoons extra-virgin olive oil

1 medium onion, thinly sliced

1 large carrot, julienned

1 celery stalk, julienned

1 rabbit, cut into 8 pieces

Fine sea salt to taste

Freshly ground black pepper to taste

1 tablespoon unbleached all-purpose flour

1 pound mushrooms, sliced

1 garlic clove, peeled and crushed

1 cup dry white wine

½ cup tomato puree (page 208)

½ cup brown stock (page 55)

1 tablespoon finely chopped flat-leaf parsley

1. In a large, deep skillet with a lid or a Dutch oven, heat 3 tablespoons of the oil over medium-high heat. Add the onion, carrot, and celery; cook, stirring frequently, until the vegetables are softened, about 7 minutes.

2. Generously season the rabbit with salt and pepper. Add the pieces to the skillet and cook, turning them several times, until they are golden, about 5 minutes per side. Sift the flour over the meat in the skillet.

3. In another skillet, heat the remaining 2 tablespoons oil over medium-high heat; add the mushrooms and garlic; cook, stirring frequently, until the mushrooms are tender, about 5 minutes.

4. Add the cooked mushrooms and the wine to the pan with the rabbit. Increase the heat to high and cook until the liquid is reduced by half, 12 to 15 minutes.

5. Stir in the tomato puree. Add the stock and a generous pinch of salt and pepper. Reduce the heat to maintain a simmer, cover, and cook, stirring occasionally, until the rabbit is very tender, about 1 hour. Sprinkle with the parsley and serve hot.

SERVES 6   COOKING TIME: 1 HOUR 30 MINUTES

COOKED SAUCES

*A*ny of these five simple-to-make classic cooked sauces will liven up a simple piece of roasted or sautéed meat or poultry. Ladle a little over each serving, or pass on the side and let diners add any amount they wish.

SALSA CON GLI CHAMPIGNON (MUSHROOM SAUCE)

Sauté 4 large button mushrooms, trimmed and thinly sliced, in a little olive oil **[1]**. Cook until they have given up their liquid. Meanwhile, in a second pan, make a white roux (page 57) of 2 tablespoons butter and 2 tablespoons flour, then whisk in 1½ cups clear stock (page 55) in a thin stream. Pour the resulting sauce over the mushrooms **[2]**. Cook for 3 minutes, stirring constantly, to thicken and combine, and then add a little minced parsley.

SALSA ALL'AGLIO
(GARLIC SAUCE)

Place 8 peeled garlic cloves in a medium pan and add enough whole milk to cover. Dilute with about ½ cup water [1]. Cook over very low heat for 10 minutes, then strain out the garlic, discard the liquid, and repeat 3 times with fresh milk and water. The garlic should become very soft. Meanwhile, prepare a white roux (page 57) with 1 tablespoon butter and 1 tablespoon flour and whisk in ¾ cup clear stock (page 55) in a thin stream. Cook for a few minutes until thickened. Transfer the cooked garlic to a blender with the white sauce [2]. Process until perfectly smooth.

SALSA AL VINO BIANCO
(WHITE WINE SAUCE)

Place 1 quartered shallot, 1 sprig thyme, 2 bay leaves, and 2 cups dry white wine in a small pot [1]. Boil until the liquid is reduced by half. Meanwhile, in a second pot, melt 1 tablespoon butter with 1 minced shallot and add 2 tablespoons flour [2]. Cook, stirring constantly, for a couple of minutes, then add 1 cup clear stock (page 55). Strain the reduced wine, discarding the herbs and shallot, and pour it into the pot with the flour mixture [3]. Simmer for an additional 10 minutes, stirring frequently. Whisk in a tablespoon or so of butter and ¼ cup heavy cream.

COOKED SAUCES

SALSA AL TARTUFO (TRUFFLE SAUCE)

Make a white roux (page 57) with 2 tablespoons butter and 2 tablespoons flour, then add 1¼ cups clear chicken stock (page 55) in a thin stream and whisk to combine. Stir in 1 tablespoon truffle paste. Add ¼ cup heavy cream and simmer gently to thicken, about 3 minutes.

SALSA ALLE ERBE (HERB SAUCE)

Place a quartered shallot, 1 sprig chervil, 1 sprig tarragon, 1 sprig marjoram, and 1 sprig parsley with ½ cup white wine in a pot. Boil until the wine is reduced by half. Strain the liquid, discarding the shallot and herbs. Meanwhile, make a white roux (page 57) of 1 tablespoon butter and 1 tablespoon flour and add 1¼ cups clear stock (page 55) in a thin stream. Whisk in the reduced wine. Cook for 10 minutes, stirring frequently, then remove from the heat. Add the minced leaves of 1 sprig chervil, 1 sprig marjoram, and 1 sprig parsley, and about 1 tablespoon butter. Whisk until melted and combined.

COLD SAUCES

*C*old sauces can be prepared very quickly and are great for making a weeknight meal a little special. They are particularly delicious with simple grilled fish or boiled shellfish. These sauces aren't literally meant to be served ice-cold; the term simply means that they don't require any cooking.

GREEN BAGNET PIEMONTESE

This sauce from the Piedmont region is excellent with boiled meats, such as those left over after you've made broth (see page 56), and roasted or grilled fish of all kinds. It is made by combining parsley, stale white bread soaked in vinegar, anchovy fillets, garlic, and oil in a blender. Use any proportions you like.

**SALSA VERDE
(GREEN SAUCE)**

Mince together 1 clove garlic, 1 hard-boiled egg, 1 drained and rinsed anchovy fillet, 1 tablespoon drained and rinsed capers packed in salt, and ¼ cup flat-leaf parsley. Add to a medium bowl. Slowly add extra-virgin olive oil while whisking until the sauce is the thickness of sour cream. Taste and add salt if necessary (with the capers and anchovy, it may not be).

**SALSA FREDDA ALL'AGLIO
(COLD GARLIC SAUCE)**

In a mortar and pestle, grind 5 peeled garlic cloves (remove and discard any bitter green sprouts) with a little coarse salt **[1]**. Add 2 slices of white bread softened with vinegar and a raw egg yolk. Drizzle in ¾ cup extra-virgin olive oil in a thin stream while stirring **[2]**. This cold garlic sauce is often served with hard-boiled eggs and simply cooked poultry or fish, and it is especially good with grilled meats.

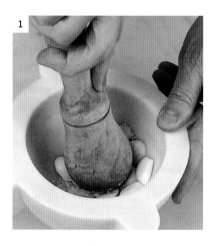

65

THE BEST KNOWN AND MOST BELOVED PASTA IN THE WORLD IS *spaghetti*. The word spaghetti means "little strings," which is obviously a reference to the characteristic shape. But while the origin of the name may be fairly clear-cut, the food has a tangled history. It is justly identified with Naples, or more specifically, the small town of Gragnano near Naples that is famous for its production of dried pasta. But the name comes from the north of Italy. The word spaghetti first appeared in print in a dictionary of the dialect of the city of Piacenza, published in 1836 by Lorenzo Foresti. Even today, in Naples, the word vermicelli is more commonly used for these long, thin strings of dried pasta. Of course, spaghetti pasta is just one among a multitude. Satisfying dried semolina pasta comes in an endless variety of shapes. Bucatini, linguine, paccheri, fusilli, conchiglie, penne, pennette, rigatoni—the list goes on and on.

In Italy, dried pasta is divided into two groups: long (such as spaghetti) and short (such as penne). Each shape marries best with certain sauces: trenette with pesto, spaghetti with clam sauce, paccheri with Genoese sauce (which, despite its name, is native to Naples), penne with four cheeses, rigatoni with ragù. And that is but a small sample of the suitable pairings.

Dried pasta is made from semolina flour, created by grinding select varieties of durum wheat. Pasta dough is extruded through a mold that shapes it into the desired form, but not all pasta is equal. Seek out pasta from companies that still use traditional bronze molds. These produce pasta with a rough surface, which is superior, because sauce clings to it more effectively. After being shaped, pasta is dried and cooled and, finally, packaged for sale.

From a nutritional point of view, pasta is simple and healthful. It provides necessary carbohydrates and a fair amount of protein (11 or 12 percent). It is also extremely low in fat (less than 1 percent). Most important, it tastes delicious. It's no wonder that it is such an international favorite.

DRIED PASTA

Dried pasta is Italy's ambassador and represents the country around the world. Pasta–in the form of spaghetti, rigatoni, penne, fusilli, and countless other shapes–plays a key role in the Mediterranean diet.

DRIED PASTA

WHEN PURCHASING DRIED PASTA (WHICH IS NEVER MADE AT HOME), look for a product that has been made using bronze molds. It will have a rough surface that allows it to marry perfectly with its sauce. The pasta you buy should be free of black dots, irregularities in shape, or white spots, which might indicate that soft wheat was used to make it. You will find semolina pasta in varying shades of yellow; a darker or lighter color does not indicate anything about the quality of the pasta—just the types of wheat it contains. Pasta should cook to that perfect al dente stage, meaning that it is tender and elastic (see page 72), but after it is drained in a colander, the pieces remain separate from one another and don't turn gluey.

1] SPAGHETTI The most popular dried pasta. Like trenette and other long, narrow pastas, it marries best with oil-based sauces.

2] FUSILLI Works beautifully with both meat- and vegetable-based sauces. Try whole wheat fusilli, which is rich in fiber and has a more assertive flavor.

3] ORECCHIETTE From the Puglia and Basilicata regions, orecchiette is traditionally served with broccoli rabe, with garlic and ricotta, or with tomato or lamb sauces.

4] MEZZE MANICHE Literally, "half sleeves." One of the most versatile shapes, this pasta goes with meat or vegetarian sauces and is also delicious baked in a casserole or tossed in a pasta salad.

PENNE Short "quills" of pasta that are perhaps the most versatile shape. They work with both smooth and chunky sauces.

BUCATINI Like thick, hollow spaghetti. This pasta is traditionally paired with sardines (page 40) or tomato and guanciale (page 48).

SPAGHETTI AGLIO E OLIO

spaghetti with garlic and oil

This dish, eaten throughout the center and the north of Italy, appears simple, and in a sense, it is. You probably have all the ingredients on hand. But in order to make a perfect garlic spaghetti, you've got to watch it carefully so that none of the ingredients burns—if you overcook the garlic, you risk unpalatable bitterness. The most common version of this basic recipe, provided below, calls for sautéing hot pepper along with the garlic. If you like, you can dress up this humble dish with a sprinkling of minced parsley after it's been plated.

Hold the spaghetti vertically in your hand and drop it into boiling salted water all at once **[1]**. This way, the individual strands distribute themselves evenly in the pot **[2]**. In the meantime, in a pan, heat 3 to 4 thinly sliced garlic cloves, and 1 minced fresh chile pepper in 3 to 4 tablespoons extra-virgin olive oil. Do not allow the garlic to brown. Add about ¼ cup pasta cooking water to the pan with the garlic **[3]**. Stir to combine thoroughly **[4]**. Take the pan off the heat. When the spaghetti is cooked, drain it in a colander, transfer it to the pan with the garlic oil, and toss **[5]**. Serve immediately.

BAKED PASTA and PASTA SALAD

MEZZE MANICHE GRATINATE (BAKED MEZZE MANICHE)
Cook 12 ounces of mezze maniche (or substitute ziti or penne) until al dente and drain. Place it in a bowl with 7 ounces (about 1 generous cup) classic ragù (see page 34). Add abundant grated aged cheese, such as Parmigiano Reggiano or Grana Padano, and 2 beaten eggs, and stir to combine **[1]**. Mix and transfer to a buttered casserole. Toss in some slices of fresh sheep's cheese (pecorino fresco) and stir gently to combine **[2]**. Top with additional sauce, thin curls of the sheep's cheese, and additional grated cheese, distributing them evenly **[3]**. Drizzle a little oil over the whole dish and bake at 375 to 400 degrees F until the cheese has melted, about 20 minutes **[4]**.

PASTA SALAD WITH VEGETABLES
Cook boccole or any other short, cylindrical pasta al dente and drain. Toss immediately with a little oil to keep it from sticking **[1]**. Spread the cooked pasta in a single layer and set it aside to cool to room temperature **[2]**. Once it has cooled, toss it with pesto, chopped marinated tomatoes, cooked peas, or other vegetables **[3]**.

Spaghetti con fragolini in umido

spaghetti with baby octopus

¼ cup extra-virgin olive oil

1 clove garlic, peeled

14 ounces baby octopus, cleaned, tentacles cut into strips

3 ripe tomatoes, seeded and diced

Fine sea salt to taste

1 pound spaghetti

1 tablespoon minced fresh marjoram leaves

1. Bring a large pot of water to a boil and salt it.

2. In a pan, heat the olive oil over medium heat. Add the whole garlic clove and cook it in the oil until it turns golden. Add the octopus bodies and tentacles, stir to combine, and cook over medium heat for 4 minutes.

3. Add the diced tomatoes to the octopus, along with a pinch of salt, and remove the pan from the heat. Cook the spaghetti al dente (see page 72), drain it, and add it to the pan with the octopus. Toss over medium heat for about 1 minute to combine the flavors.

4. Transfer the pasta to individual plates, sprinkle with the marjoram, and serve immediately.

SERVES 4 AS A FIRST COURSE COOKING TIME: 20 MINUTES

Water, salt, and semolina flour—these three simple ingredients combine to make Italy's national dish. Perfect pasta is boiled just until al dente, because it continues to cook as it is being combined with sauce and brought to the table. Cooking times vary, depending on the shape and quality of the pasta you are using, so you would be wise to taste test frequently as you reach the end of the cooking time.

Cooking Perfect Pasta

When cooking spaghetti or any other type of pasta, use a generous amount of water. Some of the water will be absorbed by the pasta, and the pasta needs to remain completely submerged in order to cook evenly.

Begin by filling a large pot with water and placing it over high heat. Once the pot comes to a rolling boil, add about 2 tablespoons salt (preferably coarse sea salt). This amount will not make the pasta taste salty. Rather, it brings out the flavor of the pasta itself; when cooked in unsalted water, pasta tastes flat.

Hold the spaghetti in your hands and roll your palms in opposite directions, as if you were setting up a game of pick-up-sticks. Let the spaghetti fall into the boiling water. Scattering the pasta like this will keep the pieces from sticking to one another. When adding short pasta to the water, shake it in so it doesn't clump.

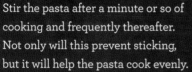

Stir the pasta after a minute or so of cooking and frequently thereafter. Not only will this prevent sticking, but it will help the pasta cook evenly.

Cooking time is key. Use the cooking time indicated on the package as a baseline, but check the pasta frequently, starting well before the printed time has elapsed. The center or heart of the pasta should remain lighter in color than the rest. Because pasta continues to cook in the sauce and on the plate, it should be drained before it reaches its ultimate doneness or it will overcook and become mushy.

When you are tossing pasta with sauce, add a small amount of pasta cooking water. Pasta cooking water contains a great deal of starch, so it serves as a creamy binder. This is especially useful when you are using an oil-based sauce. If you are planning to toss the pasta with its sauce over heat, don't drain it too thoroughly, as this does tend to dry it out. And always toss the pasta with the sauce as soon as possible after draining it—hot pasta absorbs more sauce and more flavor than pasta that has cooled.

PASTA E FAGIOLI TRADIZIONALE
traditional pasta and bean soup

Plan on serving 1¾ to 2 ounces beans—that is, about ¼ cup dried or 3½ ounces fresh shelling beans—per person. A few tips for cooking beans in general: Whether you start by sautéing the beans with some aromatics or simply boil them, cook them in a covered pot at a very gentle simmer so that not too much water evaporates. Always salt beans after they are cooked, just before combining them with pasta. The best pasta shapes for use with beans are smaller types, such as ditalini. For this dense and filling soup, use 1 to 1¾ ounces of dry pasta per person. This soup is also delicious when served at room temperature. If you prefer that option, simply keep the soup on the liquid side and leave the pasta very al dente. As the soup cools—and it will cool quickly if you ladle it into individual serving bowls—the pasta will finish cooking and the soup will become more dense.

Place 8½ ounces or about 2 cups dried cranberry beans in a bowl and add cold water to cover by several inches **[1]**. Let the beans soak overnight. (About 8 hours is usually best, but if they are on the large side or you've had them in the cupboard for a while, let them soak as long as 12 hours.) The beans will double in size and volume. Skim off and discard any broken beans that rise to the surface, then drain and rinse the beans **[2]**. Cut a 5-ounce piece of pork rind into large pieces **[3]**. Place the rind in a pot and add cold water to cover **[4]**. Bring to a boil and cook at a vigorous simmer for 1½ hours from the time the liquid comes to a boil. In another pot, combine the drained beans and 2 quarts cold water **[5]**; bring this to a boil, then cover the pot and turn down the heat to maintain a simmer.

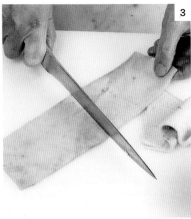

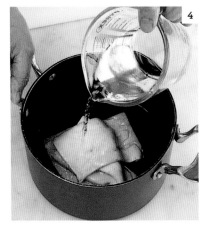

(If you prefer a more liquid, less dense soup, bring the water to a boil before adding the beans.) Mince 1 stalk celery, 1 small onion, and 1 medium carrot. Add the minced vegetables to the beans after they have been boiling for 10 to 15 minutes [6]. Cook for an additional 10 minutes, then add the boiled pieces of pork rind [7].

Cook the soup for 1 hour and 15 minutes (or longer if you prefer a denser soup), then remove the pork rind pieces with a slotted spoon and dice them [8]. Press about a third of the beans through a food mill, letting the pureed beans drop back into the soup pot [9]. Stir the diced pork rind into the soup. Bring the soup back to a boil, season with salt (taste first—the pork rind may have made it salty enough), and stir in 7 ounces dried ditalini pasta [10]. Cook, stirring frequently to prevent sticking, until the pasta is done. Drizzle on a little oil, season with pepper, sprinkle with minced parsley, and serve [11].

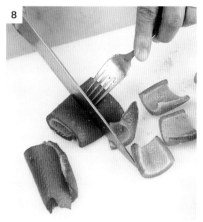

*P*ASTA HAS A LONG AND FASCINATING HISTORY. INDEED, IT REACHES all the way back to the puls of the ancient Romans, a very liquid porridge made with fermented barley and farro flour. The earliest form of true fresh pasta arrived soon after that, in the pre-Christian era, and was a thin square made with water and flour. During the Middle Ages, fresh pasta was made all over Italy, and over time, it took on specific regional characteristics. Those sharp differences can even be seen in the ingredients used to make pasta in different places. Eggs are the norm in central and northern Italy, while in the South, pasta tends to be made with only flour and water.

Almost all the regions of central and northern Italy have their own egg pasta specialties. No region can even begin to compete, however, with Emilia-Romagna, where freshly made egg pasta comes in an incredible number of varieties: tagliatelle, fettuccine, garganelli, tortellini, anolini, cappelletti, cappellacci—not to mention baked lasagne with fresh sheets of egg pasta and meat ragù.

Italians also make numerous types of fresh pasta without eggs. These include the malloredus of Sardinia (sometimes called Sardinian gnocchi), made of a dough that often includes saffron. Liguria has trofie, served with either pesto or walnut sauce.

Most of these types of pasta are ancient and were created in rural areas. As such, they match beautifully with local products. There is a logic to the rules for pairing pastas and sauces—you can never go wrong with a classic match.

FRESH PASTA

The tagliatelle of Emilia, Piedmont's tagliolini, as well as orecchiette and cavatelli from the South—fresh pasta represents the best of Italian regional cooking.

MAKING EGG PASTA DOUGH

Homemade egg pasta is completely different from commercially manufactured egg noodles. It's not difficult to make, though it may take a few trial runs before the process comes naturally to you. Egg pasta dough is made with flour and eggs, and a little time and patience. You don't need a lot of fancy equipment—just a large wooden board and a rolling pin. The work surface must be wood, however, in order for the finished pasta to take on the necessary rough surface, and the rolling pin should be the long, thin dowel type in order to put equal pressure all over the sheet of pasta. Egg pasta can be prepared a day or two in advance, but it does contain eggs and is therefore perishable—make it in advance only if you have a nonhumid and well-ventilated place where it can be allowed to dry completely. It really is best when cooked within a few hours of being rolled.

Arrange flour in a mound on a wooden work surface (use 1 cup of flour per serving) [1]. Make a well in the center that is wide enough to hold the eggs [2]. For each cup of flour used, crack 1 whole egg into the well [3]. First, break up the egg yolks with a fork [4].

Some advice

- *Eggs for making pasta should be room temperature and graded large.*

- *Using 20 percent semolina flour makes pasta that stands up a little better to cooking but is still soft.*

- *As you knead, frequently wet your hands and keep the work surface lightly floured.*

- *Resting time for the dough is key, because it gives the ingredients time to combine and allows the gluten to relax.*

- *Fresh pasta cooks extremely quickly, in 2 to 5 minutes, depending on the thickness.*

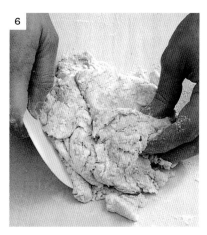

Whisk together the eggs and whites. Using the fork, push the flour a little at a time into the center and mix it with the egg until you have a crumbly dough **[5]**. If your dough seems excessively sticky, add a little more flour at this point. Use a bench scraper to collect the dough from the work surface **[6]**. Knead it by hand at length. First push the dough down toward the surface, then fold it in half toward you **[7]**. Rotate it a quarter turn. Continue pushing, folding, and turning like this until the dough is very smooth and elastic and looks completely uniform **[8]**. Set the dough aside, covered (an inverted bowl works well), and let it rest for at least 30 minutes **[9]** before rolling it out and cutting it (see pages 80 to 81).

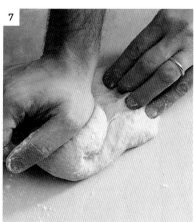

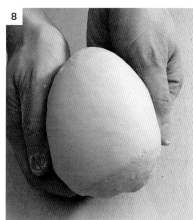

ROLLING OUT PASTA DOUGH

*f*reshly made pasta dough, whether made with eggs or without, must rest for at least 30 minutes. After this, it will be less elastic, but still soft enough to be rolled by hand into a very thin sheet. This requires some strength and, above all, patience. (You can, of course, roll out pasta dough and cut it using a pasta machine, though an aficionado will be able to tell the difference.)

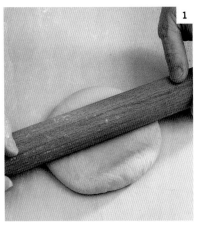

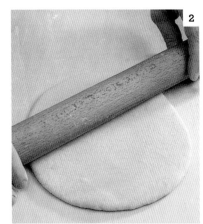

Begin by placing the dough on a lightly floured wooden work surface and rolling it into a disk using a dowel-type wooden rolling pin **[1]**. As you roll, rotate the pasta, lightly flouring the surface of the dough and the work surface. To be sure the pasta sheet is perfectly even, always work from the center out to the edge **[2]**. Keep rolling until the sheet of pasta is less than ⅟₃₂ inch thick (slightly thinner than a dime) **[3]**. At this point, it should be almost transparent. You can check by draping it over your hands **[4]**. It is now ready to be rolled and cut into noodles or used in a variety of ways.

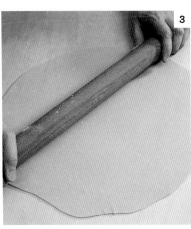

CUTTING PASTA DOUGH INTO NOODLES

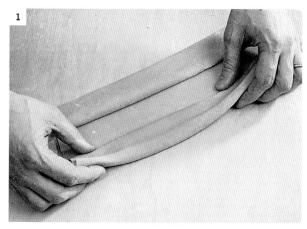

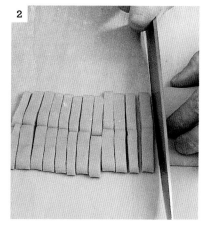

To cut long noodles by hand, first loosely roll up a thin sheet of pasta dough [1]. Next, use a very sharp chef's knife to cut the dough crosswise into ribbons ¼ inch wide for tagliatelle [2], ⅛ inch wide for fettuccine, ¹⁄₁₆ inch wide for tagliolini, and ⅝ inch wide for pappardelle.

To pick up the noodles, slide the chef's knife, flat side down and blade facing out, under half of the strands [3]. Lift while turning the blade down so that the noodles drape over the dull edge [4].

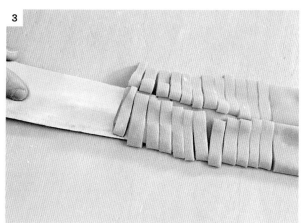

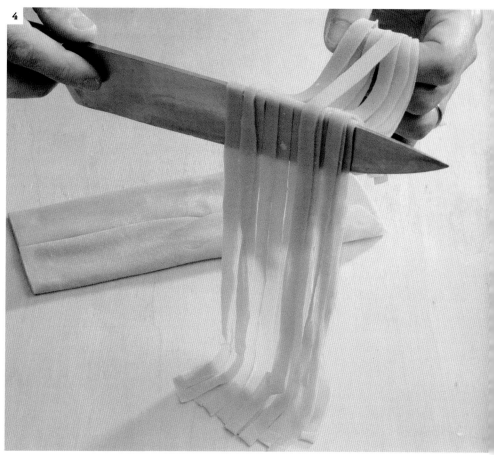

Tagliolini al burro tartufato

tagliolini with truffle butter

5 tablespoons dry white wine

⅓ cup thinly sliced shallot

8 tablespoons (1 stick) unsalted butter, cut into small pieces

½ teaspoon white truffle paste (see note)

1 cup freshly grated Grana Padano cheese

Egg tagliolini made with 4 eggs and 4 cups flour (page 78)

Flaky coarse sea salt

1. Bring a large pot of water to a boil and salt it.

2. Meanwhile, in a medium skillet, combine the wine and shallot. Heat over medium-high heat, stirring occasionally, until the wine has reduced by half, 3 to 4 minutes. Add the butter and truffle paste; continue to cook, stirring, until the butter has melted. Add ¼ cup water and stir to combine, then remove the pan from the heat. Add the cheese and stir to combine. Set the sauce aside.

3. Cook the pasta in the boiling water until tender, about 2 minutes. Reserving ½ cup of the pasta cooking liquid, drain the pasta and transfer it to a large serving bowl. Add the sauce and ¼ cup of the pasta cooking liquid; toss to combine well, then let sit for 1 to 2 minutes. Add more pasta cooking liquid to moisten, if necessary. Season with flaky coarse sea salt to taste. Serve immediately.

NOTE: *With this pasta, looks are deceiving. To the eyes, it's plain as can be, but its aroma tantalizes, and the flavor amazes. The butter sauce with white truffle paste really showcases the delicate taste of freshly made tagliolini. One bite and you will swoon. White truffle paste can be purchased at specialty food stores or online. See Sources on page 454.*

SERVES 4   COOKING TIME: 20 MINUTES (PLUS TIME TO MAKE THE TAGLIOLINI)

MACCHERONI ALLA CHITARRA

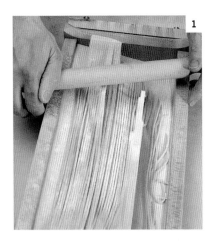

Make a dough of 2 cups semolina flour and 2 eggs, following the instructions on page 78. Set a large pot of water on the stove to boil. Let the dough rest for 10 minutes, then roll it out to a sheet ⅕ inch thick. Set a chitarra, a special tool with thin wires across the top used to make maccheroni, on a floured sheet pan and place the pasta sheet on the wires. Roll over the pasta with the rolling pin to press the noodles through the wire and onto the sheet pan [1]. To cook the pasta, salt the boiling water and add handfuls of the pasta to the pot; cook for 1 additional minute after the noodles rise to the surface [2]. Drain the pasta, reserving a little cooking water, and toss it with the sauce of your choice, using the cooking water to moisten the mixture as needed [3].

TAGLIATELLE CON PISELLI E PROSCIUTTO

tagliatelle with peas and prosciutto

Sauté 2 ounces diced prosciutto cotto in a large pan with about 1 tablespoon butter. Add 1 cup heavy cream and 3 ounces (about ¾ cup) cooked peas, and simmer until the cream has thickened slightly. Then add tagliatelle made with 4 eggs and 4 cups flour (page 78), cooked and drained, along with a ladleful of the pasta cooking water **[1]**. Remove the pan from the heat, toss the pasta in the sauce **[2]**, and serve immediately.

TROFIE AL PESTO

trofie in pesto with potatoes and green beans

To make trofie, mound 3 cups unbleached all-purpose flour in a large bowl and make a well in the center. Add 1 cup warm water (100 to 110 degrees F) to the well. Using a fork or your hand, slowly combine the flour and water. Continue until the liquid is absorbed, then knead the dough in the bowl until it forms a complete mass. Transfer it to a lightly floured work surface and knead until smooth, about 5 minutes. Wrap the dough in plastic and let it rest for 30 minutes. Line a baking sheet with parchment paper. Divide the pasta dough into 8 pieces. Cover 7 pieces with plastic wrap. On a clean surface, form 1 piece of dough by hand into a ½-inch-thick rope. Cut the rope crosswise into ¼-inch disks. Roll each disk between your hands to form a thin rope with tapered ends and transfer it to the prepared baking sheet. Repeat with the remaining dough.

Peel 12 ounces potatoes and cut them into slices. Boil them until they are just cooked through and then add the trofie to the same cooking water. When the pasta is al dente (3 to 4 minutes), add 10 ounces cooked green beans **[1]**. Place the pesto (page 52) in a warm serving bowl and thin it with a small amount of the pasta cooking water. Drain the pasta and the vegetables, transfer them to the bowl, toss with the pesto, and serve **[2]**.

85

GNOCCHI DI PATATE CLASSICI
classic potato gnocchi

To make gnocchi, cook potatoes with the skin left on in abundant boiling salted water; you will need about 2 pounds potatoes to serve 5 to 6 people [1]. Alternatively, you can steam the potatoes, but be sure they do not absorb too much water or overcook. Mash the potatoes with a potato ricer while they are still warm. (There's no need to peel them—the ricer will remove the skin for you.) Let the riced potatoes fall directly onto a work surface where you have mounded 1½ cups unbleached all-purpose flour [2]. Let the potatoes cool just until you can handle them comfortably, then mix them with the flour, using a bench scraper to help you. If the dough is so soft that it's impossible to handle, add a small amount of flour, but be careful not to add too much, as this can make the gnocchi heavy and dense [3]. Flavor the gnocchi dough with a pinch of grated nutmeg [4]. Knead vigorously. When the dough is smooth and the ingredients are well combined, cut the dough into several pieces and roll each one into a rope about ½ inch in diameter. Use a knife to cut each rope into gnocchi about ½ inch long [5]. Gently pressing down with your thumb, roll each piece along a wooden comb made for this purpose, the tines of a fork, or the back of a grater with small holes in order to create the classic grooved surface [6].

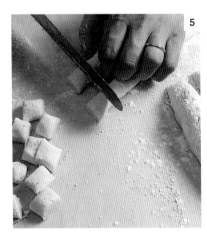

GNOCCHI DI ZUCCA

winter squash gnocchi

Seed about 1½ pounds winter squash, wrap in aluminum foil, and roast until soft. (See page 212 for more on preparing winter squash.) Mash the flesh with a potato ricer, along with ½ pound boiled potatoes **[1]**. Knead 2 cups unbleached all-purpose flour, ground cinnamon, grated nutmeg, and salt into the squash and potato mixture. (The dough for these may seem a little soft, but don't add any extra flour or they will become unpleasantly tough.) Shape the dough into ropes **[2]**, cut it, and create grooves on the surface of the gnocchi as described opposite **[3]**.

GNOCCHI DI SPINACI

spinach gnocchi

Boil 1 pound potatoes and rice them into 1¼ cups unbleached all-purpose flour **[1]**. Add 3½ ounces cooked spinach, squeezed dry and chopped; salt; and ¾ ounce grated Parmigiano Reggiano or Grana Padano cheese **[2]**. Knead to make a block of dough, then cut the dough into logs **[3]** and cut the logs into gnocchi.

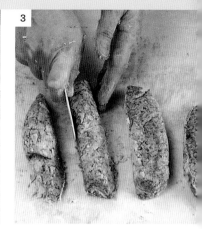

COOKING GNOCCHI

To cook gnocchi, bring a large pot of water to a boil, then salt it lightly (because the gnocchi dough is also salted). Toss in the potato or other gnocchi **[1]**. At first, the gnocchi will sink to the bottom of the pot. When they rise to the surface of the water, they are cooked. Use a slotted spoon or skimmer to remove them from the cooking water **[2]**. Transfer the gnocchi to a serving bowl **[3]**, topping each layer of gnocchi with grated Parmigiano Reggiano or another aged cheese **[4]** and the sauce of your choice. The simplest option for topping gnocchi is a generous amount of melted butter.

Gnocchetti primavera

small gnocchi with spring vegetables

1 leek, thinly sliced

2 tablespoons extra-virgin olive oil

1 cup thin ribbons of butter lettuce

Fine sea salt to taste

½ cup shelled peas

½ cup sliced asparagus

3 tablespoons unsalted butter

1 tablespoon minced fresh sage leaves

1 tablespoon minced fresh rosemary leaves

1 tablespoon minced fresh basil leaves

1 batch potato gnocchi dough (page 86), cut into ¼-inch gnocchetti

1. In a skillet, sauté the leek in the olive oil until softened. Add the lettuce and sauté until wilted, another minute or so. Season with salt and set aside.

2. Bring a large pot of water to a boil and salt it lightly. Blanch the peas and the asparagus until tender, about 3 minutes. Using a slotted spoon, transfer the vegetables to a plate and let the water return to a boil. In a small skillet, melt the butter and toss the minced herbs in the melted butter to flavor it.

3. Cook the gnocchetti in the boiling water, removing them with a slotted spoon or skimmer once they float to the top, about 3 minutes. Transfer them to a warm serving dish.

4. Add the asparagus and peas and the lettuce mixture to the gnocchetti. Pour the herb butter over them. Toss gently to combine and serve immediately.

SERVES 6   COOKING TIME: 20 MINUTES (PLUS TIME TO MAKE THE GNOCCHETTI)

CUSCUS

couscous

ouscous—semolina pasta that so closely resembles small grains that many people mistakenly believe couscous is a grain—was originally an Arab dish. It has long been a specialty in the Trapani area of Sicily, which was under Arab rule from 965 to 1072 and still exhibits a strong Arab influence today. In Sicily, couscous is frequently served with fish and shellfish. You can buy packaged couscous in a variety of sizes, and it needs only to be reconstituted with boiling water, but couscous that you make by hand is cooked by steaming. Making couscous isn't really difficult, though it is a bit time-consuming (mostly because of the steaming) and can get a little messy. It can be a fun communal activity, and the difference in taste and texture is noticeable. It's worth trying at least once.

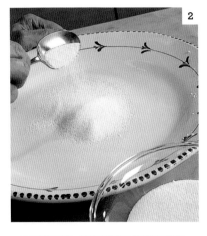

To make your own couscous, you will need a large plate or pan **[1]**. Spread out 2 or 3 tablespoons of semolina flour, depending on the size of the plate **[2]**, and shake it into a single even layer. Lightly salt about ¾ cup water and drizzle a little of this onto the flour (use 1 tablespoon for every 2 tablespoons of flour) **[3]**. Moving your open hand in a wide, spiral motion, spread the liquid through the flour **[4]**. Continue to move your hand in the same direction; rub the plate with your fingertips to dislodge any semolina that may stick there **[5]**.

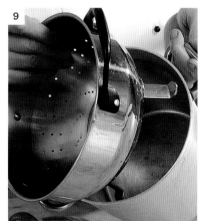

As you work, you will begin to see tiny clumps forming—about ¹⁄₁₆ inch in diameter **[6]**. Transfer this finished couscous to a clean dish **[7]** and repeat the process with more semolina flour and water. If you use 1½ cups semolina flour, you should get enough couscous for 3 to 4 portions of a main dish or 5 to 6 portions to serve as a side dish. Spread out the finished couscous in a single layer and drizzle on 2 to 3 tablespoons extra-virgin olive oil. Distribute the oil using your fingers **[8]**. If you have a traditional couscous steamer, use that to steam the couscous, but a reasonable facsimile can be created using a colander, cheesecloth, and a pot that is large enough to completely enlose the colander and that has a tight-fitting lid **[9]**. First fill the pot with enough water to reach just below the bottom of the colander. (It is important that the water not boil away completely after simmering for 2 hours.) Bring the water to a boil, line the colander with cheesecloth, and pour the couscous onto the cloth. Lower the heat to maintain a simmer, place the colander inside the pot, cover, and cook for 2 hours, fluffing up and mixing the couscous every 30 minutes **[10]**.

Umido di molluschi e cuscus

couscous with shellfish

12 green beans, cut into ½-inch lengths

1 pound small littleneck clams, scrubbed

1 pound Manila clams, scrubbed

¾ pound mussels, scrubbed and beards removed

9 tablespoons extra-virgin olive oil, plus more for drizzling

2 medium tomatoes, cut into ¼-inch dice

2 garlic cloves, gently smashed and peeled

1 teaspoon dried oregano

1 teaspoon finely chopped serrano chile

½ cup finely chopped carrot

½ cup finely chopped zucchini

½ cup finely chopped onion

⅓ cup drained canned chickpeas

About 1¾ cups steamed homemade couscous (page 90), or ¾ cup dried packaged couscous prepared according to package instructions

1. Cook the green beans in a saucepan of salted boiling water until crisp-tender, about 2 minutes. Drain and set aside.

2. In a large saucepan or heavy pot, combine the littleneck clams, Manila clams, mussels, and 3 tablespoons of the oil. Cook over medium heat, covered, just until the clams and mussels open wide, checking frequently after 3 minutes and transferring the open shellfish to a bowl using a slotted spoon. (Discard any shellfish that remain unopened after 10 minutes.) Strain the shellfish juices through a fine-mesh sieve into a second bowl.

3. Add 2 tablespoons of the oil and the tomatoes to same pot; bring them to a gentle simmer and cook, stirring occasionally, until the tomatoes are fragrant and slightly reduced, about 10 minutes. Stir in the shellfish juices, then remove the pot from the heat.

4. In a large skillet, heat the remaining ¼ cup oil over medium-high heat until hot but not smoking. Add the garlic, oregano, and chile; cook, stirring constantly, until the garlic just begins to brown, about 1 minute. Add the tomato mixture, carrot, zucchini, ¼ cup of the onion, and 1¼ cups water; cook, stirring occasionally, until the vegetables are tender, about 3 minutes. Stir in the green beans, chickpeas, both types of clams, and mussels; cook 1 minute, then remove the skillet from the heat and cover it to keep the contents warm.

5. Divide the couscous among serving bowls, then spoon shellfish, vegetables, and broth into the bowls. Drizzle with oil.

SERVES 4　　COOKING TIME: 30 MINUTES (PLUS TIME TO MAKE THE COUSCOUS)

Flavorful meat agnolotti, sweet squash tortelli, ravioli filled with ricotta and spinach. These little pasta packages containing various types of fillings are synonymous with holidays and celebration.

Stuffed Pasta

Stuffed pastas are almost all made using fresh egg pasta. They come in a wide variety of regional types and different shapes and fillings. The names used for the various types of filled pasta can be confusing, to say the least. Parma, for example, offers anolini, shaped like little broad-brimmed hats, and square tortelli that outside of that area are called ravioli. Bologna's cappelletti are known as agnolini in Mantua, while the agnolotti of Piedmont may be round or square. Panzerotti are usually half-moons and are often stuffed with ricotta and fresh herbs. But then there are oval ravioli and stuffed pasta in many other shapes as well.

All of this variety is enticing, but tortellini have long been the standard bearer of stuffed pasta. Tortellini hail from Bologna and are mentioned in Alessandro Tassoni's seventeenth-century poem *The Stolen Pail* and as far back as Giovanni Boccaccio's fourteenth-century *Decameron*. There is also a mention of tortellini in a fourteenth-century cookbook, where they are rendered as *torteleti de enula* and stuffed with enula, an herb that grows widely in the Emilia region. Tortellini are shaped like small rings and are said to be a representation of Venus's belly button.

Stuffed pasta should always be cooked gently—stir the pot too vigorously and the little pouches may open up and leak filling into the cooking water. Cook them in batches carefully removing them with a slotted spoon or skimmer shortly after they rise to the surface of the water.

TORTELLINI

PASTA

Pour 2¾ cups unbleached all-purpose flour onto a work surface and make a well in the center. Into the well add 3 eggs, 2 teaspoons extra-virgin olive oil (this makes the pasta easier to fold), and a pinch of salt [1]. Begin to combine the ingredients in the well, incorporating the flour a little at a time (for more detailed instructions, see page 78) [2]. When you have a uniform dough, knead it energetically until it is very smooth and elastic [3]. Wrap the pasta in plastic or cover it with an overturned bowl and allow it to rest for about 30 minutes before rolling it out.

FILLING

Brown 3½ ounces pork loin, cut into chunks, in 1 tablespoon or so of butter. Sprinkle in a few fresh sage leaves, the leaves from 1 sprig rosemary, a little sliced onion, and a pinch of freshly ground black pepper [1]. If desired, add a generous splash of dry white wine and allow it to evaporate. Sauté until the meat is cooked through, about 15 minutes [2]. Grind the cooked meat in a food processor fitted with the metal blade, along with 1 tablespoon of the pan juices, 4 ounces prosciutto crudo, and 4 ounces mortadella [3]. Add 6 ounces grated Parmigiano Reggiano cheese, 1 egg, and grated nutmeg; mix to combine [4].

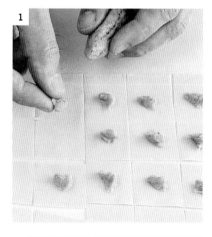

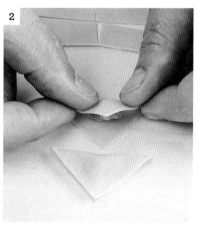

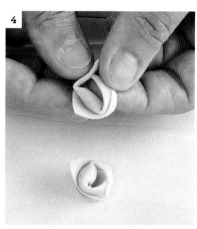

SHAPING

Roll the pasta into a very thin sheet and cut the sheet into 1½-inch squares. Place ¼ teaspoon filling in the center of each square [1]. Fold each square in half to form a triangle and seal the edges firmly. (If the pasta is dry, brush the edges with a small amount of water before folding.) [2] Fold up the base of each triangle to create a cuff [3], then wrap the base around the tip of your index finger with the fold on the outside to make a ring. Seal the two pointed ends together (again using a bit of water if needed), overlapping them slightly [4].

COOKING

Make a broth with 1½ pounds beef, ½ capon, celery, carrot, onion, salt, and 4 quarts water (see page 56). Skim the fat, filter the broth, and bring it to a low boil. Add the tortellini a few at a time. About 1 minute after they rise to the surface (this should happen fairly quickly), remove them with a slotted spoon and transfer them to serving dishes. Ladle broth over the cooked tortellini and serve.

CAPPELLETTI

The name of this stuffed pasta literally means "little hats" and refers to its resemblance to hats from the Middle Ages. The filling used for cappelletti is generally a little lighter and more delicate than the filling used for their cousins, tortellini. Cappelletti filling combines capon and fresh sheep's cheese with a bit of lemon zest. These are usually served floating in shallow bowls of broth, preferably made with capon.

 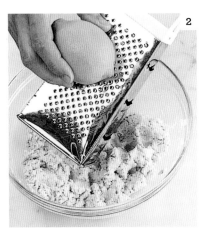 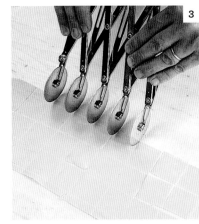

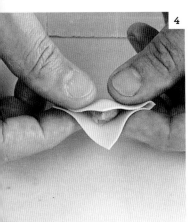 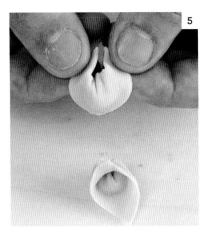 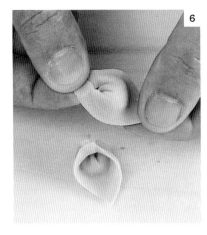

For the filling, season 1 pound boneless capon breast and 4 ounces pork loin to taste with salt, freshly ground black pepper, sage, and rosemary. Brown it in a large pot or Dutch oven in a combination of oil and butter. Cover and cook for 6 minutes. Turn the meat and cook it for an additional 10 minutes. Once the meat is cooked through, grind it very finely. In a bowl, combine the ground meat, 2 ounces crescenza cheese, 2 ounces ricotta cheese, 2 ounces grated Parmigiano Reggiano cheese, and 1 egg **[1]**. Add a little grated lemon zest, salt, and pepper, and mix to combine thoroughly **[2]**.

Prepare the pasta as for tortellini (page 96) using 2¾ cups unbleached all-purpose flour, 3 eggs, 1 tablespoon oil, and salt. Roll out the pasta very thin and cut it into 1½-inch squares. This can be accomplished more easily and quickly, not to mention more accurately, by using a pantograph **[3]**. Place a small amount of filling in the center of each square and fold each in half to make a triangle, sealing the sides together **[4]**. Bring the two ends of the base of each triangle together, overlapping slightly, and press gently to seal **[5, 6]**. Boil the freshly made cappelletti in capon or chicken broth (page 56). Remove them 1 minute after they float to the surface. Serve the cappelletti with the broth in which they are cooked.

ANOLINI

*T*he term *anolini* is used only in Parma, where it refers to a meat-filled pasta cut into circles with smooth edges. Anolini are served at the start of every Christmas and New Year's meal in the area, most traditionally in broth, but sometimes they are cooked in broth, then served with melted butter and grated aged cheese.

For the filling, in a heavy pot or Dutch oven, brown 1 pound cubed lean beef with oil, butter, and a soffritto (page 260) made of 1 carrot, 1 onion, and 1 stalk celery, all minced **[1]**. Add 1 tablespoon tomato paste, 1 cup red wine, 2 cloves, a pinch each of ground cayenne pepper and grated nutmeg **[2]**, and about 1 cup beef and capon broth (page 97). Bring the liquid to a boil, turn the heat down to maintain a simmer, and cook, covered, until the meat is extremely tender, about 1½ hours. Check occasionally and add ¼ to ½ cup broth if the pot is getting dry. When the meat is cooked, grind it. Then combine the ground meat with 3½ ounces grated Parmigiano Reggiano cheese, 1½ cups bread crumbs, 1 egg, and sea salt to taste.

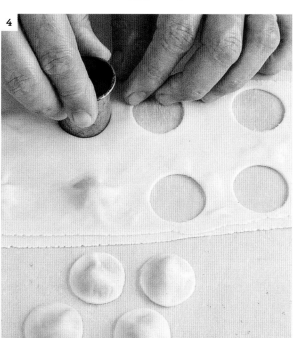

Prepare and roll out pasta as for tortellini (page 96). Cut it into strips and spoon small amounts of the filling onto one strip, making two rows and leaving 1½ inches between each portion of filling. Brush each strip with water, and place the water-brushed side down on the strip with the filling. Press around the filling to seal **[3]**. Cut out the anolini with a 1¼-inch round cutter **[4]**. Cook the anolini in the broth, using a slotted spoon or skimmer to remove them from the broth 1 minute after they float to the surface.

RAVIOLI DI PESCE

fish ravioli

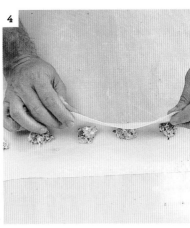

Fillet a 1-pound sea bass and skin the fillets, reserving the scraps and bones **[1]**. Cut the fillets into chunks and sauté them in a pan with oil and minced shallot and 1 small minced celery stalk until just cooked through, 2 to 3 minutes. Remove the cooked fillets with a slotted spoon and set aside. Add the scraps and bones to the pan and cook them briefly, then add ¼ cup white wine **[2]**. Add ¾ cup water and salt to taste and simmer for 15 to 20 minutes. Filter the resulting broth and reserve.

Mince the cooked fish fillets and combine them with minced parsley, ¼ cup bread crumbs, and salt and freshly ground black pepper to taste **[3]**. Prepare and roll out pasta as for tortellini (page 96). Cut the pasta into wide strips and arrange small amounts of the filling in a line down one side. Fold the empty half of the pasta strip over the filling **[4]**. Cut out the ravioli into half-moons using a small round cutter and leaving the folded edge of the pasta intact by aligning it with the diameter of the cutter **[5]**. Cook the ravioli in boiling salted water and remove them with a slotted spoon when they rise to the surface. While the ravioli are cooking, combine ½ cup heavy cream with the fish stock in a skillet and reduce the mixture. Add the drained ravioli to the skillet with the sauce and toss to combine **[6]**. Serve hot **[7]**.

OTHER FILLINGS FOR PASTA

VEGETABLE FILLING
Dice 2 trimmed artichokes, 2 large zucchini, 1 large carrot, ½ medium onion, and 1 bell pepper [1]. Cook the vegetables in oil, and add ½ cup heavy cream [2]. Cover the pan and simmer for 15 minutes. The mixture should be fairly dry. Season to taste with salt and freshly ground black pepper. Grind the cooked vegetables in a food processor fitted with the metal blade, or mince very fine by hand. Combine with grated Parmigiano Reggiano cheese [3].

Storing filled pasta

You can prepare very dry fillings, such as the filling used for cappelletti (page 98) a day in advance, but no sooner. Store the filling in the refrigerator. All stuffed pastas except those that contain fish can be frozen. Arrange the pieces in a single layer on a baking sheet and freeze. Once the individual pieces are thoroughly frozen, transfer them to plastic freezer bags for longer-term storage; they will keep for up to 3 months. Cook frozen pasta by adding it directly to boiling broth or water without defrosting. Cook the pieces for 2 to 3 minutes after they float to the surface.

RICOTTA AND SPINACH
Push 1 pound ricotta cheese through a sieve into a bowl [1]. Combine it with 7 ounces spinach that has been cooked, squeezed dry, and minced, preferably in a blender [2]. Season to taste with salt, freshly ground black pepper, and freshly grated nutmeg. Stir in 2 eggs and 2 ounces grated Parmigiano Reggiano cheese [3]. Fill the ravioli, cook them, and serve with butter and sage or tomato sauce.

Ravioli di borragine
borage ravioli

1 pound veal roast

Fine sea salt to taste

Freshly ground black pepper to taste

7 tablespoons extra-virgin olive oil

1 stalk celery, minced

1 small onion, minced

1 carrot, minced

1 sprig fresh sage

1 sprig fresh rosemary

3½ cups unbleached all-purpose flour

4 large eggs

Pinch saffron, crumbled and dissolved in 1 teaspoon room-temperature water

1 shallot, sliced

Leaves of 1 sprig thyme

1½ pounds borage (or other greens)

1 tablespoon grated Parmigiano Reggiano cheese, plus more for serving

5 tablespoons unsalted butter

1 tablespoon minced flat-leaf parsley

3 scallions, cut into quarters lengthwise

Leaves of 1 sprig marjoram, minced

1. Preheat the oven to 375 degrees F. Season the veal with salt and pepper. Combine ¼ cup of the oil with the minced celery, onion, and carrot. Spread in a Dutch oven. Add the sage and the rosemary, place the veal breast on top, cover, and roast for 50 minutes.

2. Meanwhile, mound the flour on a work surface. Make a well in the center, and add the eggs and the saffron. Beat the eggs with a fork, then begin working in the flour. When the mixture resembles a paste, knead by hand for 10 minutes, adding more flour as you work. Form the dough into a ball, wrap it in plastic, and let it rest for 30 minutes.

3. In a skillet, heat the remaining 3 tablespoons oil and cook the shallot and thyme until the shallot is transparent. Stir in the borage, cover, and cook for 5 minutes. Let the greens cool enough to be handled, then squeeze them dry and chop them, reserving their cooking liquid.

4. Remove the meat from the oven and set it aside to cool, covered, for 20 minutes. Reserve the pan juices. Chop the meat, then grind it in a food processor fitted with the metal blade. Add the borage and grated cheese and process again to combine.

5. Divide the pasta dough into 4 parts. Roll out each piece into sheets (page 80). Cut the dough into strips about 3 inches wide. Place 1 teaspoon of filling at regular intervals along a strip, brush the edges with water, and top with another strip of dough. Press out any air, and seal between the filling using your fingers. Use a 3-inch oval pasta cutter to cut oval ravioli (or use a knife or fluted pastry wheel to cut square ravioli). Set them aside on a floured surface.

6. Bring a large pot of water to a boil and salt it. To prepare the sauce, combine the borage cooking liquid with the pan juices from the meat and reduce by half. Stir in 3 tablespoons of the butter until it melts and season to taste with salt and pepper. Strain this sauce, discarding the solids, into a large serving bowl. Stir in the minced parsley. Meanwhile, in a small skillet heat the remaining 2 tablespoons butter and cook the quartered scallions until golden. Cook the ravioli in the boiling salted water, 3 to 4 minutes; transfer them to the serving bowl and toss gently with the sauce. Drizzle the scallion mixture over the ravioli, sprinkle with minced marjoram, and serve, passing additional grated cheese on the side.

SERVES 6　　COOKING TIME: 1 HOUR 30 MINUTES

 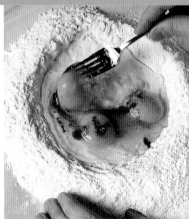 

R

ICE HAS LONG BEEN ONE OF THE BEST SOURCES OF NUTRITION
for man. Research shows that wild rice, the ancestor to the varieties we eat today, was a major food
source for prehistoric populations in a large area that stretches from eastern India to southern China.
Rice was already widely used in the Near East before the fourth century B.C., and from there, it spread
to Egypt and then the Mediterranean. Rice was originally considered medicinal, and it remained in
that role through the Middle Ages and the Renaissance, until Ludovico Sforza offered incentives
for growing it as food during the late fifteenth century. As a result, swampy areas in Lombardy were
transformed into rice farms. Rice became a star of Milanese cuisine, where it appears not only in the
famous Milanese risotto with saffron, but also in delicious riso al salto, a crispy rice patty traditionally
made with leftover risotto. In Italy, short-grain rice is grown almost exclusively, rather than long-grain
types, such as basmati. There are many varieties grown in Italy, but the most common are Carnaroli,
Arborio, and Vialone Nano, all of which share a unique characteristic that makes them perfect for
risotto: the outside of the grains gives off a substantial amount of starch when cooked, contributing
to the creaminess of the dish.

Rice is extraordinarily versatile, delicate, and pleasantly sweet, though its flavor is not overpowering,
so it beautifully reflects the taste of any ingredients paired with it. The combination of rice and saffron
is a classic, but risotto made with such additions as mushrooms, sausage, or seafood has many fans as
well. Rice can be used for more than risotto, of course—it is a key ingredient in refined dishes such as
sartù, a Neapolitan rice timbale; it can be used to create stuffings for vegetables; and it is used for the
justly famous arancini of Sicily, one of Italy's most beloved street foods.

RICE

Satisfying, healthy, and nutritious, rice has long been one of the major food sources on Earth and is widely grown. In Italy, rice is served mainly in the North.

VARIETIES of RICE

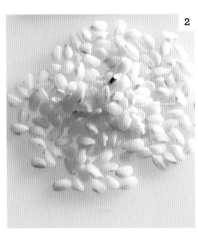

1] ORIGINARIO Plain short-grain white rice, with its small, round, pearly grains, is ideal for making rice pudding, because it absorbs a lot of water and because, when fully cooked, it is slightly gluey and its grains are not distinct from one another. Unlike rice used for risotto, this type of rice should be rinsed briefly before cooking.

2] VIALONE NANO This variety of rice has a strong aroma that increases in intensity as it cooks. The small, round grains absorb both liquid and flavorings, and it releases just the right amount of starch for a perfect risotto. Vialone Nano is often used in recipes from the area around Mantua, where it is grown. Local favorites include risotto with winter squash and risotto alla pilota, a hearty dish made with local salami that was created for workers in rice mills.

3] CARNAROLI This variety is the king of risotto. As it cooks, its large tapered grains stay firm, remain separate, and absorb so much liquid that they are visibly enlarged at the end of cooking. Because Carnaroli rice can absorb so much, it has a somewhat longer cooking time, allowing it to take on more intense flavoring.

4] PADANO This round-grained, medium-sized rice is good for making creamy risotto that is on the soft side. It also is an excellent choice for rice croquettes and riso in cagnone, a simple dish of boiled rice with garlic, butter, and sage.

5] BALDO This is another excellent choice for risotto, and its slightly longer grains ensure that the results will be creamy, yet the grains will remain separate from one another. Baldo is very versatile, and in addition to risotto, it can be used in soups, rice tarts, and timbales.

ARBORIO This short-grain rice has a center that remains very firm even after long cooking, making it ideal if you prefer a more al dente risotto. It is named for the town of Arborio, in the Po river valley.

BOILED RICE

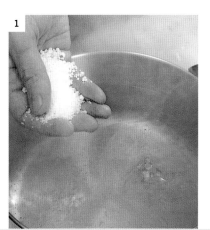

Simple boiled rice may be eaten with a little butter or oil and grated cheese (preparations that are particularly soothing for overworked stomachs) or used in more complex dishes. To boil rice, bring a large amount of water (at least twice the volume of the uncooked rice) to a boil in a large pot. Salt the water and add the rice. After the water returns to a boil, turn down the heat to maintain a simmer and cook for 12 to 15 minutes, stirring occasionally. Drain and serve.

TOASTED RICE

If you want to prepare a good risotto, always start by toasting the rice in butter or oil over medium heat for 2 minutes **[1]**. The rice should be very hot, almost too hot to touch—you can test it by touching it briefly with the back of your hand **[2]**. You should not be able to keep your hand near it for more than a second. If you listen carefully, you'll also hear the sound that the rice makes as it toasts. When it is properly toasted, it emits a kind of squeaking noise.

RISOTTO BIANCO AL PARMIGIANO

risotto with parmesan cheese

Mince ½ small onion very finely. Sauté it over low heat in a small amount of oil until it is just golden and all the liquid has evaporated. The lighter the color of the onion, the more delicate the flavor of the risotto will be [1]. Add 1½ cups Carnaroli rice. Toast the rice (see page 107) for 1 to 3 minutes, stirring continuously so that it doesn't stick [2]. As soon as the rice begins to stick to the bottom of the pan, add ½ cup dry white wine and continue to cook, stirring continuously, until it has evaporated [3].

Add a ladleful (about ½ cup) hot beef broth (it's best to keep the broth in a small pot at a simmer while you work) and continue to cook, stirring continuously, until almost all the broth has been absorbed. Add another ladleful and repeat this process, always waiting until the previous addition has been almost completely absorbed before adding more broth. The rice should be fully cooked after 16 to 20 minutes [4]. Remove the risotto from the heat and add 3 to 4 tablespoons butter, stirring until it melts [5]. Add 1½ ounces grated Parmigiano Reggiano cheese, and stir to combine [6]. Serve immediately.

Risotto alla milanese

milanese risotto

8¼ cups beef stock (page 55)

Pinch saffron threads

5 tablespoons unsalted butter

1½ ounces marrow

1 small onion, sliced

2½ cups Carnaroli rice or other rice for risotto

½ cup dry white wine

⅔ cup freshly grated Parmigiano Reggiano cheese

Fine sea salt to taste

1. Place the broth in a small pot. Bring it to a boil, then turn down the heat to maintain a simmer. Ladle out ¼ cup of the broth into a small bowl, crumble the saffron into the broth, and set it aside.

2. In a large skillet or saucepan, melt 2 tablespoons of the butter over low heat. Add the marrow and onion and cook over very low heat for 15 minutes. Do not allow the onion to brown.

3. Remove the onion with a slotted spoon and discard it. Add the rice to the pan. Toast (see page 107), stirring, until the rice becomes translucent. Add the wine and cook, stirring, until it is mostly absorbed. When you draw a wooden spoon across the diameter of the pan, very little liquid should run into the space. Then add 1 cupful of the hot broth. Simmer, stirring frequently, until the broth is almost absorbed. Continue adding broth in ½ cupfuls, stirring constantly and allowing each addition to evaporate almost completely (use the spoon test above, but don't let the pan get so dry that the rice sticks) before adding the next, until the rice is tender but still slightly firm to the bite and the mixture is creamy.

4. When the rice is al dente and almost done, add the saffron liquid, straining it through a fine-mesh strainer.

5. Stir in the remaining 3 tablespoons butter, the Parmigiano Reggiano, and salt. Add 1 cup of broth, stir to combine, and serve immediately.

SERVES 6 ⬩ COOKING TIME: 30 MINUTES

Riso al Salto

Crispy Rice Cake

Whether you're using leftover risotto or you've made risotto just for this dish, crumble it with your fingers to separate the grains before beginning.

For best results, use a cast-iron or nonstick pan that is 6 to 8 inches in diameter. Heat the pan, add 1 or 2 tablespoons of butter over medium-high heat, and when it begins to sizzle, add 3 to 4 tablespoons of the cooked risotto, spreading it out so that it covers the bottom of the pan and is ½ inch to ¾ inch thick.

Cook, shaking the pan occasionally to move the rice cake. It is done when the edge is golden brown.

This crispy, savory cake is made with risotto alla Milanese (page 109) or risotto bianco al Parmigiano (page 108). It is an excellent way to use up leftovers, and the preparation is quick, too—just a few minutes in a hot pan, and it is ready in all its golden simplicity. It is so good that you may find yourself making risotto just so that you can have riso al salto. If that's the case, spread the freshly cooked risotto on a baking sheet and allow it to cool before continuing with the recipe.

To flip the rice cake, use a plate that is slightly smaller than the pan and turn the cake out onto it.

Slide the cake back into the pan and rub a small amount (about 1 table-spoon) of butter around the edge until it has melted.

Cook the cake for an additional 2 minutes, then invert it onto a serving plate. Serve it sprinkled with grated Parmigiano Reggiano cheese.

Sartù

neapolitan rice timbale

1 ounce dried wild mushrooms

5 tablespoons extra-virgin olive oil

1 small onion, thinly sliced

2 tablespoons tomato paste concentrate (from a tube)

7 cups chicken or beef broth (page 56), heated to a simmer

1 cup frozen peas

Fine sea salt

Freshly ground black pepper

⅓ pound pork sausage, in casing

⅔ pound ground beef

1 large egg

5 tablespoons freshly grated Parmigiano Reggiano cheese

5 tablespoons fine plain bread crumbs, plus more for the mold

3 tablespoons unbleached all-purpose flour

6 tablespoons unsalted butter, plus more for greasing the mold

4 ounces chicken livers, cut into small pieces

2½ cups Arborio rice

4 ounces fresh mozzarella cheese, cut into cubes

1. Soak the mushrooms in 2 cups hot water for 20 minutes; drain them, reserving the liquid, and finely chop.

2. Preheat the oven to 350 degrees F.

3. In a large saucepan, heat 2 tablespoons of the oil over medium-high heat. Add the onion and cook, stirring occasionally, until softened, about 5 minutes. Dilute the tomato paste in 1 cup of the broth, then add it to the pan with the onion. Add the mushrooms, peas, and a pinch of salt and pepper; bring the liquid to a simmer. Add the sausage and simmer, covered, until it is nearly cooked through, about 10 minutes. Transfer it to a cutting board and slice it into ¼-inch pieces. Return the pieces to the saucepan and simmer, uncovered, until the liquid is mostly evaporated, about 10 minutes more. Remove the pan from the heat.

4. In a bowl, stir together the beef, egg, 1 tablespoon of the Parmigiano Reggiano, 1 tablespoon of the bread crumbs, ¼ teaspoon salt, and ¼ teaspoon pepper. Form the mixture into 1½-inch balls.

5. In a large skillet, heat the remaining 3 tablespoons oil over medium-high heat until hot but not smoking. Dust the meatballs lightly with flour and, working in 2 batches, fry them until golden on all sides, about 5 minutes. Drain on paper towels. Drain the oil from the skillet and wipe it clean with paper towels. Melt 1 tablespoon of the butter in the skillet over medium-high heat. Add the chicken livers and a pinch of salt; cook, stirring occasionally, until the livers are cooked through, about 2 minutes. Add these and the meatballs to the pan with the sausage; stir to combine.

6. Bring the remaining 6 cups broth and the mushroom liquid to a boil in a large saucepan. Add the rice, reduce the heat to medium-low, and cook until the rice is al dente, about 8 minutes. Drain the rice and transfer to a large bowl. Stir in 4 tablespoons of the butter and the remaining 4 tablespoons Parmigiano Reggiano while still warm.

7. Grease a 2-quart mold or ovenproof bowl with butter and dust it with bread crumbs. Put 1½ cups of the rice mixture into the bowl and press it into the base and up the sides, forming a well in the center. Pour the meat sauce into the well, top it with mozzarella, then cover it with the remaining rice. Dot the rice with the remaining 1 tablespoon butter, cut into small pieces, and sprinkle it with the remaining 4 tablespoons bread crumbs. Bake for 1 hour.

8. Transfer the mold to a wire rack and let it cool for 10 minutes. Run a knife around the edges of the mold to loosen the rice, then invert it onto a large serving plate. Serve immediately.

SERVES 6   COOKING TIME: 2 HOURS

RICE CROQUETTES, ARANCINI, and RICE TIMBALE USING LEFTOVER RISOTTO

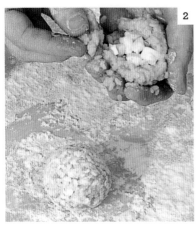

CROQUETTES AND ARANCINI

Combine 2 tablespoons grated aged cheese such as Parmigiano Reggiano and 1 egg with about 10 ounces cold leftover risotto alla Milanese (page 109) or risotto bianco al Parmigiano (page 108). Stir to combine [1]. Form some of the rice mixture into a ball, about 1½ inches in diameter. Use your thumb to make an indentation; press diced mozzarella and pieces of prosciutto cotto into the indentation, then seal it up with a little more of the rice mixture [2]. Repeat until you have used all of the rice mixture. Round the balls again between your palms and dredge them in flour, then egg, and then bread crumbs [3]. Brown the rice croquettes in a generous amount of hot oil, drain them, and blot them on butcher's paper or paper towels. Serve cold or hot [4]. To make arancini, use ragù and grated pecorino Romano cheese for the filling in place of the mozzarella and prosciutto.

TIMBALE

Preheat the oven to 400 degrees F. Butter a mold (6 inches in diameter and 4 inches high) and line the bottom with a disk of parchment paper. Arrange diced prosciutto cotto, slices of scamorza cheese, and cooked peas on the bottom. Cover with a generous amount of cold risotto bianco al Parmigiano (page 108), spreading it out to the edge so that it creates a wall around the perimeter of the mold [1]. In the center, arrange two layers of scamorza cheese slices (9 ounces) and diced prosciutto cotto (5 ounces). Cover with additional cold risotto and smooth the top to make it even [2]. Cook the timbale in a bain-marie (a large, shallow pan of warm water) in the oven for 20 to 25 minutes. Unmold and serve hot.

RISOTTO CON LE VERDURE
vegetarian risotto

Mince 3 trimmed scallions and 1 ounce celery; dice 5 ounces zucchini, 5 ounces carrots, and 3 stalks asparagus, reserving the tips. Heat about 5 cups vegetable broth to a simmer, then blanch the asparagus tips in it and set them aside; return the broth to a simmer. Cook the scallions and celery in a small amount of extra-virgin olive oil until they have given up all their liquid. Toast 1½ cups Vialone Nano rice for a minute or so (see page 107), then add ½ cup white wine **[1]**. When the wine has evaporated, add the diced vegetables and 3 ounces fresh shelled peas or snap peas **[2]**. Cook as for risotto (page 108) using the hot vegetable broth. When the rice is cooked, stir in 7 tablespoons butter **[3]**. After the butter has melted, add 2 ounces grated Parmigiano Reggiano cheese and serve with the blanched asparagus tips.

The right tool

A COPPER POT

A tin-lined copper pot is ideal for cooking risotto. The thick bottom retains heat and makes it easy to brown the rice without scorching it. As you add broth by the ladleful, the uniform distribution of heat allows it to evaporate slowly. If you do purchase a copper pot, however, keep in mind that when copper comes into contact with acidic foods, dangerous amounts of the metal may leach into them. That's why a high-quality pot will have a copper exterior for better distribution of heat, but it will be lined with tin. Always read labels carefully—look for a pot that has been lined manually using pure tin. It is important to use only wooden or rubber utensils in such pots to avoid scratching the lining. A copper pot with a stainless steel lining is an acceptable alternative.

115

THE FOODS WE CALL GRAINS INCLUDE MANY PLANTS IN THE GRAMINEAE, or Poaceae, family of grasses (an exception is buckwheat, which belongs to the Polygonaceae family). Since ancient times, man has valued grain as a food source that can be stored long term, is easy to transport, is highly nutritious, and can be eaten whole or ground into flour to make bread and flatbreads. After rice, the oldest cultivated grain is barley: Traces of it have been found in a prehistoric village in France dating back 10,000 years. Wheat was first cultivated in 3000 B.C. in Egypt. Cultivation of grains quickly spread, though the various grains grown depended on climatic and environmental aspects—something that is still true today when it comes to growing, processing, and consuming grains: Oats and rye are more popular in colder areas, while wheat, barley, and rice are more common to more temperate areas.

Many traditional Italian recipes, both savory and sweet, employ whole grains. Sicily's *cuccìa* is a traditional dish of Palermo. It features boiled wheat sweetened with ricotta, sugar, chocolate, and candied fruit; it also exists in a savory version flavored with oil, salt, and pepper. Naples has its own ricotta and wheat pie, called *pastiera*, an Easter specialty, while barley appears in soups in the Veneto, and farro is widely used in Tuscany and Umbria. Even buckwheat appears in the form of buckwheat polenta and *pizzoccheri*, or buckwheat noodles, in Valtellina.

OTHER GRAINS

Farro, barley, and buckwheat are not seen on the Italian table as frequently as rice, but they are traditionally cooked in certain regions.

GRAIN BASICS

WITH THE EXCEPTION OF FARRO AND BARLEY, which may be sold pearled, that is, stripped of the hull and bran, whole grains should be soaked for several hours before cooking. Unless otherwise indicated, rinse them under running water to eliminate any dust and, especially if you buy your grains in bulk, do a quick check for any extraneous pieces. Once they've soaked, whole grains are ready to be boiled, usually in two to three times as much water as grain, since they absorb a lot of liquid. They may also be cooked in broth or milk.

1] FARRO This ancient grain has seen a renaissance in Italy in recent decades after being largely forgotten for years. Farro with the hulls still on should be soaked and will cook in 45 minutes; pearled farro will cook in 30 minutes without soaking. Farro is delicious in soups and also makes a wonderful base for vegetable salads. It is also ground into flour that is used to make hearty whole grain pasta.

2] CORN Corn is a highly versatile grain prized around the world. In Italy, corn is most commonly seen in the form of polenta, which is made of the dried, ground kernel. When cooked, polenta transforms into a hearty, smooth dish that pairs beautifully with earthy toppings such as sausages or mushrooms.

3] BARLEY With the hulls on, barley cooks in 45 minutes after it is soaked. Pearled barley does not need to be soaked and will cook in about 30 minutes. Barley is excellent in soups and salads and is also cooked risotto style to make orzotto.

4] BUCKWHEAT Buckwheat is actually not a grain, but since it is always treated as one, it's included here. Buckwheat groats (the kasha of Eastern Europe) are not commonly eaten in Italy, but buckwheat is ground into flour that is used in the North to make a type of polenta known as polenta taragna and flat noodles called pizzoccheri that are traditionally paired with potatoes, cabbage, and cheese.

POLENTA

Polenta isn't complicated, but it is time-consuming. Standard Italian polenta is labeled polenta bramata. In gourmet and Italian import stores, you may also see polenta taragna, with buckwheat (good with very hearty toppings); polenta bianca, a more delicate and finely ground white corn polenta; and polenta integrale, or whole-grain corn polenta.

To cook polenta, bring 13 cups of water to a boil in a Dutch oven or other strong, heavy pot. When the water is boiling, add 1 tablespoon salt and turn the temperature down to maintain a simmer. Drizzle in 3 cups polenta very slowly. Stir constantly with a wooden spoon as you do this, making sure no lumps form. (If they do, smash them against the side of the pot with the back of the spoon.) After you are sure the polenta is completely smooth, cook at a simmer, stirring constantly, until it is very thick, pulls away from the side of the pot, and tastes cooked rather than raw, about 45 minutes. As the polenta thickens, it will bubble like lava and may splash up and burn you, so you may want to wear oven mitts or protect your hands and wrists in some other way as you cook it.

Serve polenta hot with ragù or sausages. It needs a sauce or accompaniment hearty and substantial enough to stand up to it.

Leftover polenta

Because making polenta can be a chore, it's sensible to cook the entire package at one time, though you probably won't be able to eat it all unless you're serving a crowd. (Polenta is very filling.) Leftover polenta, however, is a treat. Spread any leftover polenta into a thin layer on a sheet pan or plate while it's still warm and allow it to cool; it will form a solid cake that will lift off in one piece.

You can cut the cooled polenta into slices and crisp them up in a pan with a little oil or brush them with oil and grill. Slices of toasted or grilled polenta can be used in place of bread with crostini, served with baccalà mantecato (see page 337) spread on top, or topped with sauce and eaten. They can even be sprinkled with cinnamon and sugar and eaten for breakfast. Thin slices of cooked, cooled polenta can also be layered with ragù and béchamel, topped with grated cheese, and baked in the style of the lasagne on page 36.

FARRO and WHEATBERRIES

FARRO SOUP

Cook 4 ounces diced pancetta with a clove of garlic until the pancetta renders its fat, then add 1 sliced onion and sauté until golden **[1]**. Add 10 ounces (2 to 3) chopped tomatoes, parsley, basil, and salt. Cook the tomatoes until soft, then add ¾ cup farro **[2]**. Pour in 6 cups broth (page 56) and simmer until the farro is soft, about 30 minutes for pearled farro and 45 minutes for soaked hulled farro **[3]**. Serve hot with a generous amount of freshly ground black pepper **[4]**.

BOILED FARRO FOR SOUPS

If the farro is not pearled, soak it in cold water for 4 to 5 hours. Drain and rinse **[1]**. Boil the soaked farro in salted boiling water with a bay leaf until tender but not fully cooked, 20 to 45 minutes, tasting frequently **[2]**. Drain, add the partially cooked farro to the soup of your choice (chickpea soup and vegetable soup are two traditional options), and finish cooking **[3]**.

PASTIERA (NEAPOLITAN RICOTTA AND WHEAT PIE)

Combine the contents of a 1-pound jar cooked wheat-berries (available in Italian and gourmet groceries), 1 cup whole milk, 1 vanilla bean, and 1 cinnamon stick in a small pot and cook until very creamy and dense. Remove and discard the vanilla bean and cinnamon stick and set the pan aside to cool to room temperature **[1]**. Combine 14 ounces fresh ricotta cheese with 5 egg yolks, ¾ cup sugar, 4 ounces diced candied orange and citron peel, grated lemon zest, and a splash of orange flower water **[2]**. Add the cooked wheat mixture **[3]** and then beat 2 egg whites into stiff peaks and fold them into the wheat mixture. To make the crust for the pie, cut 2 tablespoons butter and 2¾ ounces lard into 5 cups unbleached all-purpose flour mixed with a pinch of salt until the combination has the texture of very fine meal. Add ¾ cup sugar, 1 egg, and 1 egg yolk. Knead to combine, shape the dough into a ball, wrap it in plastic, and refrigerate until firm, at least 30 minutes. Roll about two-thirds of the dough into a disk and gently fit it into the bottom of a 10-inch springform pan. Make a thick rope of one-half of the remaining dough and press it around the border of the dough in the pan, then use your fingers to build it up the side, making it an even thickness and height. Pour in the filling and spread it evenly over the dough. Roll the remaining half of the dough into an oblong shape 10 inches long and cut it into strips. Arrange the strips into a lattice on top of the pie and bake at 350 degrees F until the filling is set (a knife inserted into the center should come out clean) and the crust is nicely browned, about 1 hour and 30 minutes. If the crust begins to look too dark and the filling is not set yet, cover the pan loosely with aluminum foil **[4]**.

Orzotto

risotto-style barley

4 cups chicken stock (page 55)

3 tablespoons extra-virgin olive oil

1 clove garlic, crushed

1 pound Catalogna chicory or escarole

Fine sea salt to taste

1 small onion, minced

4 ounces pancetta, diced

1½ cups pearl barley

½ cup dry white wine

Freshly ground black pepper to taste

2 tablespoons unsalted butter

¼ cup freshly grated Parmigiano Reggiano cheese

1. Place the stock in a small pot, bring it to a boil, then turn down the heat to maintain a simmer. In a large pot, heat 1 tablespoon of the olive oil. Add the garlic and then the chicory or escarole. Season with salt and cook until wilted, about 5 minutes. Set aside to cool.

2. In a heavy-bottomed pot over medium heat, heat the remaining 2 tablespoons olive oil. Add the onion and pancetta; sauté until the onion is transparent. Add the barley and toast for 2 minutes, stirring occasionally.

3. Add the wine and cook, stirring constantly, until it is absorbed. Season with salt and pepper, and begin adding the stock in ½-cup increments, stirring constantly. Wait until the liquid is absorbed before adding more stock. (If you run a wooden spoon through the barley, very little liquid should run into the empty space.) After 20 minutes, squeeze as much water as possible from the chicory, chop it, and add it to the barley. Continue to cook until the barley is al dente, about 30 minutes.

4. When the orzotto is done, remove the pan from the heat and adjust the seasoning with salt and pepper. Stir in the butter and cheese, and mix well. Serve immediately.

SERVES 4   COOKING TIME: 35 MINUTES

ORZOTTO with SAUSAGE

Cook a soffritto (page 260) of minced onion, celery, carrot, and a bay leaf in extra-virgin olive oil until softened. Add 4 ounces Italian sausage, casings removed, in chunks [1]. Cook, stirring continuously, until browned. Add 1½ cups pearl barley (no need to soak) and cook, stirring constantly, for 2 minutes [2]. Add about ½ cup dry white wine and then cook as directed opposite with vegetable broth until tender [3]. Stir in a tablespoon or so of butter and some grated Grana Padano cheese.

*L*EAFY GREENS ARE NUTRITIOUS AND DELICIOUS. Perhaps the most difficult part of cooking them is simply getting them clean. To do this, soak the greens in several changes of water until the water is perfectly clear and no grains of sand settle to the bottom. (A salad spinner is very useful for this.) Take heart from the knowledge that dirtier greens are probably local—they haven't had a chance to shake off the soil in which they were grown.

In Italy, cooked spinach and other greens (either cultivated or foraged in the wild) provide one of the most common side dishes. They are cooked in the water that clings to their leaves after they are cleaned, squeezed dry, and chopped, and served either *all'agro*—with lemon juice and oil—or sautéed *all'aglio e olio*—with garlic and oil. Spinach, chard, and the like are also used in savory tarts and as filling for ravioli. Lettuce and very tender greens are often featured in salads. Indeed, it's the rare meal in Italy that doesn't include a salad of some kind, whether as a side dish or—usually with the addition of cheese, canned tuna, or hard-boiled eggs—as a light entrée in its own right. Italians also prepare dishes with cooked lettuce, which transforms it.

LEAFY GREENS

Leafy greens range from spinach and chard to all kinds of crisp lettuce. More delicate leafy greens grow in the spring, but winter offers hardier types, like kale, which is terrific in soup or sautéed for a side dish.

CHARD AND SPINACH

CHARD (Swiss chard is the most common type available in the United States) is a type of green with white, red, or orange stalks. The leaves are usually green in color, but red chard is also available. Chard is actually beet greens grown for the greens—in other words, without the edible beetroot attached. Spicy mustard greens can be substituted, as can kale. Unless they are extremely tender, these greens are best cooked at least briefly. Because the leaves cook more quickly than the stems, many recipes will instruct you to cut away the stems and cook them separately. If you find yourself with some chard stems left over after preparing a recipe that uses leaves only, sauté or braise them on their own for a quick and interesting side dish. Spinach can be eaten both raw in salads and cooked. It wilts very quickly when cooked, so it can be used to make an easy, fast vegetable side dish.

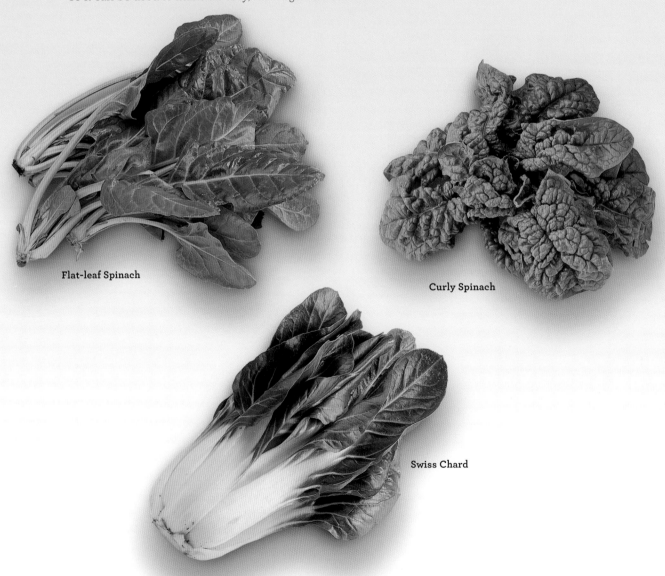

Flat-leaf Spinach

Curly Spinach

Swiss Chard

WORKING WITH LEAFY GREENS

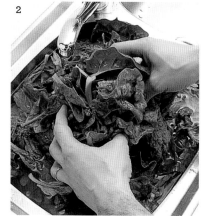

CLEANING SPINACH AND OTHER GREENS

Greens, and especially spinach, must be cleaned very thoroughly to remove sand and grit. Fill a sink, large bowl, or salad spinner with a generous amount of cold water [1]. Swish the leaves around with your hands, let them rest for a moment (you want any dirt to fall to the bottom), and then lift them out (or lift up the basket from the salad spinner) [2]. Repeat until you no longer see even one grain of sand in the sink or bowl when you lift up the greens—this can take three or more rounds. Once the greens are clean, they're ready to be used [3]. For most cooked preparations, there's no need to dry the greens—they will steam in the water that clings to the leaves after washing.

STEMMING BUNCH SPINACH

By hand, break the external spinach leaves off of the bunch, discarding any that are yellow or damaged [1]. When only the small inner leaves remain, cut away the root end of the bunch with a paring knife and discard it [2]. Hold the larger external leaves together in one hand and use a paring knife in the other to cut away their thick stems [3].

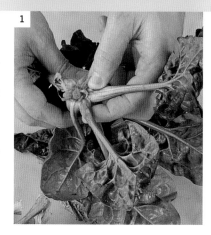

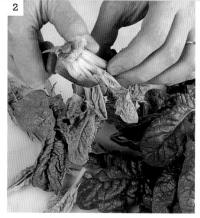

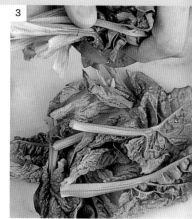

WORKING WITH LEAFY GREENS

STEMMING LOOSE-LEAF SPINACH AND OTHER GREENS
Hold the leaves in one hand, all facing in one direction, and with the other, use a paring knife to cut away the stems at the base of the leaves. Stemmed greens will weigh about one-third less than whole greens.

 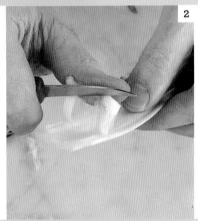

REMOVING RIBS FROM GREENS
The central ribs of larger greens usually require longer cooking times than the leaves, so you'll want to cut them out and cook them separately. First, use a sharp paring knife to make a V-shaped cut along the sides of the ribs. There's no need to remove the narrow part at the top, just the thick stalk **[1]**. If the rib is so thick that it feels fibrous, peel away and discard the stringy outer layer **[2]**.

 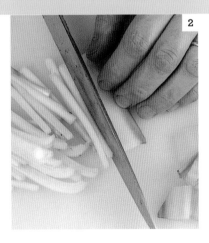

CUTTING GREENS INTO CHIFFONADE AND JULIENNE
To cut chiffonade, stack the leaves together and use a chef's knife to slice them into very thin ribbons **[1]**. To julienne the ribs, cut them into 2-inch chunks with a chef's knife, then into matchsticks **[2]**.

FREEZING SPINACH

Blanch spinach in boiling salted water for 1 minute, then remove it with a slotted spoon [1] and transfer it immediately to a bowl of ice water to preserve the color and stop the cooking process [2]. Drain but do not squeeze the spinach. Blot it dry on paper towels. At this point, the spinach can be frozen. See additional instructions for freezing vegetables on page 196.

Purchasing spinach

Freshness is always essential when buying vegetables, but doubly so when purchasing spinach, which can turn rather quickly. Look for leaves that are a deep green color with no yellowing, a minimum of torn leaves, and no dark or soft spots. Fresh spinach should be refrigerated no longer than two days, but really it's best to use it within a day of purchase. Spinach is also available frozen. While fresh is best, of course, and you wouldn't want to use frozen spinach in a dish where the spinach flavor and texture are front and center, such as a side dish of sautéed spinach, frozen spinach can be useful in dishes where the spinach will be chopped up and combined with other ingredients. Look for a high-quality brand, organic if possible. Avoid canned spinach completely. Frozen spinach doesn't need to be cooked before it is used in a recipe. Simply thaw it and continue as instructed.

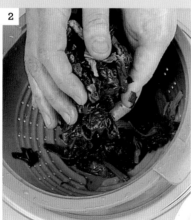

STEAMING SPINACH

Place washed spinach with water still clinging to its leaves in a pot, cover, and steam until soft, 4 to 5 minutes [1]. Drain the spinach and squeeze it with your hands to remove as much water as possible [2]. You can refrigerate cooked spinach for 2 to 3 days. Place a plate upside down in the storage container and rest the spinach on top of it—that will allow any remaining water to drain off so that the spinach doesn't get soggy [3].

SPINACH TARTS, BAKED SPINACH, and SPINACH DUMPLINGS

TORTA VERDE PIEMONTESE (PIEDMONT RICE AND SPINACH TART)
In a pot, heat ¼ cup extra-virgin olive oil and 5 tablespoons butter, and sauté
1 minced onion, 2 ounces diced fatback or pancetta, and 2 pounds cleaned,
chopped spinach until the spinach wilts. Add ¾ cup short-grain Italian rice
and cook about halfway, until the rice is soft on the inside but still has a hard
center, by adding hot broth in small amounts and letting it simmer to incorporate between additions. You will need about ¾ cup broth total. Remove the rice
mixture from the heat. Once it's cool, stir in 4 eggs, ½ cup grated Parmigiano
Reggiano cheese, a little nutmeg, and salt to taste [1]. Oil a pie plate or other
baking dish and coat the surface with a generous amount of bread crumbs.
Transfer the rice mixture to the pie plate, smooth the top with a spatula, sprinkle with more bread crumbs and grated cheese, and bake at 350 degrees F until
set, about 1 hour [2].

TORTA ALLE ERBE (SAVORY TART WITH GREENS)
Steam 2½ pounds spinach or other greens and squeeze
dry (page 129) [1]. Make a dough with 1¼ cups unbleached
all-purpose flour, a few tablespoons lard or butter, and
enough water to make it pliable and soft. Divide the dough
into 2 pieces, one slightly larger than the other. Roll out the
larger piece into a disk and place it on a lightly oiled pizza
pan or parchment-lined baking sheet. Chop the greens and
moisten them with some extra-virgin olive oil, then combine them with grated Parmigiano Reggiano cheese and
salt to taste. Spread the filling over the bottom crust, leaving a 1-inch margin. Roll out the smaller piece of dough to
a disk, place it on top of the filling, and fold the edge of the
bottom disk of dough up over the top disk, crimping as you
go and pressing to seal the pastry. Bake at 350 degrees F
until golden, about 1 hour. Serve at room temperature [2].

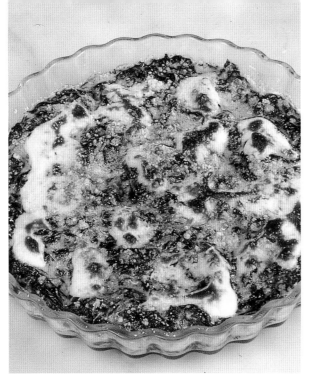

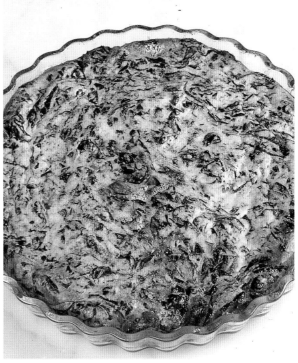

SPINACH FLORENTINE

Make 1¼ cups béchamel (see page 57). Steam 2 pounds spinach and squeeze it dry (see page 129). Chop and sauté the spinach in a skillet with extra-virgin olive oil and minced garlic. Salt to taste. Stir the spinach together with ¼ cup of the béchamel and ¾ cup grated Parmigiano Reggiano cheese. Transfer the mixture to a baking dish, top it with an additional ½ cup to 1 cup béchamel, and bake at 400 degrees F until the top is brown, 15 to 20 minutes.

ERBAZZONE

Steam and squeeze dry 2 pounds greens of any kind (see page 129), sauté them in a little butter, and combine them with 1 cup bread crumbs, 1¼ cups grated Parmigiano Reggiano cheese, 2 eggs, ½ cup unbleached all-purpose flour, and salt and freshly ground black pepper to taste. Transfer the mixture to a baking dish and bake at 350 degrees F until browned and set, 20 to 25 minutes.

MALFATTI

Steam 1¾ pounds spinach, squeeze it dry (see page 129), and mince it. Stir in 1 cup ricotta cheese, ½ cup grated Parmigiano Reggiano cheese, 2 eggs, 1¼ cups unbleached all-purpose flour, and a generous amount of grated nutmeg. Form the mixture into oval dumplings and cook them in boiling salted water, following the instructions on page 88 for cooking gnocchi. Serve with browned butter (butter cooked over low heat until a light brown color) and additional grated cheese.

AUTUMN GREENS

THE DIFFERENT VARIETIES OF CHICORY, which include radicchio and dandelion, are cold-weather greens. They are very popular in Italy and deserve to be better known in the United States. Most of these greens can be eaten either raw or cooked, and their flavors mutate greatly from one state to the other. Raw, they have a pleasantly bitter edge (sometimes the greens are soaked to leach out some of the bitterness), while when grilled or sautéed or steamed, they turn sweet. They are also excellent when not cooked completely, but served in a raw salad topped with hot dressing that wilts them slightly.

When buying chicory, look for firm, smooth leaves and try to use it within a day or two of purchase. Keep in mind that, in general, the larger the leaves, the more bitter the flavor. If you are planning to serve the greens raw, seek out tender, young leaves, and even if you plan to cook them, stay far away from anything that looks overgrown or tough.

Escarole

Belgian Endive

Puntarelle

Curly Endive

Treviso Radicchio

Castelfranco Radicchio

Chicory

WORKING WITH CHICORY

TRIMMING THICK-STEMMED CHICORY

Eliminate the outside leaves if they are tough or damaged [1]. Use a sharp knife to cut off the base [2], then cut the leaves into thirds or in half, depending on how long they are. Rinse and soak the chicory in cold water [3] to eliminate some of the bitterness. When you trim 1 pound of thick-stemmed chicory (Catalogna chicory is pictured here), you'll end up with about 12 ounces of greens to cook.

PREPARING THIN-STEMMED CHICORY

On a work surface, spread the leaves from one bunch, facing in the same direction. Pick out and discard any damaged ones [1]. Cut off the stems and then slice the leaves thinly [2]. Place the prepared chicory in a bowl of cold water and cover it with a damp dish towel [3]. Set the bowl in the sink and run cold water into it to release grit.

133

PREPARING BELGIAN ENDIVE and PUNTARELLE

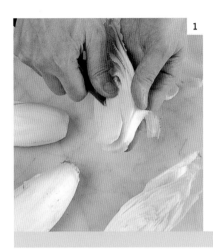

BELGIAN ENDIVE
Cut the head in half, then cut away and discard the heart. It is now ready for cooking **[1]**. If you are going to eat it raw, separate the leaves and cut them into slices.

PUNTARELLE
Discard the outer stalks, then break apart the stalks and discard the base. Cut the puntarelle bunches lengthwise and soak them in cold water **[2]**. To make a classic puntarelle salad, remove the leaves from the cold water and pat them dry. Make a strongly flavored dressing by pounding rinsed, drained, and minced anchovy fillets, minced garlic, lemon juice, and extra-virgin olive oil with a mortar and pestle. Pour the dressing over the leaves, toss to combine, and serve.

TRIMMING RADICCHIO
Scrape the base to remove any soil. Separate the leaves, discarding those that are damaged. If you purchase 3½ ounces of radicchio, you'll have about 2½ ounces after you clean and trim it.

Dandelion greens

Common dandelions are very closely related to wild chicory. Dandelion greens are edible—though, like their cousins, they are fairly bitter. Local farmers' markets may sell them. They make a nice addition to a mixed salad, or they can be dressed with a hot bacon or pancetta dressing. Larger leaves make a nice addition to soups.

BLANCHING and DRAINING THICK-STEMMED CHICORY

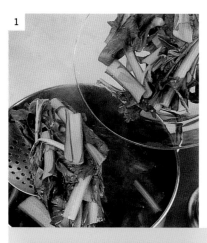

Blanch trimmed and cleaned Catalogna or other thick-stemmed chicory in boiling salted water for 1 minute **[1]**. Drain it, bring a fresh pot of water to a boil, salt it, and boil the chicory again for 10 minutes **[2]**. It may seem like a lot of work to change the boiling water, but the process makes the greens much less bitter.

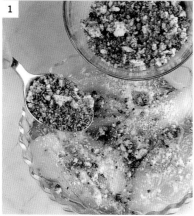

OTHER METHODS FOR COOKING AUTUMN GREENS

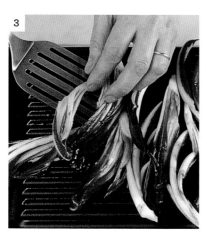

BELGIAN ENDIVE GRATIN [1]

Top trimmed, cooked heads of endive (cut in half if large) with melted butter, grated Parmigiano Reggiano, and a mixture of bread crumbs, minced flat-leaf parsley, and minced hard-boiled egg. Broil until browned on top and serve immediately.

SAUTÉED ESCAROLE [2]

Sauté minced pancetta in extra-virgin olive oil, then add a few slices of garlic and trimmed and chopped escarole and sauté over high heat for a few minutes, shaking the pan to keep the greens from sticking.

GRILLED TREVISO RADICCHIO [3]

Trim red Treviso radicchio and cut each head into quarters or eighths, depending on the size. Drizzle with extra-virgin olive oil and season with salt and freshly ground black pepper. Transfer to a hot grill and cook for a few minutes until the radicchio has grill marks and has wilted only slightly—don't let it soften too much.

BRAISED RADICCHIO [4]

In a small amount of extra-virgin olive oil, sauté minced pancetta and minced onion. Add whole radicchio leaves that have been rinsed but not dried, season with salt to taste, cover, and cook over low heat for 10 minutes. If the pan appears to be drying out, add a tablespoon or two of water.

135

Insalata tricolore

three-color salad

1 to 2 small heads Belgian endive

1 medium head radicchio

1 bunch arugula

½ cup extra-virgin olive oil

Juice of ½ lemon

Fine sea salt to taste

Freshly ground black pepper to taste

1. Peel off and discard the external leaves from the endive. Separate the leaves. Soak them in ice water while you prepare the other greens.

2. Peel off and discard the external leaves of the radicchio. Separate the leaves of the rest of the head. Discard the fibrous core. Stack the radicchio leaves and cut them into ribbons. Place them in a large bowl.

3. Soak the arugula in at least three changes of cold water to clean it. Discard any thick, tough stems. Tear the leaves into small pieces and add them to the bowl with the radicchio.

4. Drain the endive leaves. Stack and cut them crosswise into thin ribbons.

5. In a small bowl, combine the olive oil and lemon juice. Season to taste with salt and pepper. Whisk vigorously, then pour over the salad and toss. Taste and adjust the seasoning. Serve immediately.

SERVES 4   PREP TIME: 20 MINUTES

Insalata tricolore

The tricolore, or three-color, is the nickname for the red, white, and green Italian flag, and this salad mimics those colors. One of the great qualities of this salad is that the three greens used are available as the weather begins to turn colder, when more delicate lettuces are out of season. You can vary this in numerous ways: add a handful of toasted nuts or seeds for additional crunch, later in the fall replace the arugula with very tender kale, or cut the leaves into shreds for more of a coleslaw texture. Don't skip the step of soaking the endive in ice water, though—that extra crispness gives the dish its refreshing bite.

ARUGULA, WATERCRESS, and VARIOUS TYPES of LETTUCE

A SIMPLE GREEN SALAD OF SEVERAL VARIETIES OF LETTUCE makes frequent appearances on the Italian table, and for good reason—there are few dishes more satisfying, healthful, and refreshing. Salad is served as a side dish alongside the second course of an Italian meal, not at the start. Italians often forage for wild greens to include in their salads. Arugula and watercress are the cultivated descendants of those wild greens.

Wild Arugula

Butter Lettuce

Romaine Lettuce

Watercress

Arugula

TRIMMING and CUTTING LETTUCE

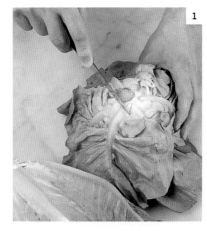
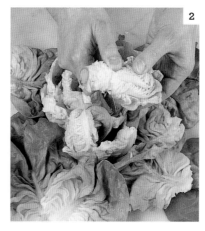

Use a sharp knife to make a deep cut around the stem **[1]**. Separate the leaves. When you get to the core, discard it **[2]**. Also discard any leaves that look wilted or damaged **[3]**.

CLEANING WATERCRESS

Soak watercress in abundant cold water, separating the stems and discarding any extraneous material **[1]**. Remove the stems one at a time and transfer the leaves to clean cold water **[2]**. From 7 ounces of watercress, cleaned, the yield will be about 3 ounces.

Italian cooks excel at elevating simple dishes to great heights by employing the best possible ingredients and treating them with care and respect—an Italian salad, whether an insalata verde (green salad) or an insalata mista (mixed salad), is perhaps the best example of this.

Salad

THE GREENS

An Italian green salad consists of mild lettuce, with some more assertively flavored greens such as arugula or watercress. Inspect the greens carefully and be sure to use only healthy, vibrantly colored leaves. Greens should be washed very thoroughly (see the instructions on page 127) and either spun dry in a salad spinner or blotted thoroughly and gently with a clean dish towel. Wet leaves will result in an inferior salad, as the water will dilute the dressing. With the exception of endive (see page 136 for an insalata tricolore featuring endive), salad greens should not be cut with a knife. Tear greens into bite-sized pieces with your hands. For a mixed salad, include tomato wedges and carrots grated on the largest holes of a four-sided box grater. Place torn greens and other ingredients in a large bowl. You want these to fill the bowl only about two-thirds of the way, in order to allow for tossing.

THE DRESSING

Italians are perplexed when they visit the United States and are presented with a choice of salad dressings—and they're even more puzzled when they see something labeled "Italian dressing." Italians dress salads almost exclusively with a vinaigrette made with extra-virgin olive oil and red wine or balsamic vinegar, though there are some salads that marry better with lemon juice than with vinegar. Purchase the best Italian extra-virgin olive oil you can afford. It should be cold-pressed and unfiltered (cloudiness in olive oil is a good thing). High-quality olive oil is expensive, no doubt about it, so you may want to buy two kinds, both of them extra-virgin: a flavorful oil for dressing salads and using raw, and a milder, somewhat less expensive one for cooking. Purchase olive oil from a shop that will allow you to taste it before you buy it. To taste olive oil properly, curl your tongue, cupping the oil, and inhale sharply, then swallow. You'll get a truer impression this way (though you may also get some funny looks).

Choose a good-quality vinegar as well—if purchasing a balsamic, buy a commercial variety. True, traditional, certified balsamic vinegar is aged for at least twelve years and is wildly expensive—as much as $400 for a small bottle. Assuming you can't get your hands on a bottle of that, look for a good-quality non-certified balsamic vinegar imported from Italy. It should be labeled as aceto balsamico di Modena (the birthplace of true balsamic vinegar), and the ingredients should be vinegar and perhaps grape must, but no sweeteners, which are often added to inferior vinegars to mimic the complex sweet and sour taste of true balsamic, and certainly no coloring. Commercial balsamic vinegars that have aged longer will cost more, and they are worth the difference in price.

Make a vinaigrette of about three parts oil to two parts vinegar, adjusted to your own personal taste. (You should be able to eyeball this, as the vinegar and oil will remain separate until you whisk them together.) You may be tempted simply to drizzle some oil and some vinegar onto the salad and toss it, but combining the oil and vinegar in a small bowl to emulsify it is important and really not much work. Add a pinch of salt and whisk until the ingredients are thoroughly combined.

FINISHING THE SALAD

Dip a salad leaf into the dressing and taste to be sure you're satisfied with your work. Then, pour the dressing over the salad, and toss the salad well with a large spoon and fork or even with clean hands. The leaves should be coated, but there shouldn't be any dressing collected at the bottom of the bowl. Serve the salad immediately after dressing it.

DRYING HERBS

*J*ust like vegetables, herbs are seasonal. Here's how to preserve different kinds of herbs so that you can have them on hand when the mood strikes all year round.

AIR DRYING

Make bouquets of herbs, tie the stems together with kitchen twine **[1]**, and hang them upside down in a dark, humidity-free place where they can dry naturally. Once dried, the herbs will keep in a tightly sealed container for about 1 year.

DRYING IN THE MICROWAVE

Wash and dry sprigs of fresh thyme, or other herbs, place them between two paper towels **[2]**, pat them dry again, and microwave them for about 2 minutes, turning them after 1 minute. Once they are dry, remove the leaves from the sprigs **[3]**.

SOME HERBS SUITABLE FOR DRYING

1] THYME—with its distinctive scent, thyme is perfect for slow-cooking meats such as lamb and rabbit and also complements oily fish such as mackerel. Thyme is often combined with rosemary.

2] MARJORAM—closely related to oregano, but a little sweeter. Marjoram pairs with red meat, game, and fish.

3] SAGE—roasted meat, poultry, and rabbit all are good sage candidates. Dried sage is actually more aromatic than fresh. Sage is also combined with parsley, rosemary, oregano, bay leaf, and thyme.

FREEZING HERBS

Mince fresh herbs very fine, dry them with a flat-weave dish towel very thoroughly, spread them in a single layer on a tray, and freeze them. Once they are frozen, transfer them to a container with a lid and store them in the freezer. Herbs suitable for this method include:

1] BASIL
Tender basil is always added to dishes at the last minute, and it is a good choice with vegetables, fish, and shellfish. It is often accompanied by thyme, parsley, rosemary, and oregano.

2] PARSLEY
Flat-leaf parsley is easier to handle and more flavorful than curly-leaf varieties. It is the workhorse of herbs and can be paired with fish, poultry, vegetables, and eggs.

3] CHIVES
The chive is a very delicately flavored onion. It is usually snipped with kitchen shears and sprinkled over dishes containing meat, vegetables, eggs, or cheese at the last minute. It pairs well with parsley and tarragon.

BOUQUET

A simple bouquet adds flavor to sauces and is easy to fish out and discard when the dish is completely cooked. To make one, use kitchen twine to wrap together a carrot, a celery rib, 2 bay leaves, and a sprig of parsley. Of course, the components can vary, depending on the recipe, your personal taste, and what's available.

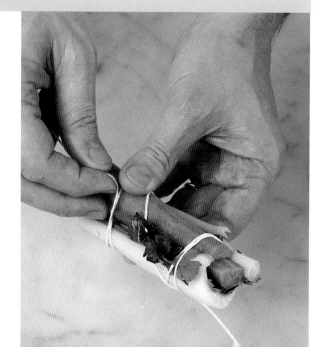

CLEANING and MINCING HERBS

CLEANING

All herbs must be cleaned before they're used. Pull off and discard any soft or damaged leaves or stems. If they are looking a little limp, soak them in cold water for 30 minutes or so to perk them up **[1]**. Clean herbs just as you would leafy greens in several changes of water (see page 127). Pat them dry with a dish towel or paper towels **[2]**.

MINCING

Place the cleaned, towel-dried herbs on a work surface. Place a chef's knife on top of them, holding the tip of the knife between the fingers of one hand and the handle with the other hand. Rock the blade up and down, changing the angle of the knife frequently and pausing to push the herbs back together into a pile **[3]**. Repeat this motion until the herbs are cut as finely as you like **[4]**.

Herbs

Fresh aromatic herbs are used in hundreds of savory preparations in the Italian repertoire. A tablespoon of minced parsley or a few torn basil leaves are often a cook's final touch before serving, especially for lighter summer dishes.

AROMATIC SALT

Combine fine sea salt with minced herbs and ground spices [1] and rub this mixture into meat [2] before cooking. You can prepare aromatic salt with dried herbs in larger quantities and store it in a sealed jar at room temperature.

ROSEMARY SKEWERS

Use a sprig of rosemary as an aromatic skewer for grilled meat. Choose thicker stems and strip the leaves off the part of the sprig you want to use as a skewer, but keep some rosemary leaves at one end. Simply poke the stem through the pieces of meat or vegetables and cook as indicated in the recipe.

STEAMING with HERBS

Tarragon and other herbs can be used when steaming fish. The heat releases the aroma of the herbs and infuses the fish lightly. Place the herbs directly on the fish. Do not put them in the cooking water—they won't flavor the fish at all that way.

PUREE, PESTO, SOUP, and BRAISE

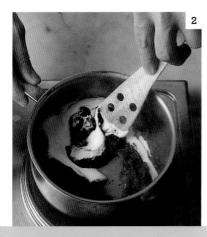

WATERCRESS PUREE

In salted water, blanch about 1 pound of cleaned watercress for 2 minutes, remove it with a slotted spoon or skimmer [1], then squeeze it dry and mince it. In a pot, combine the minced watercress with 2 to 3 tablespoons heavy cream [2] and season to taste with salt and pepper. Cook over medium heat until the liquid has thickened.

ARUGULA PESTO

Trim 1 bunch arugula and place the leaves in a food processor fitted with the metal blade [1]. Add pitted black olives, rinsed capers [2], 1 peeled clove garlic, grated Parmigiano Reggiano and pecorino Romano cheeses, and extra-virgin olive oil. Puree to combine. Use in the same way as a traditional basil pesto.

ARUGULA TART

Blanch 7 ounces arugula, squeeze it dry, and mince it; combine the greens with 1 cup ricotta cheese, 7 ounces diced Taleggio cheese, 2 eggs, 2 tablespoons bread crumbs, salt, and pepper [1]. Line a tart pan with a removable rim with savory tart dough, such as the one on page 163. Spread the arugula mixture evenly into the tart shell [2]. Bake at 350 degrees F until the filling is browned and set, about 40 minutes [3]. Serve warm.

PANCOTTO (BREAD SOUP)

Chop 1 pound peeled potatoes and boil them. When the potatoes are tender but still hard in the center—about half-way cooked—add 1 pound cleaned arugula [1]. Continue cooking until the potatoes are soft enough to be pierced easily with a paring knife, then add 4 slices of day-old rustic bread [2]. As soon as the bread is softened, remove the pan from the heat. Use a skimmer or slotted spoon to transfer the bread and vegetables to soup plates, along with a little of the liquid. Drizzle with extra-virgin olive oil and sprinkle with minced garlic and crushed red pepper.

GENOESE SOUP

Blanch lettuce and borage (an herb that tastes somewhat like cucumber), then squeeze them dry and chop. Cook the chopped greens in oil with minced onion for 30 minutes [1]. Season the sautéed greens to taste with salt and pepper. Let the sautéed greens cool, then combine them with 3 lightly beaten eggs and grated Parmigiano Reggiano. Cook this mixture in a baking dish set in a bain-marie (a large, shallow pan of warm water) until firm. Cut the mixture into squares and serve in broth (page 56) [2].

BRAISED LETTUCE

Wrap 5 stacked lettuce leaves in 1 to 2 slices of pancetta [1] and secure the bundle with a toothpick. Repeat with additional lettuce and pancetta. In a pan, sauté a soffritto (page 260) of minced shallot, carrot, and pancetta in some butter. Add the lettuce bundles to the pan [2]. Add about ¼ inch of broth to the pan [3], cover, and simmer for 10 minutes. Season the lettuce with salt to taste, dot it with butter, and continue cooking, uncovered, until the liquid has evaporated and the pancetta browns.

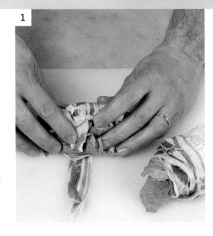  

_V_EGETABLES HAVE LONG TAKEN CENTER STAGE ON THE ITALIAN TABLE. From season to season, Italian cooking relies on a range of different vegetables and vegetable cooking techniques. (As a rule of thumb, winter vegetables require longer cooking, while summer vegetables cook quickly or may even be served raw.) The seasons set the pace for garden vegetables commonly grown in Italy. Spring brings tender asparagus and zucchini. Summer sees an explosion of the colors and flavors that are so important to Mediterranean cooking: Cucumbers, tomatoes, bell peppers, and eggplants are truly sun-kissed. Then, in the fall, winter squash appears, and winter is the time for light green fennel and darker green, almost purple, kale.

In many parts of the world, vegetables are relegated to side dishs, but in Italy, they are so much more. They make wonderful main courses, can be added to all kinds of sauces, and serve as toppings for pizzas, as well as fillings for savory tarts and stuffed pasta. Vegetables are also natural partners for eggs and cheese. The activity of canning at home has regained popularity in recent years, and if you take time during peak season to can tomatoes and other vegetables, you can enjoy them all winter long.

Interestingly, as vegetable-centric as Italy is, many of the country's most beloved vegetables originally came from elsewhere. Tomatoes and peppers are from the Americas; artichokes hail from the Middle East; eggplants are from the Far East. All have found an ideal growing environment in Italy and have become symbols of Italian cooking.

There are plenty of regional varieties of produce in Italy. Now-ubiquitous San Marzano tomatoes are a phenomenon of the Campania region. The eggplant grown in Palermo is long and thin, while in Florence, it is round and squat. Bassano is known for its white asparagus. In short, Italy has not just delicious products, but plenty of varieties that have yet to be widely discovered. Keep an eye out for these newly available choices at your local farmers' market and, most of all, try to keep pace with the seasons and buy as locally as possible. That's how Italians approach grocery shopping, and it's the best way to be sure that vegetables go from farm to table as quickly as possible. This not only helps them maintain their nutritional value, but also guarantees that they will taste their best.

GARDEN VEGETABLES

Vegetables, whether served raw or cooked, follow the rhythm of the seasons. You will find different colors and flavors depending on what time of year it is, each vegetable offering a healthy serving of vitamins, minerals, and fiber.

ARTICHOKES

AN ARTICHOKE IS THE HEAD OF A SPINY THISTLE PLANT. Only a small part of it is edible—basically, its heart. In the United States, cooks regularly steam artichokes and diners scrape a small amount of edible flesh off the leaves with their teeth, but Italians discard the leaves (properly termed *bracts*). Different artichoke varieties have different leaf shapes, and their colors range from gray to purple, though most of them have a greenish tint. The vast majority of artichokes grown in the United States are the globe type, but Italy boasts a wider variety. Tuscany has its own artichokes (sometimes labeled Siena artichokes in the United States), as do Liguria, Sardinia, and Puglia. The islands in the Venetian lagoon are known for castraure artichokes, which are quite small and tender and are usually preserved in oil. The most common artichoke in Italy is the Romanesco, which is large and round. But for the most part, the various types of artichokes are interchangeable. For many Italian dishes, you will want smaller artichokes, sometimes sold as "baby artichokes." These are not any particular variety, but just less developed flowers from lower down on the artichoke plant.

Artichokes feature heavily in Italian folk medicine and are believed to have curative powers. It is at least true that they are rich in minerals and vitamins A, B, and C. Best of all, they are tasty, as well as attractive.

Castraure Artichokes

Ligurian Artichoke

Pugliese Artichoke

Tuscan Artichoke

Sardinian Artichoke

Romanesco Artichoke

SELECTING and TRIMMING ARTICHOKES

SELECTING

Look for firm specimens with freshly cut stems and shiny leaves that show no sign of wilting. Smaller artichokes will be more tender. You will want two or three smaller artichokes per person. There's no difference in taste between thornier artichokes and their less pointy cousins—you're going to trim away and discard the tips of the leaves in any case. Wearing gloves when working with artichokes is always a good idea, because artichokes can stain your hands. They also turn brown very quickly when cut, so it's best to keep a bowl of water with lemon juice at hand and drop the artichokes into it immediately after you've trimmed them.

TRIMMING

First remove any leaves from the stems, then cut off the stems, leaving an inch or two **[1]**. Pull off and discard any hard, dark-colored leaves **[2, 3]** around the heart, which is the edible portion. Look for the lighter green color that will indicate you've reached the heart. When you have revealed the light green heart of the artichoke, peel any tough skin off of the outside of the stem **[4]**. Cut off the top of the artichoke completely, whether the leaves are pointy and sharp or dull and rounded **[5]**. As soon as you cut an artichoke, drop it into water acidulated with lemon juice **[6]**. Cut the artichokes in half and use the tip of a paring knife to dig out the fuzzy part in the center **[7]**.

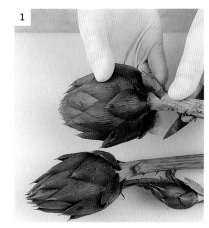

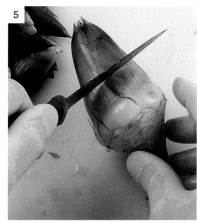

149

ARTICHOKE STEMS

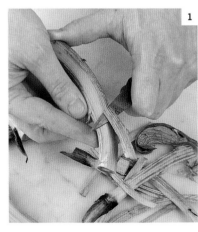

Artichoke stems make a great stuffing for whole fish and chicken, or filling for a savory tart. They are also delicious in pasta and risotto dishes. First, trim off the fibrous, bitter skin [1]. Next, slice the stem into rounds. (You can slice several at once.) [2] Cook the rounds in a pan in oil, along with minced shallot [3]. Add white wine and salt and simmer over low heat until the artichoke stems are tender.

The right tool

A SMALL PARING KNIFE

Cleaning artichokes is a somewhat tedious task that can be made easier if you use a small paring knife. It's the best tool for taking off the outer leaves without hurting yourself; it's also good for peeling the stem, because it gives you a great deal of control and allows you to be precise as you remove the fibrous portion, leaving the tender part intact. A small blade is also perfect for extracting the hairy choke that forms at the center of each artichoke; this must be removed at all costs—it is extremely unpleasant to eat.

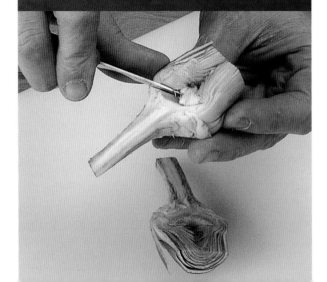

BRAISED and BOILED ARTICHOKES, and ARTICHOKES ALLA GIUDÌA

BRAISED [1]
Clean and trim the artichokes but leave them whole, then place them in a pot with cool water, oil, garlic, white wine, and lemon juice. Cook, covered, over medium heat until tender, about 20 minutes.

BOILED [2]
Clean and trim the artichokes and cut them into quarters, or leave them whole if they're quite small. Cook them in boiling water with lemon wedges and a small amount of oil.

ALLA GIUDÌA [3]
This classic preparation calls for using Romanesco or other artichokes without sharp tips. Thoroughly clean and trim the artichokes, but leave them whole. Then smash them so that they open up like flowers and fry them in a generous amount of oil.

TRIFOLATI and ROMAN-STYLE ARTICHOKES

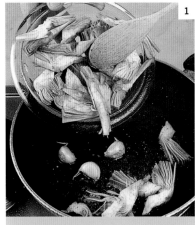

TRIFOLATI

When something is cooked trifolati style, it is prepared with minced garlic and parsley. To cook artichokes in this manner, cut cleaned and trimmed artichokes into wedges. Heat a pan over high heat and add some oil and garlic, along with the artichoke wedges. Sauté until the artichokes look dry and are starting to crisp [1]. Add some white wine. When the artichokes are tender, add additional minced garlic and parsley, and toss to combine [2].

ROMAN STYLE

Use larger artichokes for this dish, but they should still be tender and compact. Choose Romanesco artichokes, which do not have the sharply pointed leaves, if you can find them. Clean and trim the artichokes, leaving them whole and with an inch or two of their stems attached. Use your fingers to gently pry apart the leaves, so that you can more easily access the hairy choke and remove it [1]. Then stuff the half-open artichokes with a mixture of garlic, parsley, and fresh mint [2]. Brown the artichokes in extra-virgin olive oil with a couple of anchovy fillets added to it for flavor [3]. Finally, place the artichokes upside down (stems pointing up) in a baking dish, season them with salt, and drizzle them with a generous amount of oil [4]. Add water to cover, place a lid on the dish (or use aluminum foil if the dish doesn't have a tight-fitting cover), and bake at 350 degrees F until the artichokes are tender, about 1 hour.

ASPARAGUS

ASPARAGUS IS ORIGINALLY FROM CHINA and reached Italy during the Roman era. It has been highly regarded ever since (perhaps in part because for many years asparagus was believed to be an aphrodisiac). The plant grows in the wild and is also farmed. The asparagus season begins in March and continues until May or June; asparagus that appears in the grocery store at other times of the year is grown in greenhouses or imported from afar and should be avoided. Wild asparagus has a stronger, slightly more bitter flavor than farmed asparagus. Also farmed is white asparagus, which owes its color—or lack thereof—to the fact that it is never exposed to light. Most recipes can use white, green, or purple asparagus, depending on which you prefer and what's available to you, but asparagus soups and frittatas are best made with thinner asparagus.

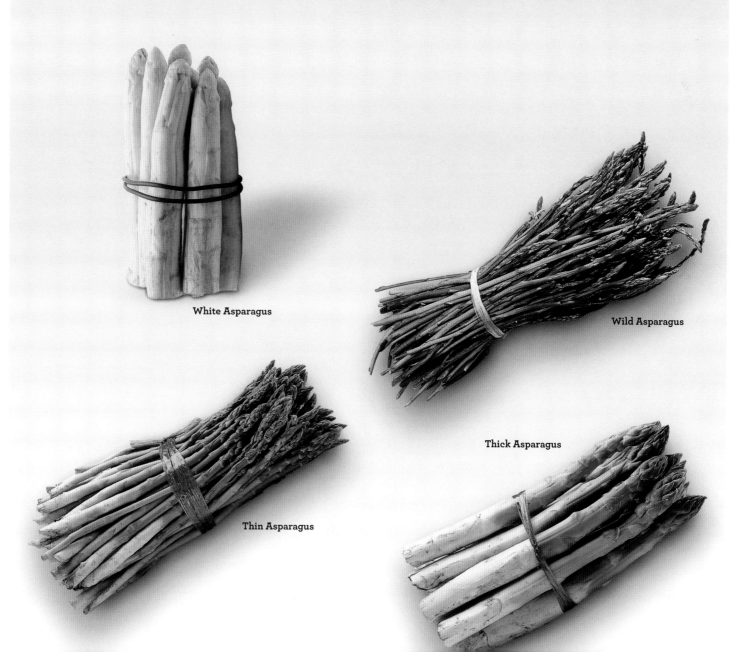

White Asparagus

Wild Asparagus

Thin Asparagus

Thick Asparagus

SELECTING and PREPARING ASPARAGUS

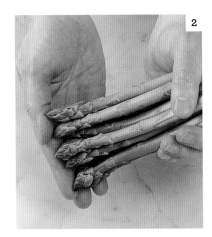

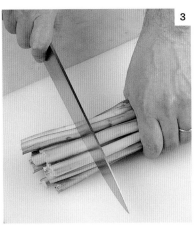

SELECTING

Asparagus is usually sold in bunches that weigh about 1 pound. When buying it, look for spears with tightly closed tips. If the leaves are opening out from the stalks, it is not as fresh as it should be. If you can, break one of the stalks—it should snap audibly and break off cleanly. The stalks should be smooth and firm, free of scratches or pits. Asparagus wrapped in a damp paper towel will keep in your crisper in the refrigerator for 3 to 4 days. If you plan to use it within a day, you can store it at room temperature, arranged upright (like a bouquet of flowers) in a glass of cold water.

PREPARING

Rest each stalk on a work surface and use a vegetable peeler to remove the skin from about half the stalk toward the bottom [1]. After peeling all the stalks, hold them together with their tips even [2]. Cut off the bottom quarter or so of the stalks, which is tougher and more fibrous [3]. Rinse the asparagus in a generous amount of cold water, changing the water several times [4]. Tie the asparagus into individual portions (plan for 6 or 7 ounces per person) using kitchen twine [5]. Asparagus can be either steamed or boiled in this manner. An asparagus pot is a tall, narrow pot designed to allow the asparagus to stand up vertically so that the tips, which cook more quickly, don't overcook. It's not absolutely necessary, but it is useful. To boil asparagus, submerge all but the tips in salted simmering water for 5 to 10 minutes, depending on the size [6].

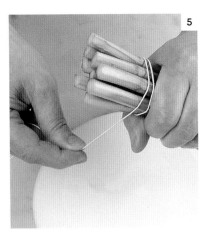

CUTTING ASPARAGUS

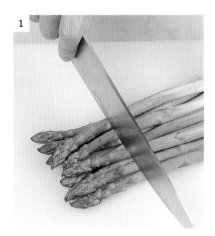

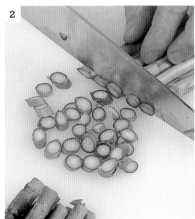

Asparagus spears are not always used whole. For some dishes, after cleaning, the tips of the spears need to be cut off [1]. The stalks are excellent in risotto and can be thinly sliced into rounds with a chef's knife [2] or they may be cut lengthwise into either julienne or thin strips [3]. (Don't throw out the asparagus tips. They are often tender enough to eat raw and, when thinly sliced, make a delicious salad.)

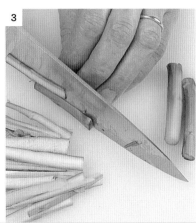

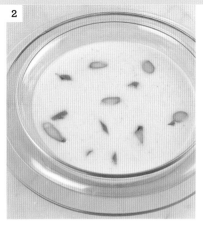

CREAM OF ASPARAGUS SOUP

The bottom ends of asparagus stalks, normally discarded because they are fibrous, can be used to make an excellent cream of asparagus soup. Sauté some minced onion in oil and butter, add the thick ends of the asparagus stalks, chopped, and brown them [1]. Add a tablespoon or so of flour and then enough broth to cover (in a pinch, add water and a bouillon cube). When the asparagus stalks are soft, puree them, along with their cooking liquid and heavy cream, egg yolk, salt, and pepper [2]. Garnish with thinly sliced rounds of asparagus that you have quickly sautéed.

Asparagi al cartoccio
asparagus in parchment

2¼ pounds asparagus, trimmed

3 tablespoons unsalted butter

2 tablespoons unbleached all-purpose flour

1¼ cups whole milk, heated to a simmer

Pinch freshly grated nutmeg

Fine sea salt to taste

Freshly ground black pepper to taste

2 ounces Emmental cheese, thinly sliced

3½ ounces thinly sliced prosciutto, cut into 1-inch pieces

½ cup freshly grated Parmigiano Reggiano cheese

1. Preheat the oven to 425 degrees F with racks positioned in the upper and lower thirds. Cut 8 pieces of parchment paper into rectangles measuring 13 by 14 inches.

2. Steam the asparagus, covered, in a steamer set over boiling water or using an asparagus pot until crisp-tender, 3 to 5 minutes. Transfer the stalks with a slotted spoon to a bowl of ice and cold water to stop cooking, then drain and pat them dry.

3. Put one-quarter of the asparagus in the center of a piece of parchment paper. Repeat with the remaining asparagus, using 4 of the 8 pieces of parchment all together. Reserve the remaining paper.

4. To make a béchamel, heat 2 tablespoons of the butter in a 2-quart heavy saucepan over medium-low heat until melted, then add the flour and cook over low heat, whisking, for 3 minutes. Add the hot milk little by little, whisking to incorporate between additions, then bring the mixture to a boil, reduce the heat, and simmer, whisking, until the béchamel is thickened, 3 to 4 minutes more. Add the nutmeg and season with salt and pepper.

5. Spoon the béchamel over the asparagus, then top with the Emmental and prosciutto; cut the remaining 1 tablespoon butter into small pieces and scatter them over the asparagus; sprinkle Parmigiano Reggiano over all. Top each portion with one of the reserved parchment pieces, then crimp the edges to form sealed packets. Put the packets on baking sheets and bake until heated through, 12 to 15 minutes. Transfer the packets to plates, cut them open, and serve immediately.

SERVES 4   COOKING TIME: 20 MINUTES

BRAISING, STEAMING, and SAUTÉING ASPARAGUS

*A*sparagus is versatile and can be used in everything from risotto to pasta (it makes wonderful lasagne), from soups to frittatas. It also stands on its own baked with butter and some grated cheese—topping asparagus cooked this way with a fried egg gives you what Italians call asparagus alla Bismarck. Asparagus is equally delicious when steamed and drizzled with a little extra-virgin olive oil and lemon juice or with melted butter. A finely chopped hard-boiled egg also makes a fine topping. Before cooking wild asparagus, always blanch it briefly in boiling water to remove some of its bitterness and to develop the flavor.

BRAISING
Asparagus can be braised in a covered saucepan in either water or broth with a tablespoon or so of butter, some salt, and any aromatic herbs you like [1, 2]. It will cook in 7 to 8 minutes.

STEAMING
Asparagus can be steamed in a steamer or steamer basket set over boiling water. When prepared this way, asparagus gets soft without any loss of its delicate flavor. It will cook in 4 to 5 minutes [3].

SAUTÉING
Julienne asparagus stalks and cook in a little extra-virgin olive oil, sprinkle them with salt, and serve them as a side dish or use them as an ingredient in pasta dishes, frittatas, or savory tarts [4].

ASPARAGUS FRITTATA, SOUP, and RISOTTO

FRITTATA

To make an asparagus frittata, julienne the stalks and sauté them in a small amount of oil until tender, 7 to 8 minutes. Season with salt, and then pour beaten eggs into the pan **[1]**, shaking it to distribute the eggs evenly and cover the bottom **[2]**. Cook on one side, then flip the frittata and cook the other (or, if you don't feel comfortable flipping the frittata, use an ovenproof pan to cook it in and run it under the broiler for 2 to 4 minutes to set the top, keeping a close eye on it to make sure it doesn't burn).

SOUP

Sauté blanched wild asparagus in oil with garlic and shallot. Season to taste with salt and pepper and add water to cover **[1]**. Bring to a boil, then whisk in beaten egg, grated pecorino Romano cheese, and minced herbs **[2]**. Serve with toasted slices of rustic bread.

RISOTTO

Toast rice for risotto (see page 107) in a base of oil, butter, and minced onion. Add diced or thinly sliced asparagus **[1]**. Cook as for risotto, using simmering broth (page 56); at the end, stir in butter and grated Parmigiano Reggiano cheese **[2]**.

BROCCOLI and CAULIFLOWER

BROCCOLI AND CAULIFLOWER ARE WINTER VEGETABLES, although some varieties are now available year-round. The boundaries between broccoli and cauliflower, which are close relatives in the family of cruciferous vegetables, can somtimes become blurred. Standard snowball cauliflower is white, but there are also green varieties, as well as the deep purple violetto di Sicilia. Of special note is Romanesco broccoli, also known as Roman cauliflower, which sports light green cone-shaped rosettes all over its head. Dark green broccoli (which used to be called Calabrese in the United States because of its roots in that Italian region) has a longer stalk and more distinctively floral-looking florets. Both broccoli and cauliflower are terrific for making soups, pasta sauces, and side dishes that support meat and fish. They are also nutritional powerhouses, rich in antioxidants, vitamins A and C, iron, calcium, phosphorous, and beta carotene. When purchasing broccoli and cauliflower, look for tightly closed heads without dents or bruises. Broccoli florets should be dark green, without a hint of yellow or any sprouting flowers. Both vegetables will keep in the refrigerator for several days; you can also chop them into florets, boil them, dry them thoroughly, and freeze them. These vegetables do have a sulfurous odor when cooking that some people find objectionable. If you are one of these people, place a cotton pad soaked in vinegar on the pot lid or add a small piece of bread soaked in vinegar and lemon juice to the cooking water, and you will find that the odor dissipates.

Broccoli

Cauliflower

Romanesco Broccoli

Broccoflower

Violetto di Sicilia

SELECTING, PORTIONING, and TRIMMING BROCCOLI and CAULIFLOWER

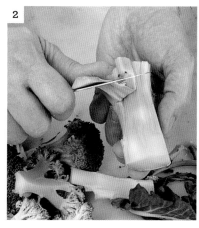

SELECTING
When purchasing broccoli, look for compact florets. Plan to serve 5 to 7 ounces of trimmed broccoli or cauliflower per person. If you buy fresh broccoli, there shouldn't be much waste. Keep in mind when purchasing cauliflower that you will discard about half of the weight of a typical head.

PORTIONING AND TRIMMING BROCCOLI
Pull off larger stalks and mark the end of each with an X, then cut the stalks in quarters the long way [1]. Cut off the florets, and if they are large, cut them in half. If the end of the stalk is very tough and fibrous, trim it away. Using a paring knife, peel off any fibrous skin and discard it [2]. Chop the remaining tender heart into pieces.

PORTIONING AND TRIMMING CAULIFLOWER
Begin by slicing off the base to remove most of the leaves [1]. Any leaves that don't come away with the stalk can be pulled off by hand [2]. Cut around the head to detach the florets from the tough central core, leaving them still attached to one another [3]. Then simply pull apart the individual florets [4]. Cauliflower leaves can be cooked along with the florets or used in vegetable soup.

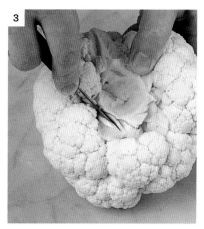

161

BOILING CAULIFLOWER IN SALTED and ACIDULATED WATER

To cook an entire head of cauliflower, after trimming the base, cut an X into it [1]. If you are cooking green cauliflower, you don't need to add acid to the salted water [2]. But if you are cooking white cauliflower, you want to make the water acidic with some vinegar or lemon juice in order to keep the cauliflower from discoloring [3]. Cauliflower florets [4] should be ready in about 10 minutes, while a whole head will take 25 to 45 minutes to be fully cooked, depending on its size.

Tip

THE VERSATILITY OF BROCCOLI AND CAULIFLOWER

Broccoli and cauliflower are a great resource, as they can serve as side dishes or as ingredients in pasta dishes. They can also be the base for baked dishes, puddings, and more. And while broccoli and cauliflower are usually served cooked, if they are very fresh they can be eaten raw, either in salads or pinzimonio, a traditional Italian appetizer of mixed crudités and lightly blanched vegetables served with a small bowl of top-quality extra-virgin olive oil for dipping.

Tartellette gratinate con cavolfiore
savory cauliflower tartlets

DOUGH

2½ cups unbleached all-purpose flour

10 tablespoons (1¼ sticks) cold butter, cut into small pieces

Fine sea salt to taste

FILLING

1 pound trimmed cauliflower florets (about 1 head)

1 teaspoon white wine vinegar

2 large eggs

½ cup heavy cream

¼ cup grated Grana Padano cheese

Pinch ground cinnamon

Fine sea salt to taste

Freshly ground black pepper to taste

1 tablespoon minced shallot

½ cup bread crumbs

2 tablespoons minced flat-leaf parsley

2 tablespoons extra-virgin olive oil

1. To make the dough, place the flour in a bowl. Toss in the butter pieces and pinch or cut the butter into the flour until the mixture resembles coarse meal. Stir the salt into ¼ cup water and pour this into the bowl while stirring with a fork to form a dough. Shape the dough into a ball, wrap it in plastic wrap, and refrigerate for at least 20 minutes. Preheat the oven to 350 degrees F.

2. For the filling, cook the florets in boiling salted water with white wine vinegar for 10 minutes. Drain the cooked florets and spread them on a baking sheet to cool.

3. Reserve 18 cauliflower florets. Puree the rest with the eggs, cream, 2 tablespoons of the Grana Padano cheese, the cinnamon, and salt and pepper. In a small bowl, combine the shallot, bread crumbs, parsley, and the remaining 2 tablespoons Grana Padano.

4. Roll out the dough to ⅛ inch thick and use it to line six 5-inch fluted tart pans; arrange these on a baking sheet. Divide the pureed cauliflower filling evenly among the tartlets. Bake for 12 minutes, then remove the baking sheet from the oven and arrange 3 of the reserved whole florets on each tart, sprinkle with the bread crumb mixture, drizzle a little olive oil on the top of each, and return them to the oven to bake until the bread crumb topping is golden and crisp, 5 to 7 additional minutes.

SERVES 6　　COOKING TIME: 1 HOUR 10 MINUTES

STEAMING, FRYING, and SAUTÉING BROCCOLI and CAULIFLOWER

STEAMING
Florets can be placed in a steamer basket **[1]** and cooked for 10 minutes **[2]**.

FRYING
Florets that have been blanched in boiling acidulated water **[1]** and dried thoroughly can be tossed in a batter of flour, egg, and milk (or simply dredged in flour) and fried in a generous amount of oil, preferably peanut oil **[2]**.

SAUTÉING
In a pan, sauté a couple of chopped cloves garlic in 2 tablespoons extra-virgin olive oil **[1]**, then add a generous amount of bread crumbs. Cook until the bread crumbs are crisp and golden **[2]**. Then add boiled broccoli or cauliflower florets (see page 162) **[3]**. This makes a tasty topping for pasta.

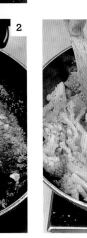

COOKING BROCCOLI and CAULIFLOWER WITH BÉCHAMEL and IN CREAM SOUP

WITH BÉCHAMEL

Sauté boiled broccoli or cauliflower florets in oil with minced garlic and grate on a little Grana Padano cheese and some nutmeg [1]. Stir in an egg whisked with a little milk and seasoned with salt. Break up the florets into smaller pieces as you stir [2]. Transfer the mixture to a buttered baking dish. Make a béchamel (see page 57) mixed with a little heavy cream and an egg yolk and pour it over the top. Bake at 450 degrees F until browned, about 15 minutes.

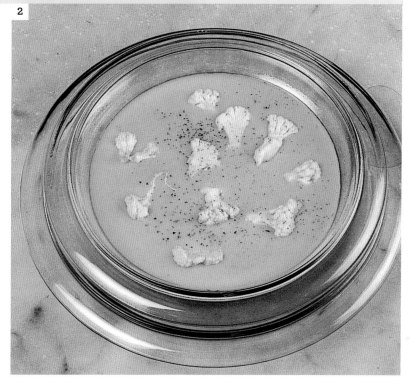

CREAM SOUP

Brown an onion in some oil and add cauliflower florets. Cook until tender, then sprinkle on some flour and whisk in milk and broth [1]. Cook for approximately 30 minutes, then puree and serve with a few whole boiled florets (see page 162) scattered over each serving, along with a generous grinding of pepper [2].

CABBAGES, KALE, and BRUSSELS SPROUTS

CABBAGES ARE CRUCIFEROUS VEGETABLES, harvested in late autumn and winter. Savoy cabbage, with its bumpy leaves and dark green color, is very common in Italy and worth discovering. Green cabbage is smoother and has a waxier-textured leaf. These compact heads may be cut into wedges or shredded into ribbons. Brussels sprouts are a very small variety of cabbage, and Napa or Chinese cabbage is long and white, while red cabbage is as brilliantly colored as its name implies. Lacinato or Tuscan kale has long, bumpy leaves and is used in Tuscany's famous ribollita and many other traditional dishes from the area. Kohlrabi is also a member of the cabbage family, though normally the kohlrabi stalk is eaten and not the leaf. No matter which kind of cabbage you buy, look for firm leaves that are not wilted or yellowed. Lacinato kale, red cabbage, and Brussels sprouts are usually cooked, while Napa cabbage, green cabbage, and kohlrabi may be cooked or eaten raw. The firm yet pliable leaves of savoy cabbage can be used as wrappers for stuffed cabbage and other dishes. Cabbages are particularly strong choices healthwise and offer a good dose of minerals and vitamins, especially vitamins A and C.

Red Cabbage

Savoy Cabbage

Lacinato Kale

Green Cabbage

Napa Cabbage

Kohlrabi

Brussels Sprouts

CLEANING and TRIMMING SAVOY CABBAGE

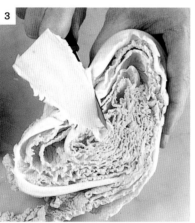

TRIMMING
Trimming savoy cabbage (and most other types of cabbage) and preparing it for cooking begins with cutting the leaves at the base to remove them from the core **[1]** and then pulling them off and separating them **[2]**. Any damaged leaves should be discarded. When you have removed all the leaves, cut the heart in half, remove the core with a V-shaped cut, and discard it **[3]**. If you want whole leaves, as for stuffed cabbage, make a V-shaped cut at the base of each leaf, using a sharp paring knife, to remove the thick, hard portion of the center rib **[4]**.

CUTTING CABBAGE INTO RIBBONS
Cabbage is often cut into ribbons either before it is cooked or to be used in salads. Use a sharp chef's knife and either thinly slice the entire head or stack up several leaves and slice them all at once **[5]**.

TRIMMING BRUSSELS SPROUTS

To prepare brussels sprouts for cooking whole, peel off any damaged leaves on the outside, then cut off any stem that remains, along with a little bit of the core [1]. Next, cut an X into the base of each one to help it to cook evenly [2]. You can also detach all the little individual leaves [3] and sauté them—a little more work, but delicious (see opposite).

SAUTÉING BRUSSELS SPROUTS

Brussels sprouts are usually cooked whole, but you can bring out a whole new flavor dimension and tenderness by separating them into individual leaves and then browning those leaves in a skillet with some oil, diced pancetta, and minced onion **[1]**. Sprinkle with minced flat-leaf parsley before serving **[2]**.

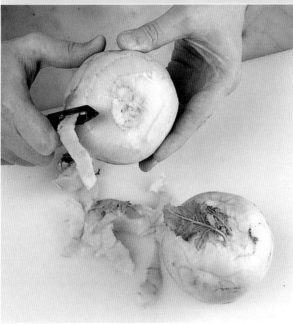

TRIMMING and PREPARING KOHLRABI

Kohlrabi should be trimmed like a root vegetable: Cut off the ends and peel it. With a grater or mandoline, cut it into thin slices and make a salad by dressing it simply with extra-virgin olive oil, salt, and pepper. For a richer preparation, cut the trimmed kohlrabi into cubes and braise it with butter, sugar, and water. Add a little cream at the end and let it reduce.

CARDOONS

THE CARDOON IS A WINTER VEGETABLE THAT LOOKS LIKE CELERY, but is actually closely related to the artichoke. It tastes something like an artichoke, too, though it's a little sweeter. Cardoons are grown using a technique called blanching, which consists of protecting the plants from light and air for ten to twenty days before harvest by covering them almost completely with paper or straw. This way, the cardoon's base, which otherwise would be hard and fairly bitter, comes in sweet, crunchy, and tender after the late-autumn frost. Light ivory-colored cardoon varieties are particularly wonderful.

It can be a bit tricky to trim cardoons, as many varieties are prickly. You may want to wear gloves; this will not only protect you from getting pricked, but will also keep your fingers clean—like artichokes, cardoons contain a substance that stains the skin brown. To stop the vegetable itself from turning an unappetizing brown, rub it with a cut lemon or drop it into ice water with a little lemon juice as you work on it.

Cardoons are almost always eaten cooked, not raw, and it's best to briefly parboil or blanch them before you bake, fry, or sauté them to leach out some of the bitterness. Raw cardoons are, however, an indispensable ingredient in Piedmont's famous bagna caôda appetizer, which is raw vegetables, including cardoons, served with a hot garlic fondue for dipping. If you plan to serve raw cardoons, it's worth seeking out the curved cardoons (called *gobbi,* or "hunchbacks," in Italian), which are extra sweet. They should be soaked for 3 to 4 hours after being sliced to guard against bitterness. Cardoons are a good source of fiber and potassium, and they are low in calories. They may be a little trouble to prepare, but they are well worth the effort.

Cardoon

Curved Cardoon

TRIMMING and PEELING CARDOONS

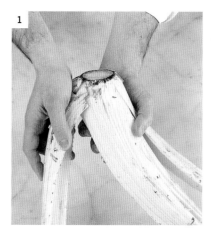

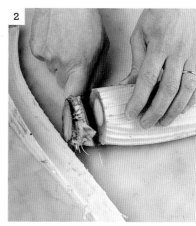

TRIMMING CARDOONS

Detach any outside stalks that are hard and fibrous [1] and all the leaves. Cut off and discard the bottom ½ inch of the root [2]. Continue to pull off stalks until just the heart remains. Cut the stalks into pieces about 2 inches long [3] and then immediately drop them into cold water mixed with lemon juice to keep them from darkening. You will end up discarding about two-thirds of the weight of the cardoons as you trim them.

PEELING CARDOONS

Large cardoon stalks should be peeled to remove the prickly, tough skin and strings [4]. You will be left with only the tender heart after you are done. If you have younger, more tender stalks, you can peel them if there are any strings and scrape them with the blade of a knife to remove any fuzz [5].

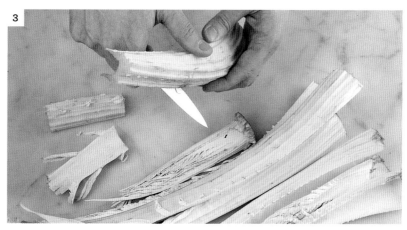

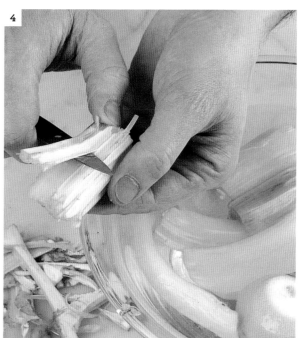

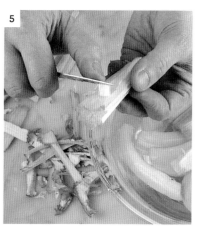

CUTTING CARDOONS INTO JULIENNE and THIN SLICES

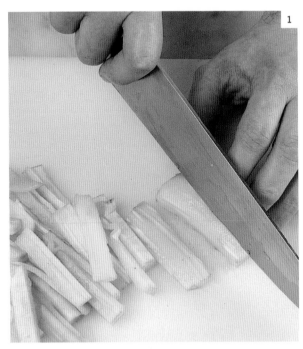

1

After cardoons have been trimmed, cut into 2-inch lengths, and thoroughly cleaned, they are usually cut into smaller pieces. You can cut them into medium julienne **[1]** or thin slices **[2]**. The former are used in various hot dishes, while the latter, blanched until tender, make a delicious addition to winter salads.

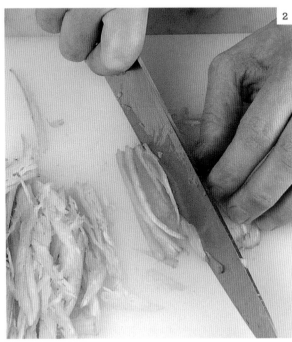

2

Curved cardoons

The curved cardoons grown in the Belbo valley in Piedmont are known for their excellent quality. Most cardoons grown in this area are the Spadone variety, and they are planted in spring in the sandy soil along the river. The cardoons do not curve on their own, but are grown using a special technique. When the plants reach a certain size, a second row of holes is dug next to them, then the tops are bent over and buried in the sand.

PARBOILING and BLANCHING CARDOONS

Even if cardoons will be cooked in a dish, they should be parboiled or blanched first to remove some of their bitterness.

PARBOILING

Drop the trimmed and sliced cardoons into salted boiling water with lemon slices in it [1]. Cook until crisp-tender, about 15 minutes, then proceed with the recipe.

BLANCHING

Fill a pot with 4 quarts water, bring it to a boil, and salt it. Add 2 tablespoons unbleached all-purpose flour whisked to a smooth paste with a little water [2] and 2 tablespoons extra-virgin olive oil [3]. Toss in the trimmed and cut cardoons [4] and boil until they are almost completely tender, about 45 minutes. The oil on the surface of the water prevents discoloration.

Ravioloni con i cardi

cardoon ravioloni

3½ pounds cardoons

½ medium onion

3 to 4 sage leaves

5 tablespoons extra-virgin olive oil

2 cups unbleached all-purpose flour

2 large eggs

7 ounces prosciutto cotto

½ cup grated Grana Padano cheese, plus more for serving

3 tablespoons bread crumbs

Fine sea salt

Pinch freshly grated nutmeg

3 shallots, minced

1¾ cups heavy cream

Freshly ground black pepper to taste

3 tablespoons minced fresh herbs, such as chives, thyme, sage, and flat-leaf parsley

1. Trim the cardoons, cut them into 2-inch pieces, and parboil them for 5 minutes (page 173). Drain and peel the cardoon pieces, then boil them in 10 cups water with the onion, sage leaves, and 2 tablespoons of the olive oil until very soft, about 1½ hours.

2. Meanwhile, make the pasta using the flour, eggs, and a small amount of salt, following the instructions on page 78. Wrap the dough in plastic and set it aside to rest for 30 minutes.

3. Drain the cardoons, discard the onion and sage leaves, and press the cardoons against a sieve with a spoon to remove as much water as possible. Mince the cooked cardoons with the prosciutto. Stir in the grated Grana Padano, bread crumbs, a pinch of salt, and the nutmeg.

4. Divide the pasta dough into 4 pieces and cover 3 of them with plastic wrap. If using a hand-cranked pasta machine, flatten the dough so that it will fit through the rollers. Feed pasta through the rollers at their widest setting three or four times, folding and turning the pasta until it is smooth and the width of the machine. Then begin decreasing the roller setting one notch at a time (do not fold or turn the pasta), until the sheet is approximately 3½ by 20 inches. Repeat with the other 3 pieces of dough. If you are rolling by hand, roll out the dough and cut it into sheets approximately that size. (See page 80 for more on rolling out pasta dough by hand.)

5. Lay a pasta sheet on a lightly floured work surface with the long side facing you. Starting from the left end of the dough, about 2 inches from a short edge, mound about 1½ tablespoons of filling onto the dough. Put four more dots of filling onto the dough, each about 4 inches apart. Fold the dough over the filling lengthwise. Gently press the edges to seal. Using a notched wheel, cut the pasta sheet widthwise between dots of filling to create 5 ravioloni. Transfer the ravioloni to a lightly floured baking sheet and cover them with a barely dampened, clean dish towel. Repeat with the remaining dough and filling to create 20 ravioloni.

6. Bring a large pot of water to a boil and salt it. Cook the ravioloni in batches of 5 until they are al dente.

7. Meanwhile, for the sauce, in a large skillet, sauté the shallots in the remaining 3 tablespoons olive oil until just golden. Add the cream, season with salt and pepper, and stir in the minced herbs. Add the cooked ravioloni and toss over medium heat until the cream has thickened. Serve with additional grated Grana Padano cheese on the side.

SERVES 8 ~ COOKING TIME: 1 HOUR 40 MINUTES

CELERY

THERE ARE FOUR TYPES OF CELERY YOU MAY FIND IN YOUR GROCERY STORE. You will definitely find stalk celery, which is grown for its ribs. It may be eaten raw as a snack or in salads and is used as a base for many cooked dishes, such as soups and sauces. White celery (the same variety as green stalk celery, but grown with the stalks covered by soil or mulch) is more tender and sweet. If you can find it, use it in raw preparations to take full advantage of those qualities. You may also find celery root, a large, round root with white flesh that has a more mellow celery taste than the ribs and can be eaten raw or cooked. Finally, you may find leaf celery, also known as cutting celery; it has thin stalks and is grown, as the name implies, mainly for its leaves, which resemble parsley but taste distinctly of, well, celery. Celery in all its forms is refreshing and low in calories. It is so ubiquitous as a muted component in many recipes that it is somewhat underappreciated, but raw and especially cooked celery—which takes on a tender texture and a completely different flavor—can be an interesting side dish on its own. On the following pages, you will find some recipes that put celery center stage.

Celery Root

Green Stalk Celery

Leaf Celery

CHOOSING, TRIMMING, and CUTTING CELERY

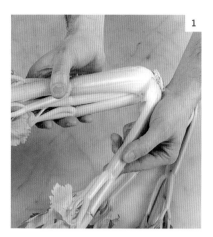

When purchasing celery, look for green, unwilted leaves. The stalks should be firm and fleshy and make a snapping sound when broken. They should also be tight against one another. To clean stalk celery, first detach the stalks at the base one by one [1]. Then remove the tops where the leaves grow [2]. Use a knife to cut and peel away any fibrous strings from the ribs; these tend to grow on the outside [3]. Place the stalks on a cutting board, flatten the ribs with the palm of your hand or the flat side of a chef's knife, and dice, mince, or thinly slice them [4].

PEELING, CUTTING, and CLEANING CELERY ROOT

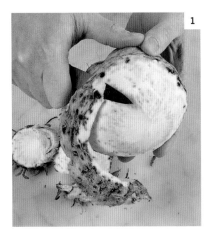

Cut off the leaves and stalks from the celery root, then peel it with a large paring knife, being careful to remove any eyes **[1]**. Cut the root into slices **[2]**, matchsticks, wedges, or other shapes. Since celery root oxidizes quickly, wash and place the cut pieces in a bowl of cold water with lemon juice in it **[3]**.

SCOOPING OUT, CARVING, SAUTÉING, and BOILING CELERY ROOT

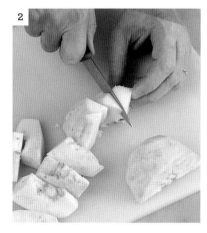

SCOOPING OUT AND CARVING
Cut a celery root in half and hollow each piece out using a small scoop. These make good containers for stuffing [1]. Celery root can also be cut into equal-sized pieces, such as half wedges, for cooking [2]. For a really professional-looking presentation, those pieces can then be carved (this is called "turning," from the French *tourner*) into small barrel-shaped pieces about 2 inches long [3]. These can be boiled or braised.

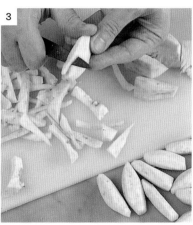

SAUTÉING
Sauté half wedges of celery root in extra-virgin olive oil with sliced onion [4]. This makes a sophisticated side dish that accompanies red meat especially well.

BOILING
Cook chopped or turned celery root in salted boiling water with a lemon slice in it to keep the root from oxidizing and turning brown [5]. Drain and dress the celery root with extra-virgin olive oil and salt.

Bastoncini di sedano all'agro con acciughe

celery with anchovies

12 ounces celery stalks
1 cup white wine vinegar
1 firm ripe tomato
Fine sea salt to taste
1 tablespoon extra-virgin olive oil
1 teaspoon minced fresh thyme leaves
12 anchovy fillets, rinsed and drained

1. Cut the celery into julienne about 2 inches long. Bring a large pot of water to a boil, salt it, and add the vinegar. Add the celery and simmer until it is easily pierced with the tip of a paring knife but not too soft, about 5 minutes.

2. Meanwhile, dice the tomato; place it in a small bowl and toss it with a pinch of salt, the olive oil, and thyme. Set aside.

3. When the celery is cooked, remove it from the pot with a slotted spoon or skimmer and transfer it to a serving bowl. Pour the tomato mixture, including all juices, over the celery and toss to combine.

4. Garnish with anchovy fillets and serve.

SERVES 4   COOKING TIME: 25 MINUTES

FRYING, BRAISING, GLAZING CELERY and CELERY ROOT, and CELERY MARINADE

FRYING CELERY ROOT

Fried celery root is a fun alternative to potatoes. Cut the trimmed celery root into matchsticks. Dredge the pieces in flour, shaking them over the bowl with your hands to eliminate any excess [1]. Fry them in a generous amount of very hot oil, drain [2], and briefly blot them on paper towels. Serve immediately.

BRAISING CELERY

A very tasty side dish: white celery stalks, cut to 3-inch lengths, then sautéed with extra-virgin olive oil, pancetta, and onion [3]. Add some tomato puree (page 208) diluted with broth or water [4] and simmer over low heat.

GLAZING CELERY AND CELERY ROOT

To glaze turned pieces of celery root with equal-sized lengths of celery stalks, brown them in a small amount of butter, then add a ladleful or two of hot broth and simmer until the liquid reduces, leaving both types of celery coated in a silky sauce [5].

CELERY MARINADE

To make an excellent marinade for red meat that you can then braise or stew, toss chopped celery stalks, chopped carrot, and chopped onion in a large bowl. Pour in enough red wine to coat the meat [6]. Marinate in the refrigerator for 8 to 12 hours. Celery's delicate flavor will come through in the finished dish surprisingly well.

EGGPLANT

THE EGGPLANT, BROUGHT TO ITALY BY ARAB TRAVELERS, comes in various shapes and sizes. You may find oval, long (sometimes called Japanese or Asian), or round varieties, and the colors can range from dark purple to violet to white. There's no real difference among the various kinds, so your best bet is to choose the healthiest-looking eggplants available. They should feel firm to the touch and have shiny skin without scarring. Their stems should be green and fresh looking. When an eggplant is overripe, it develops an abundance of seeds, which you want to avoid. Eggplants are almost always cooked, and in most cases, they are salted first in order to purge their bitter taste and eliminate excess water. Eggplants are, in and of themselves, a healthy choice, rich in vitamins and minerals and not terribly caloric. However, they can absorb virtually unlimited amounts of oil during cooking.

Long Eggplant

Oval Eggplant

Round Violetta Eggplant

TRIMMING, PEELING, and CUTTING EGGPLANTS

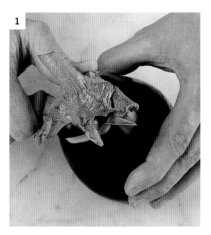

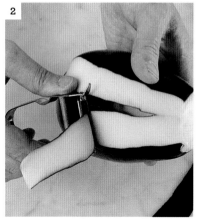

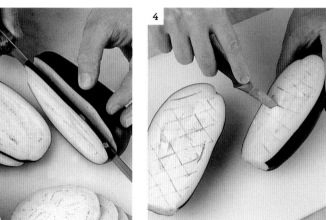

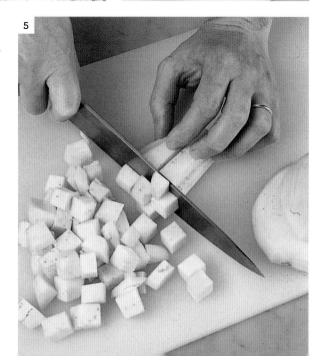

TRIMMING

To trim an eggplant, all you really need to do is cut off the green stem [1] and a little bit of the vegetable underneath. You don't discard much of an eggplant.

PEELING

Thin eggplant skin can be removed using a vegetable peeler [2]. The skin is perfectly edible, however, and if you're going to cut the eggplant lengthwise, you should leave at least some of the skin intact. It looks pretty, and it helps the slices hold their shape once they're cooked.

SLICING

No matter whether eggplants are long and narrow or squat and round, they can be sliced crosswise into rounds or lengthwise into strips [3], depending on the recipe.

CROSSHATCHING

This technique helps eggplants to cook more evenly and is especially useful if you'll be taking out the flesh and stuffing the eggplant. Using a sharp paring knife, make deep, intersecting slits into the cut side of half an eggplant [4].

DICING

When you'll be stewing the eggplant or using it in sauce, peel it completely and cut it into ½-inch cubes [5].

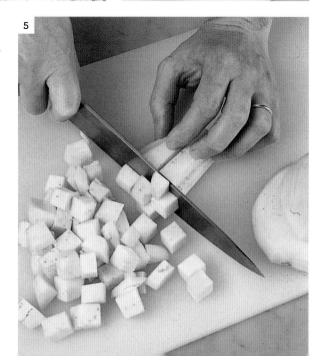

183

PURGING and GRILLING EGGPLANT

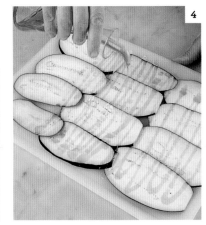

PURGING

Before an eggplant is grilled or fried, especially if it's been hanging around in the refrigerator for a while, it should be salted and drained to take away some of the bitterness. Layer slices of eggplant in a colander, salting each layer **[1]**, and set a plate on top of them. Place a weight (a can of beans or similar small, heavy item will work) on top of the plate **[2]** and let the eggplant sit for at least 30 minutes. Then, to eliminate excess water, press the eggplant gently with your hands and blot it with paper towels **[3]**. Long, thin eggplants generally don't need to be purged. You probably don't need to purge an eggplant that you'll be sautéing or stewing either, as long as it's fresh, but you can't taste eggplant when it's raw to determine its level of bitterness, so better safe than sorry is the rule.

GRILLING

Cut an unpeeled eggplant lengthwise into uniform slices about ¼ inch thick. Drizzle the slices with olive oil **[4]** and place them on a hot grill **[5]**. Turn once to cook both sides **[6]**.

Caponata

2 medium eggplants, cut lengthwise into ½-inch slices

3 tablespoons fine sea salt

3 tablespoons extra-virgin olive oil

1 small yellow onion, minced

2 stalks celery, chopped

1½ cups Italian canned tomatoes and their juices

1½ cups pitted oil-cured black olives

1 tablespoon capers, rinsed and drained

½ cup red wine vinegar

2 teaspoons sugar

¼ cup chopped basil leaves

1. Lay the eggplant slices in a single layer on dish towels or paper towels. Sprinkle both sides liberally with the salt; let them stand for at least 1 hour to allow the bitter juices to drain.

2. Preheat a grill or broiler. Rinse the eggplant slices and pat them dry. Brush the slices lightly with 2 tablespoons of the oil. Grill or broil them until they are soft and slightly charred, about 3 minutes per side; set them aside to cool.

3. Heat the remaining 1 tablespoon oil in a large sauté pan over low heat. Sauté the onion for 1 minute. Add the celery; sauté until it is soft, about 10 minutes. Add the tomatoes, olives, and capers; increase the heat to medium. Simmer, stirring occasionally, until the tomato liquid has been reduced somewhat and the ingredients are combined, about 5 minutes.

4. Meanwhile, roughly chop the grilled eggplant slices. Add the eggplant to the pan; cook for 1 minute. Pour the vinegar into the pan and sprinkle on the sugar; simmer, stirring occasionally, until most of the liquid has evaporated, about 10 minutes. Remove the pan from the heat and stir in the basil.

SERVES 8 AS AN APPETIZER ⟋⟍ COOKING TIME: 30 MINUTES (PLUS 1 HOUR FOR SALTING EGGPLANTS)

Caponata

Caponata is one of Sicily's best-known and best-loved dishes. There are probably as many recipes for it as there are cooks in Sicily, but it always includes eggplant. Grilling the eggplant makes the resulting dish a little less heavy.

Caponata may be served as an appetizer, a side dish, or a kind of relish, where its acidity really shines. Try it on top of grilled fish or spread on toasted bread. It may be eaten hot or at room temperature and can be prepared in advance, making it a great choice for picnics.

SAUTÉING, BLANCHING, and PRESERVING EGGPLANT

SAUTÉING

One of the classic ways to cook eggplant is to sauté diced eggplant in extra-virgin olive oil with garlic and parsley—as simple as that [1].

BLANCHING

Peel the eggplant and cut it into slices. Boil the slices in salted water or water with a teaspoon of white vinegar added [2]. Season the eggplant with oil, salt, and pepper and serve immediately, or follow the instructions below to preserve it in jars.

PRESERVING

Remove the boiled eggplant slices from their cooking water with a slotted spoon and drain them on paper or kitchen towels [3]. Place the eggplant in sterilized dry jars, along with whole cloves of garlic, pepper, and aromatic herbs, and add enough olive oil to cover [4]. Refrigerated, the eggplant should keep for at least 1 week.

Crazy apple

Eggplant is of Chinese and Indian origin and is commonly used in Middle Eastern cooking, but when it first arrived in the West, it was considered poisonous and was used only for ornamental purposes. The Italian word for eggplant, melanzana, comes from mela insana, which means "crazy apple."

FRIED EGGPLANT, BAKED EGGPLANT, and MARINATED EGGPLANT

FRIED

Eggplant slices that have been salted and pressed to remove excess liquid (page 184) and then dried thoroughly with paper towels are first dredged in flour [1] and then in beaten egg. Fry a few slices at a time in very hot oil, remove them with a slotted spoon [2] and drain, sprinkle them with salt, and serve immediately.

 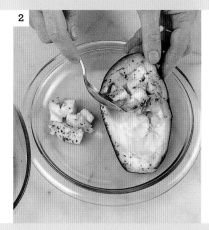

BAKED

Slice an eggplant in half, crosshatch it (page 183), and bake it with oil and minced herbs [1]. Once the eggplant flesh is soft, you can use a spoon to scrape it out, leaving the peel intact [2]. Combine the cooked eggplant with other ingredients to make a stuffing, if desired.

MARINATED EGGPLANT

Use a mortar and a pestle to grind rinsed anchovy fillets, garlic, chile pepper, and oregano. Thin the paste with a little vinegar until you have a fluid sauce. Pour this over thick slices of blanched eggplant that have cooled. Allow them to marinate (preferably overnight) before serving.

FENNEL

ORIGINALLY FROM ASIA MINOR AND THE MEDITERRANEAN BASIN—where it still grows in its wild form—fennel has been appreciated since the ancient Roman era. The fronds are used as an herb and the root as a vegetable. When raw, fennel tastes strongly of anise or licorice (as do its seeds); that flavor softens when it's cooked. Italians classify fennel as "male" (rounder bulb) and "female" (a longer bulb) and prefer the former for salads (as well as cut into sticks and eaten as a snack like carrots and celery) and the latter for cooking. There are numerous varieties of fennel grown in different areas of Italy, and they are almost always named for the areas where they are cultivated. These include sweet Florentine fennel and giant Neapolitan fennel. In a grocery store in the United States, you're unlikely to have a choice between different varieties or "genders." When purchasing fennel, which is always harvested before it blossoms, look for white, firm bulbs with tightly overlapping leaves and feathery fronds.

Fennel is believed to aid digestion. When cooking cabbage and beans, Italians often add a small amount of wild fennel to the dish for that reason. Keep in mind that while fennel pairs beautifully with lemon juice, its aromatic compounds make an unhappy match with wine and vinegar. Most of those oils disperse when fennel is cooked, but a salad with raw fennel is rarely if ever tossed with a vinaigrette and instead is dressed with extra-virgin olive oil alone or whisked with some lemon juice.

Male Fennel

Female Fennel

Wild Fennel

TRIMMING and PREPARING FENNEL

TRIMMING

Cut off and discard the cylindrical stalks that sprout from the top of the bulb [1], but keep the fronds, which can be used as herbs and as garnish. Cut away the base of the stem [2]. Remove the thickest external layer [3]. If these pieces are undamaged and firm, you can chop them and use them for soup, but they are often fibrous and should be discarded. You will lose about half the weight of a bulb of fennel in trimming.

PREPARING

If you plan to cook the fennel whole, make an X in the base of a trimmed fennel bulb, cutting about ½ inch into the bulb, to help it cook evenly [4]. If you are going to slice it into smaller pieces, cut it in half and then into quarters [5] and gently loosen the layers. This makes it easier to clean the fennel, which you can do simply by holding it under cold running water. To stop fennel from turning brown, soak it in a bowl of cold water. This will give the fennel terrific crunch if eaten raw [6].

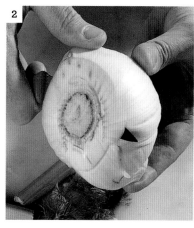

189

THINLY SLICING and CUTTING FENNEL INTO JULIENNE

*M*atchsticks of fennel are a nonnegotiable ingredient in pinzimonio, the simplest of Italian appetizers, for which raw matchsticks of vegetables are provided for dipping in extra-virgin olive oil seasoned simply with salt and pepper. But fennel is delicious in more elaborate preparations as well. It can be braised or boiled, and when baked with béchamel and grated aged cheese, it makes a satisfying vegetarian entrée.

Cut whole fennel bulbs into medium-thick slices **[1]** or separate the layers and cut them into julienne **[2]**. If you plan to eat the fennel raw, either on its own or as part of a mixed salad, cut the pieces to smaller size and in very thin slices **[3]**.

fennel seeds

Fennel seeds are actually the fruit of the wild fennel plant and are rich in the aromatic compounds that give fennel its distinctive flavor. Chief among these is a substance called anethole, also found in other plants in the same family, such as anise and caraway. Fennel seeds are used to flavor both sweet and savory baked goods, cured meats (such as Tuscany's famous fennel sausage), cheese, fresh and preserved fish, lamb, duck, and pork.

Finocchi ripieni di verdure

stuffed fennel

3 bulbs fennel of similar sizes

1 medium carrot

1 small onion, minced

6 tablespoons extra-virgin olive oil

2 tablespoons bread crumbs

Fine sea salt to taste

Freshly ground black pepper to taste

⅓ cup grated Grana Padano cheese

2 ounces provolone cheese, cut into strips

1. Trim the fennel bulbs, keeping the ends intact, and cut them in half. Make a few slits in the center of each bulb half. Steam the bulbs in a steamer basket until tender, 12 to 15 minutes. Preheat the broiler.

2. Carve out the interior of the bulbs, leaving the outsides whole, and mince the fennel pieces you removed, as well as the carrot. Sauté the onion in 3 tablespoons of the olive oil. Add the carrot and fennel to the pan with the onion and sauté until soft. Stir in the bread crumbs. Season lightly with salt and pepper.

3. Place the fennel bulbs in a baking dish. Season them to taste with salt and pepper and drizzle them with the remaining 3 tablespoons olive oil. Sprinkle the grated cheese over the fennel, then stuff the bulbs with the bread crumb mixture.

4. Place the strips of provolone on top of the fennel and broil until the cheese has melted and the bread crumbs are golden, about 3 minutes. Keep a close eye on the fennel to be sure it doesn't burn.

SERVES 6   COOKING TIME: 25 MINUTES

BLANCHED, BRAISED, and STEAMED FENNEL

BLANCHED

Fennel cut into wedges can be boiled in 10 to 12 minutes. Include a thick lemon slice in the water to avoid discoloration [1].

BRAISED

Cook shallot, onion, and pancetta in a small amount of oil. Add ¼ cup tomato paste. Add fennel cut into wedges and enough cold water to cover [2]. Simmer for 20 minutes.

STEAMED

Arrange fennel wedges in a steamer basket [3]. Remove them from the heat when they are cooked through but still firm, 12 to 15 minutes [4]. Steamed fennel wedges can be eaten plain or used in other dishes.

Wild fennel

Wild fennel is foraged all over the Mediterranean, and you can see its feathery fronds in fields throughout Italy. It is commonly used to flavor fish and lamb dishes, especially in the South. The fronds from cultivated fennel make a passable substitute.

FRIED and BAKED FENNEL, and FENNEL IN PASTRY

FRIED

Blanch or steam wedges of fennel and pat them dry as thoroughly as possible. Dredge them in beaten egg [1] and then in a mixture of grated Grana Padano cheese and bread crumbs. Fry the fennel in butter, turning the pieces to brown both sides [2]. Drain them on paper towels, season them with salt, and serve hot.

BAKED

Line the bottom of a baking dish with slices of whole wheat bread moistened with milk and arrange wedges of blanched or steamed fennel (see page opposite) on top of them [1]. Cover the fennel with slices of hard-boiled egg and Taleggio cheese [2]. Sprinkle on grated Parmigiano Reggiano cheese and bake at 350 degrees F until the cheese has melted and browned.

IN PASTRY

Blanch or steam 2 pounds fennel (see page opposite) and sauté it in butter. Season with salt and mince. Combine the fennel with 3 to 4 ounces grated Gruyère cheese, an egg yolk, and 4 rinsed, finely chopped anchovy fillets [1]. Make a double-crust savory short-crust pastry such as the one on page 163, line a pie plate with one round of the pastry, and spread the filling evenly into it [2]. Cover with a second disk of dough and bake at 375 degrees F until brown, about 15 minutes. Serve warm.

Tatin di finocchi

savory fennel tarte tatin

2 (12-by-8-inch) sheets puff pastry

¼ cup grated Parmigiano Reggiano cheese

¼ cup grated pecorino Romano cheese

2 bulbs fennel

¾ pound thinly sliced prosciutto crudo

¾ cup cooked chickpeas (canned are fine), drained

1 large egg

1 tablespoon extra-virgin olive oil

Fine sea salt to taste

Freshly ground black pepper to taste

2 tablespoons unsalted butter

2 shallots

⅓ cup sugar

1½ tablespoons apple cider vinegar

1. Preheat the oven to 375 degrees F. Brush the puff pastry sheets with a little water, sprinkle one with three quarters of the grated cheeses, place the second pastry sheet on top, and sprinkle half of it with the remaining cheeses. Fold the 2 sheets in half into a 6-by-8-inch rectangle. Using a rolling pin, roll the pastry into a square about 1/16 inch thick. Trim this into a 9-inch disk and cut a 2-inch ring around the perimeter of the disk.

2. Butter the bottom and sides of a 9-inch pan with sloping sides. Line the bottom with a piece of parchment paper and line the sides with the 2-inch ring of puff pastry, folding it at a 45-degree angle so that it covers about ⅓ inch on the bottom of the pan as well.

3. Trim the fennel and cut it into 24 wedges. Wrap 15 of the wedges with all but 1 ounce of the prosciutto slices.

4. In a food processor, puree the chickpeas with the egg, olive oil, and ½ cup water, and season with salt and pepper; process until the mixture is very smooth. Melt 1 tablespoon of the butter in a small pan. Mince the remaining prosciutto and cook it in the butter along with the minced shallots. Stir into the chickpea puree until combined.

5. In a clean pan, melt the remaining 1 tablespoon butter and sprinkle in the sugar. When the mixture begins to caramelize, add the vinegar, being careful to guard against splatters; cook for 3 additional minutes, then remove the pan from the heat. Immediately pour this caramel into the bottom of the pie plate and arrange the fennel wedges in a circle on top so that every fourth wedge is a piece of fennel that is not wrapped in prosciutto. Arrange the remaining fennel wedges in the center of the circle.

6. Pour the chickpea mixture over the fennel and place the disk of puff pastry on top. Bake in the preheated oven for 25 minutes. Place a serving platter upside down over the tart. Flip the pan and serving platter so that the tart unmolds onto the platter. Peel off the parchment paper, rearrange any components that have moved slightly, and serve immediately.

SERVES 8 ⟋ COOKING TIME: 1 HOUR

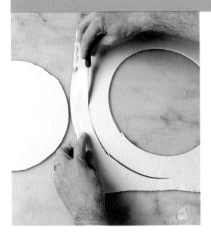

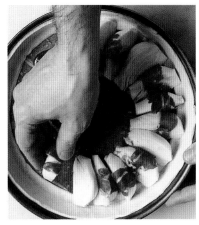

All vegetables must be trimmed and cleaned before being frozen. Most should be parboiled for a few minutes. If you freeze your vegetables quickly at the right temperature, they'll keep for up to a year. Naturally, once thawed, they need to be used in short order and cannot be frozen again.

Freezing Vegetables

Pick the best vegetables for freezing. Discard any torn or wilted parts, seeds, and if appropriate, the peel. Always wash vegetables very well. Parboil them in unsalted water for a few minutes; this will keep them from suffering freezer burn or turning yellow in the freezer. Be sure to use a large enough pot; alternatively, cook the vegetables in batches, refreshing the cooking water every two to three batches.

Remove the parboiled vegetables from the cooking water with a slotted spoon and immerse them immediately in ice water. Shocking them this way will help them keep their color.

Drain the vegetables and squeeze them dry, if appropriate. Divide them into small portions. That way they will freeze more quickly and will be more convenient to use, since small batches thaw quickly.

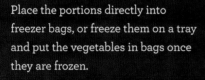

Place the portions directly into freezer bags, or freeze them on a tray and put the vegetables in bags once they are frozen.

You can freeze cut vegetables of all kinds, as long as, again, the pieces are small so that they freeze quickly.

You can also keep prepared vegetables and sauces in the freezer. Use ice cube trays or silicon muffin tins to create the portions. Good candidates for freezing include diced tomatoes, roasted peppers, and herb sauces such as pesto.

PEPPERS

THE SPANISH BROUGHT PEPPERS from Central and South America to Europe. At first, in Italy, peppers were seen only as ornamental plants, but eventually Italians discovered they were edible. The rest is history—peppers are now an important part of Italian cuisine. They are eaten raw and roasted, stewed, sautéed, and stuffed. When it comes to bell peppers, Italians favor yellow and red peppers over the green peppers often found in the United States. The variety of peppers available is mind-boggling: There are bull's horn peppers, which are long and cone shaped, and larger, fleshier varieties like quadrato d'Asti peppers. Holland peppers are round, while giant sweet peppers are elongated and, as their name implies, large. Little green friarelli peppers are sweet and perfect for frying. Peppers are spicy—or not—due to the presence—or absence—of capsaicin, which resides in both the flesh and the seeds.

Friarelli Peppers

Bull's Horn Peppers

Holland Pepper

Giant Sweet Pepper

Quadrato d'Asti Pepper

TRIMMING and PREPARING PEPPERS

There are two ways to trim peppers: You can either cut around the stem with a paring knife [1] and pull out the stem and central core, leaving the pepper intact, or cut the pepper in half and pull out the stem, core, seeds, and internal ribs [2]. There isn't much to discard with peppers, only about 10 percent of their weight.

Some recipes will instruct you to salt peppers and drain them of excess liquid. To do that, toss the pieces of pepper in a bowl with some salt, set them aside for a couple of hours, then press them gently between your hands to extract as much liquid as possible [3].

Depending on how they will be used, trimmed peppers may be cut into wedges or julienne, diced, or minced [4].

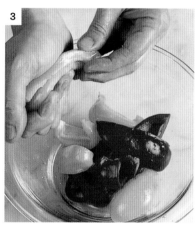

ROASTED, SAUTÉED, and PUREED PEPPERS

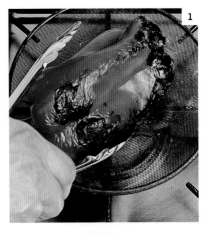

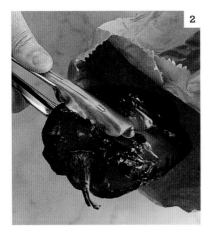

ROASTED

To roast a pepper, making it both sweeter and easier to peel, you have three choices: You can use tongs to hold it over a lit gas burner (using a flame tamer, if you like) **[1]**, cook it on a griddle, or roast it in the oven. When the pepper is black and blistered all over, place it in a brown paper bag **[2]** or in a bowl covered tightly with plastic wrap and let it cool. The skin should then peel off easily, and you can pull out the stem and core. To serve the roasted peppers as they are, cut them into strips and dress them with oil, salt, pepper, minced garlic, and herbs.

SAUTÉED

Small green frying peppers (known as friarelli peppers in the south of Italy) can be left whole or cut in half lengthwise. After trimming and cleaning them, sauté them in extra-virgin olive oil with salt **[3]**.

PUREED

Cut red and yellow bell peppers into chunks and cook them in extra-virgin olive oil with some salt, then pass them through a food mill **[4]**. The resulting puree can be used as a pasta sauce.

Purchasing peppers

No matter whether they are green, red, or yellow, when purchasing peppers, look for those that are shiny and firm, with taut skin and no visible damage. If you are going to cut up the peppers, any type will work, but otherwise consider how you intend to serve them. If you're planning to roast them, look for large and fleshy peppers; round Holland peppers are perfect for stuffing, while small green peppers such as friarelli are ideal for frying. The many varieties of bell peppers grown today are generally very sweet, but it's best to taste a little piece before cooking them to be sure.

PEPPERS IN SAUCE, PRESERVED IN VINEGAR, and STUFFED

IN SAUCE

Cut bell peppers, plum tomatoes (or other tomatoes appropriate for making sauce), and onion into dice. Cook slowly over low heat in a large pot with a few teaspoons of sugar **[1]**; add garlic, chile pepper, extra-virgin olive oil, vinegar, ground mustard seeds, ground cinnamon, and cloves **[2]**. When the mixture is very soft, puree it through a food mill. This sauce can be preserved in jars. It makes an excellent accompaniment to boiled meats and raw vegetables.

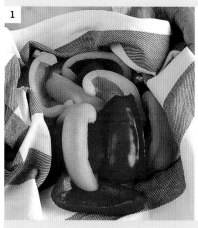

PRESERVED IN VINEGAR

Salt and drain red and yellow bell pepper wedges, then dry them with a clean kitchen towel **[1]** or paper towels. Meanwhile, boil either plain white wine vinegar or a combination of water, white wine, and white wine vinegar with black peppercorns, chile peppers, and coriander seeds **[2]**. Place the pepper wedges in jars and pour in enough of the vinegar mixture to cover them. Can to preserve safely for long-term storage according to jar manufacturer's instructions.

STUFFED

Prepare a stuffing by combining stale bread softened with a sprinkling of water with drained, flaked tuna canned in olive oil and minced parsley **[1]**; season this mixture with oil, salt, and pepper and use it to stuff cleaned and trimmed pepper halves **[2]**. Place the stuffed bell pepper halves in a lightly oiled baking dish and bake at 350 degrees F for 40 minutes **[3]**.

PEPPERS AND EGGS, FRIED PEPPERS, PEPPERS WITH BREAD CRUMBS, and PEPPERS WITH ANCHOVIES

PEPPERS AND EGGS

Cut red, green, and yellow bell peppers into strips and sauté them in extra-virgin olive oil [1]. When the peppers have softened, add 2 beaten eggs [2]. Cook, stirring, until the eggs are firm. Serve as a side dish.

FRIED PEPPERS

Remove the ribs and seeds from bell peppers and cut them into thin strips. Dredge the pieces in flour, shaking off any excess [1]. Fry them in a generous amount of oil [2], drain well, and serve hot.

PEPPERS WITH BREAD CRUMBS

Cut bell peppers into wedges and sauté them until soft. Sprinkle on a mixture of bread crumbs, grated pecorino Romano cheese, capers, oregano, and salt [1].

PEPPERS WITH ANCHOVIES

Toss wedges of peeled roasted bell peppers in a sauce made by briefly cooking minced garlic and anchovy fillets in melted butter. Sprinkle with minced parsley [2].

CHILE PEPPERS

There are hundreds of different types of spicy peppers. In Italy, hot peppers are used primarily in the South (the cuisine of Calabria is particularly spicy), and mostly in the form of long, thin red peppers, which may be fresh or dried.

FRESH PEPPERS
Fresh hot peppers should be firm and shiny. To clean, wipe them with a dry cloth or paper towel. Spiciness can vary greatly—if you are wary, remove the ribs and seeds from a fresh pepper.

DRIED PEPPERS
Crushed dried peppers will keep almost indefinitely in a cool, dark place. The whole chiles are easy to crush for use in recipes. Just place a bunch of them in a mortar (ceramic is best as it doesn't absorb odors as readily) and carefully crush them with a pestle.

DRYING PEPPERS

To dry fresh chile peppers, simply hang them from their stems in a shady, cool, ventilated place. You can tie a couple of bunches together with kitchen twine if you like.

CHILE PEPPER JAM

In a saucepan, combine 1 cup sugar with a pinch of salt and ⅔ cup water. Remove the seeds from 6 to 8 fresh chile peppers and mince them; add a tablespoon or two of minced red bell pepper. Stir the peppers into the sugar syrup and cook until they become dense and liquid. Serve the jam with pork or poultry, or alongside a cheese plate.

TOMATOES

TOMATOES MAY ORIGINALLY HAIL FROM THE AMERICAS, but Italian cuisine could hardly exist without them. The inventiveness of Italian cooking met its match in the versatility of this vegetable. (Yes, the tomato is technically a fruit, but it is never treated as one.) It seems there's nothing the tomato can't do. And there are almost as many different varieties of tomato as there are dishes using tomato as an ingredient. You'll want to keep the way you're going to use tomatoes in mind when buying them. When making salad, look for cuore di bue (ox heart) tomatoes, an heirloom variety with lots of flesh and few seeds. Plum tomatoes, especially the San Marzano variety, are great for sauce and for canning. The round Sardinian tomato, red with green shoulders, marries well with fish, while vine tomatoes and deeply lobed costoluto tomatoes are multipurpose. Small cherry tomatoes and pear tomatoes can be eaten out of hand as a snack, or halved and tossed into pasta and rice salads. They also make a juicy base for fish cooked in parchment.

Canned tomatoes are a central component in Italian cooking. They are available whole and peeled, crushed, pureed, or in the form of tomato paste (sometimes labeled tomato concentrate). Look for an Italian brand, preferably one that uses San Marzano tomatoes.

Cherry Tomatoes

Plum Tomatoes

San Marzano Tomatoes

Vine Tomatoes

Sardinian Tomatoes

Costoluto Tomatoes

Cuore di Bue Tomatoes

PREPARING TOMATOES FOR SAUCE

*T*o prepare tomatoes to be used to make sauce, you should peel and seed them.

PEELING

Cut around the stem with a paring knife to remove it [1]. Cut an X at the base of each tomato [2]. Dunk the tomatoes in boiling water for 1 minute, then remove them with a slotted spoon or skimmer [3]. The peel will now come off with a quick tug using a paring knife [4].

SEEDING AND COOKING

Cut the tomatoes in half and push the seeds and their pulp out with your thumb [5]. The tomatoes can now be diced [6] and cooked in extra-virgin olive oil with minced garlic or with a classic celery, carrot, and onion soffritto (see page 260). If you like, add aromatic herbs of your choosing.

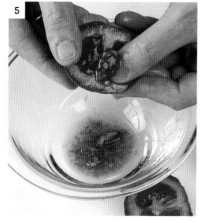

MARINATED, HOLLOWED OUT FOR STUFFING, SAUTÉED, PUREED, and DRAINED TOMATOES

MARINATED

Dice tomatoes and toss them with salt, extra-virgin olive oil, thickly sliced peeled garlic cloves, and basil [1]. Use the tomatoes as a sauce for pasta or spoon them onto toasted bread for bruschetta.

HOLLOWED OUT

If you want to stuff tomatoes, cut off the stem end with a paring knife, then, working from the top, scoop out the pulp, seeds, and core; let them fall into a bowl [2]. When you are finished, strain the contents of the bowl and use the juices to season the stuffing for the tomatoes.

SAUTÉED

Cherry tomatoes can be cut in half or sautéed whole in a pan to make the base for a sauce [3]. Larger tomatoes, cut into smaller pieces, can be sautéed as well.

PUREED

Use a food mill [4] to puree diced ripe tomatoes. The food mill will remove the seed and skins.

DRAINED

Let pureed raw tomatoes drain overnight at room temperature through cheesecloth or a paper coffee filter set in a sieve. The resulting tomatoes will be concentrated and delicious. Mix the puree with extra-virgin olive oil and finely diced mozzarella and use as a topping for crostini.

CANNING and CUTTING TOMATOES

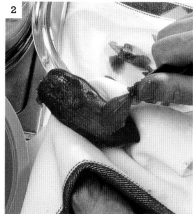

CANNING TOMATOES

Blanch San Marzano or other plum tomatoes in boiling water for a minute or two [1], then peel them [2] and transfer them to jars, layering them with basil leaves [3]. Don't press down or you'll crush the tomatoes, but try not to leave too much space between them. Can to preserve safely for long-term storage according to jar manufacturer's instructions.

CUTTING WEDGES AND SLICES

When using tomatoes in salad, you will often want to cut them into wedges or slices [1]. Don't remove the seeds.

CUTTING HALF WEDGES

Cut wedges in half crosswise [2] if you'll be cooking tomatoes in a sauce or with other vegetables.

CUTTING STRIPS

Seed the tomatoes, then cut them in half. Rest the cut side on the cutting board and quickly slice them into strips [3].

TOMATO PUREE

Cook tomatoes seasoned lightly with salt until soft, about 15 minutes [1], then put them through a food mill. If you make large quantities of sauce, you may want to invest in an automated tomato mill [2]. Transfer the tomato puree to glass jars [3], and can to preserve safely for long-term storage according to jar manufacturer's instructions. This kind of cooked tomato puree is useful for many purposes. For instance, you can heat it with garlic and basil and use it as a sauce for pasta [4].

Pomodori ripieni al forno

baked stuffed tomatoes

½ cup fine bread crumbs

1 tablespoon minced flat-leaf parsley

1 tablespoon minced basil

1 clove garlic, minced

Fine sea salt to taste

Freshly ground black pepper to taste

2 to 3 tablespoons extra-virgin olive oil, plus more for drizzling

8 ripe beefsteak tomatoes, halved and seeded

1. Preheat the oven to 350 degrees F.

2. In a small bowl, mix together the bread crumbs, parsley, basil, and garlic. Season with salt and pepper and mix in 2 tablespoons of the olive oil. The mixture should resemble wet sand. If it seems too dry, stir in a little more oil.

3. Stuff the tomato halves with the bread crumb mixture and set them on a baking sheet lined with parchment paper or in a lightly oiled baking dish. Drizzle the tomatoes with a little olive oil.

4. Roast the tomatoes until they are very soft and the bread crumbs are browned, about 30 minutes. Serve warm or at room temperature.

NOTE: *These are so easy and delicious that you may want to consider doubling the recipe. You can also cut small, thin eggplants or zucchini in half lengthwise and top them with the same bread crumb mixture. Roast until the eggplants or zucchini are quite soft, also about 30 minutes.*

SERVES 4   COOKING TIME: 45 MINUTES

Tomato tips

Tomatoes taste better when they're ripe, and they're better for you, too—that's when their vitamin C and carotene contents are at their peak. If you are going to be using tomatoes raw, look for firm ones, but if you are going to cook them, look for the ripest tomatoes you can find, which may be fairly soft. Tomato skins and seeds are perfectly edible, but some recipes instruct you to remove them for reasons of texture.

WINTER SQUASH

WINTER SQUASH, AS THE NAME IMPLIES, is harvested in the colder seasons of the year. It is a keeping vegetable and can be stored in a cool, dry place for several months. It is a staple of rustic cooking in Italy, where it is eaten on its own and also used to stuff pasta and make savory tarts, gnocchi (see page 87), soup, and risotto. Winter squash can even be sliced into thin julienne and eaten raw. It comes in a wide range of varieties with different shapes, colors, and sizes. Just consider the peel of a winter squash—it can be smooth, bumpy, ribbed, shiny, or wrinkled, and the colors range from gray-brown to orange and green. One of the more popular varieties in Italy is marina di Chioggia, which is large and round, with a very bumpy peel and yellowish pink flesh. Berettina Piacentina squash is ribbed and almost gray on the outside. Delica squash, also known as kabocha in the United States, is green on the outside with a brightly colored flesh. Fairytale pumpkin has orange skin, and butternut squash, perhaps the most widely available type in the United States, has a smooth, almost beige skin and orange flesh that is easily peeled. While all these types of squash are interesting to look at, their flavor does not vary all that widely. The texture of squash flesh may be moist or somewhat dry (or, in the case of spaghetti squash, in the form of edible strings), and some squash have thin skin that can be left in place and even eaten, while others require peeling. Feel free to substitute one for another if the type of squash indicated in a recipe isn't available to you.

Butternut Squash

Delica Squash

**Berettina Piacentina
Squash**

**Marina di Chioggia
Squash**

Fairytale Squash

CUTTING, CLEANING, and PEELING SQUASH

*A*n unpeeled, uncut winter squash will keep for months in a cool, dry place. However, once you cut it, you need to use it pretty quickly. Some large varieties are sold in halves and/or quarters. If you purchase those cut pieces, check to be sure that both the flesh and the peel are firm, with no soft spots, and use them the day you buy them.

CUTTING
Use a broad chef's knife to cut winter squash. Hold the squash firmly on the cutting board and cut off a wedge [1].

CLEANING
Use a spoon to remove the seeds and strings. Scrape with the side of the spoon to be sure you get them all [2].

PEELING
Place the wedge on its side and use the chef's knife to cut away the peel [3]. If the peel is thin, you can use a paring knife for better control [4].

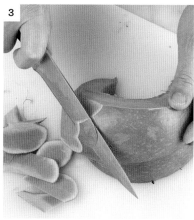

STEAMING, SAUTÉING, and ROASTING WINTER SQUASH

STEAMING

Steam squash in a steaming basket set over boiling water [1]. If you cut the squash into pieces, it will cook faster.

SAUTÉING

Diced squash can be sautéed in a pan with salt and pepper and served as a side dish [2].

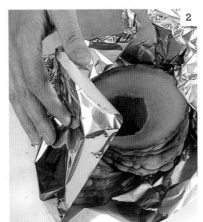

ROASTING

Many squash preparations call for cooked squash flesh. If you're cooking squash for this purpose, don't bother to peel it. Just use a spoon to remove the seeds and strings [1]. Wrap the squash wedges in aluminum foil [2] and roast them at 350 degrees F until soft, about 40 minutes. Then scoop out the flesh and discard the skin [3].

Tip

The many different varieties of winter squash are usually divided into two groups: those with compact, sweet, dry flesh and those with more fibrous moist flesh. The former are best for pureed squash and stuffing tortelli and other pastas, while the latter are best in soups and sauces.

Sformato di ceci con la zucca

chickpea tart with a winter squash crust

¼ cup extra-virgin olive oil

1 clove garlic, peeled and smashed

3 sage leaves, lightly crushed

Leaves of 1 sprig rosemary

1 small winter squash, quartered, or 1 wedge of a large winter squash, peel left on, seeds and strings removed

2 tablespoons unsalted butter

2 (15-ounce) cans chickpeas

2 large eggs

About ½ cup whole milk

Fine sea salt to taste

Freshly ground black pepper to taste

⅓ cup grated aged cheese such as Parmigiano Reggiano, grated on the large holes of a box grater

1. Preheat the oven to 350 degrees F. Combine the olive oil with the garlic, sage, and rosemary in a small saucepan. Cook gently over low heat to infuse the oil, then set the mixture aside.

2. Cut the whole squash or large wedge of squash into slices, wrap them in aluminum foil, and roast them until soft, about 40 minutes. Leave the oven on when the squash is cooked.

3. Butter a round or oval springform pan. Line the bottom and sides with parchment paper and butter the parchment paper as well. Cut the cooked squash into thin slices and use them to line the bottom and sides of the pan, bending them slightly to fit and overlapping them.

4. Drain the chickpeas, rinse, drain again, and puree in a food processor fitted with the metal blade or in a blender, along with the eggs and enough milk to make a thick puree. (Gradually drizzle the milk in through the feed tube with the machine running.) Season with salt and pepper.

5. Pour the olive oil through a small sieve to remove the garlic, sage, and rosemary. Pour the flavored oil into the chickpea mixture and puree or blend to combine.

6. Transfer the chickpea mixture to the springform pan and spread it evenly over the squash. Sprinkle on the grated cheese and bake until the top is browned and crusty and the chickpea mixture is set, about 40 minutes. Allow the tart to cool slightly before unmolding it. Serve it warm or at room temperature.

SERVES 8   COOKING TIME: 1 HOUR 30 MINUTES

SQUASH PUREE, MOSTARDA, and ROASTED SQUASH SEEDS

PUREE

Puree pieces of steamed squash using a food mill **[1]**. Over low heat, combine the pureed squash with butter, salt, and some freshly grated nutmeg **[2]**. Include one or two boiled potatoes in the puree, if you like.

MOSTARDA

Sauté diced squash with 2 or 3 shallots until browned. Add sugar, water, vinegar, and white wine and cook over low heat until very soft and syrupy **[3]**. Add a little mustard powder and cook a little while longer to combine the flavors. This homemade mostarda (a sweet-and-sour condiment similar to a chutney) pairs well with boiled meats **[4]**.

ROASTED SQUASH SEEDS

Squash seeds that have been cleaned of strings **[5]** can be spread in a Pyrex dish and baked until dry and crispy **[6]**. Shell and eat these roasted seeds—sprinkled with some salt, if you like—as a snack.

SQUASH TART, SOUP, and FRITTERS

TART

Make an olive oil dough: Place 1½ cups unbleached all-purpose flour in a bowl. Drizzle in ¼ cup olive oil and stir with a fork. Drizzle in enough water (probably ½ cup or a little more), stirring with the fork as you do, to make a soft dough. (This can also be done in a food processor fitted with the dough blade.) Knead the dough until it is smooth, then shape it into a ball, wrap it with plastic, and set it aside to rest for 30 minutes to 1 hour.

Grate 1 pound raw squash on the large holes of a box grater. Salt the squash and set it in a colander over a bowl. Place a heavy plate on top of the squash to drain it. When the squash has given up its liquid, squeeze it dry in a clean kitchen towel. Combine the squash with 1¼ cups rice cooked al dente, ½ cup ricotta cheese, 1 large egg, a few tablespoons butter, a little grated aged cheese such as Parmigiano Reggiano, and salt and freshly ground black pepper to taste [1]. Roll out a little more than half of the dough on a lightly floured surface into a very thin round (if it tears, patch it and continue) and use this to line the bottom and sides of a fluted tart pan with a removable bottom. Pour in the filling, smooth the surface, then roll out the remaining dough and place it on top of the tart. Pinch around the perimeter to seal. Bake at 350 degrees F until the tart is browned and blistering on top, 35 to 40 minutes [2].

SOUP

Sauté minced onion, celery, carrot, and fatback or pancetta in butter until golden. Add about 1 pound (a little less is fine) diced raw winter squash [1]. Add broth (see page 56) to cover and bring it to a boil, then turn down the heat to maintain a simmer and cook for 15 minutes. Stir in 1 cup short-grain rice and cook until the rice is tender [2].

FRITTERS

Soak 1 cup golden raisins in water to soften. Mash 1 pound cooked winter squash with a fork. Stir together ¾ cup unbleached all-purpose flour, 1 tablespoon baking powder, 2 tablespoons granulated sugar, a little grated lemon zest, and some salt; sprinkle this dry mixture over the squash a little at a time, mashing it together with the fork. Drain the raisins and stir them in. Form the mixture into small balls, heat a generous amount of oil or lard until it is very hot, and fry the fritters [1]. Blot them briefly on paper towels and serve them hot, sprinkled with a little confectioners' sugar [2].

ZUCCHINI

MILDLY FLAVORED ZUCCHINI, A TYPE OF SUMMER SQUASH, is one of the cornerstones of Mediterranean cooking in general and Italian cooking in particular. Zucchini was brought to Europe after the "discovery" of the Americas. It is harvested in summer and usually remains available through September, though it is grown in greenhouses these days, so you'll see it at the grocery store year-round. Italians have never developed an enthusiasm for yellow squash and tend to stick to varieties of zucchini. The verde di Milano variety (sometimes labeled black beauty zucchini in the United States) is a firm, dark green type with very white flesh, like the zucchini that is most widely available in the United States. Striata d'Italia zucchini is long and thin, with striped skin. Trombetta zucchini is a light green crookneck type of squash that resembles a trumpet. Round squash such as the tonda di Nizza is ideal for stuffing. White zucchini, though it's actually pale green, is also widely available.

Zucchini is convenient, as it cooks quickly and its neutral flavor lends itself to many uses. It is an easy side dish and also appears in savory tarts, rice timbales, pasta, and risotto. Whole zucchini can also be stuffed. Even the blossoms of zucchini are edible and are often featured in frittatas and risotto dishes, or they can be fried or stuffed and baked. Zucchini can be eaten raw, as long as it is fresh and tender.

Verde di Milano Zucchini

Tonda di Nizza Zucchini

Striata d'Italia Zucchini

White Zucchini

Trombetta Zucchini

PURCHASING, TRIMMING, and CUTTING ZUCCHINI

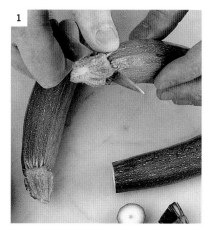

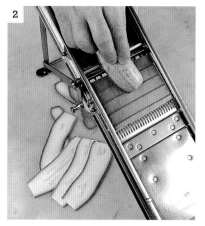

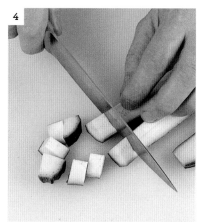

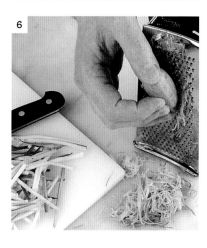

PURCHASING

There isn't a marked difference in the flavor of one type of zucchini versus another. The most important thing to look for is fresh, firm, shiny skin with no holes or brown spots. Zucchini that still has its blossom attached is assuredly fresh. (You can also purchase the blossoms separately.) The best zucchini are young and no longer than 8 inches. Larger zucchini often have more developed seeds in the center, which you'll want to cut away before cooking. With younger zucchini, there will be very little waste.

TRIMMING

If you have purchased small, young zucchini, all you need to do is cut off the ends **[1]**. You can cook baby zucchini whole without cutting them at all. If your zucchini are larger, cut them in half or in quarters lengthwise and discard the seeds.

SLICING

If you are planning to grill the zucchini, cut them into thin slices lengthwise, using either a chef's knife or a mandoline **[2]**.

MINCING

Zucchini can be cut into very fine pieces known as brunoise **[3]**.

DICING

Slice the zucchini into quarters the long way, then cut them into 1-inch dice **[4]**. Diced zucchini can be stewed or cooked in soup.

ROUNDS

Cut thin rounds of zucchini with a knife or mandoline **[5]**. Rounds can be sautéed or used in risotto.

JULIENNE

You can cut zucchini into matchsticks (julienne) by hand. These are delicious dredged in flour and fried. You can also grate zucchini on any of the sides of a box grater, depending on how you plan to use them **[6]**.

217

BOILED, GRILLED, and SAUTÉED ZUCCHINI, and ZUCCHINI FRITTATA

BOILED

Diced zucchini or zucchini chunks can be cooked in boiling water or steamed **[1]**. They will be ready in just a few minutes, so check frequently—you want them to remain crisp. To keep cooked zucchini bright green, plunge it into ice water after you remove it from the boiling water or steamer basket. Boiled and steamed zucchini can be added to a green salad or dressed with oil and vinegar and served on its own.

GRILLED

Grill thin slices of zucchini in a hot cast-iron grill pan with ridges or on a gas or charcoal grill **[2]**. Toss the grilled zucchini with extra-virgin olive oil, freshly ground black pepper, salt, and freshly chopped herbs.

SAUTÉED

Cut zucchini into rounds and sauté them with extra-virgin olive oil and minced garlic and parsley **[3]**. Season to taste with salt and freshly ground black pepper.

FRITTATA

Sautéed zucchini make a great base for a frittata. Just add beaten eggs to the pan after the zucchini are cooked **[4]**. (See page 368 for more on cooking a frittata.)

218

ZUCCHINI BLOSSOMS

Brightly colored zucchini blossoms taste faintly of the vegetable itself. They can be eaten raw or cooked. They make a wonderful garnish, but they can also be a feature of a recipe. Blossoms attached to zucchini are female; blossoms with just a stem are male. The male flowers are a little larger and less fragile and are therefore easier to stuff. Zucchini blossoms do not have a long shelf life—it's best to buy them and use them the same day. To clean them, simply check for any bugs or soil and brush them very gently with a damp paper towel. Some people find the pistils at the center of the blossoms bitter, and they can make stuffing awkward. If you want to remove them, simply pinch them off with your fingertips.

SALAD
Whole small blossoms or chopped larger blossoms can be included raw in a salad for a brilliant burst of color.

FRITTATA
Open up small zucchini blossoms or set a large one on its side on top of a frittata (page opposite) when the eggs are still soft (before running it under the broiler) for a stunning effect.

PANFRIED
Dredge stuffed or empty blossoms in a batter of unbleached all-purpose flour and water (the consistency of sour cream or a little bit thinner), then brown them in ½ inch of hot extra-virgin olive oil in a skillet, about 2 minutes per side. Serve immediately.

STUFFED
Pipe a mixture of soft cheeses such as robiola and mascarpone into the center of zucchini blossoms and either serve them raw or twist the ends closed and panfry them as described above. You can also stuff the blossoms with mozzarella cut into small dice before panfrying.

GARNISH
Place whole or chopped zucchini blossoms on cooked risotto with zucchini (or asparagus or other springtime vegetables; see pages 159 and 115).

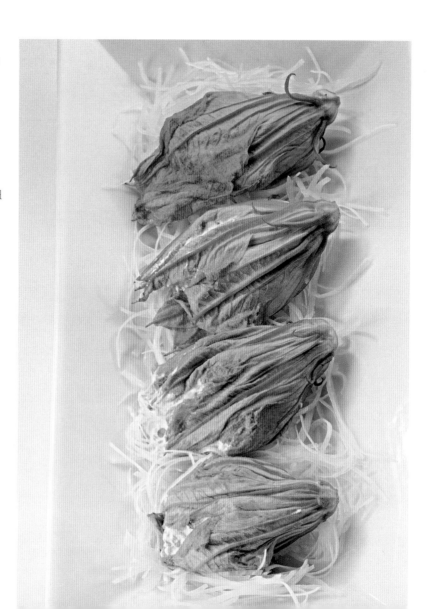

ONE OF ITALY'S GREAT CULINARY ACHIEVEMENTS HAS BEEN ITS ABILITY to raise the humblest ingredients to exalted status—a feat often made necessary by the grinding poverty of the cooks. Few ingredients offer greater nutritional bang for the buck than legumes, the edible seeds harvested from a wide variety of plants in the Fabaceae family. With their high protein content, they have stood in for pricier meat since the Middle Ages. In Italy, cannellini beans, chickpeas, fava beans, lentils, borlotti (a kind of cranberry bean), and pebblelike cicerchie beans are the most common types. Legumes are served as side dishes and used in hearty soups that, with a little rice or pasta added, make wonderful one-dish meals. Legumes also contribute to excellent pasta sauces, often in combination with some form of tomato. Some legumes, such as chickpeas, are ground into flour.

The big question when it comes to dried legumes: to soak or not to soak? It appears that soaking beans in cold water overnight or longer does not speed up the cooking time measurably, as was once believed. (Lentils don't need to be soaked, as they cook relatively quickly.) Soaking does, however, make beans much more digestible for many people, and there's no actual labor involved, so it's still recommended. Simply do a quick check for any stones or other matter in your beans, rinse them once, then place them in a bowl and add cold water to cover.

Resist the temptation to stick dried beans in the back of your pantry and forget about them. Age makes a difference with dried beans. It is ideal to buy from a source with high turnover to ensure that you are getting dried beans that are not more than a year old and to buy them in small amounts so you can use them up. While dried beans last almost indefinitely, if they are on the mature side, they will take longer to soak and longer to cook.

Bean cooking times can vary widely, based on the age of the legumes, the weather, the size of the individual beans, and so on. Start tasting them on the early side, especially for recipes that call for the beans to remain intact. If you'll be pureeing them, it doesn't much matter if they get soft and lose their shape. Finally, wait until legumes are cooked before you add tomatoes or salt; both acid and sodium can retard cooking times and may actually keep the beans from ever becoming as soft as they should be. Unlike pasta, beans should not be al dente—a properly cooked bean can be mashed easily between your tongue and your hard palate.

LEGUMES

Beans and lentils are mainstays of the Italian table and have a long tradition of innovative preparations. With their nutritional qualities and long-term storage capability, they are a perfect match for Italian cuisine's frugal yet hearty nature.

BEANS

THERE ARE ALMOST AS MANY DIFFERENT VARIETIES OF BEANS in the world as there are different kinds of pasta eaten in Italy. Additionally, recent years have seen a boom in the rediscovery of heirloom beans. You can purchase all kinds of interesting and beautifully colored "boutique" beans, and because beans are not terribly expensive, even these high-end varieties will not cost you an arm and a leg. If you're the sort of person who likes to seek out unusual ingredients, you can track down heirloom Italian varieties such as Lamon, Sarconi, and Sorana beans online and try them out.

That said, most medium-sized beans pretty much taste the same, and even their beautiful colors fade once they are cooked. If you can't find authentic borlotti in your area, swapping in cannellini beans will not change the taste of the finished dish that drastically.

Dried beans (and canned beans, obviously) are available year-round, but in late summer and early fall, you may also find fresh beans in their pods, especially if you are a regular at a farmers' market in your area. If you do, scoop them up—they're delicious and have a greener flavor than cooked dried beans. They can replace soaked dried beans in most recipes, though they do cook a little more quickly.

Cannellini Beans

Zolfini Beans

Borlotti Beans

Lamon Beans

Corona Beans

FRESH and DRIED BEANS

Fresh beans need to be shelled just before you use them or they will begin to dry out. Open each pod and run your thumb along the inside to detach the beans, letting them fall into a bowl [1]. Discard the empty pods. Dried beans should be rinsed and picked over. Discard any that are shriveled or discolored [2].

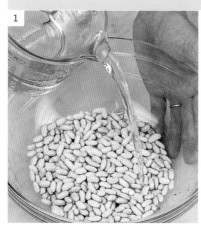

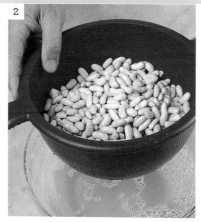

Before cooking, soak dried beans in cold water [1]. The optimal soaking time is 8 to 12 hours, so leaving them in the water overnight is the most convenient way to handle this. (If you are unsure whether your beans have soaked enough, take a paring knife and cut a bean in half—the bean should be the same color all the way through. If the center is still white and chalky, the beans are not ready yet.) After soaking, drain the beans well [2], rinse them, and drain them again. Place the beans in a pot and add cold water to cover [3], along with sage or other herbs, if desired. Bring the water to a boil, then simmer the beans, covered, until they are very tender. If the beans start to dry out before they are fully cooked, add more boiling water. Salt the beans only when they are finished cooking [4]. Depending on the age of the beans, the size of the beans, and how long you soaked them, they will take from 1½ to 3 hours to cook.

223

TRADITIONAL ITALIAN BEANS

Place dried beans that have been soaked or fresh shelled beans in a pot with water to cover. (About twice as much water by volume as dried beans, and a little less for fresh beans.) Add a couple of whole peeled cloves garlic, sage leaves, and some leaf celery or a celery stalk [1]. Bring the water to a boil, turn down the heat to maintain a low simmer, and cook, covered, until the beans are very tender and creamy, about 2 hours for fresh beans and 3 for dried. The beans should be moist, but most of the liquid should evaporate during cooking or be absorbed. If the pot begins to look too dry before the beans are finished, add a small amount of boiling water. Once the beans are cooked, season them with sea salt and freshly ground black pepper [2] and drizzle on the highest quality extra-virgin olive oil you can afford [3].

POLENTA WITH BEANS, RICE WITH BEANS, and BEAN SOUP

CAZZAGAI (POLENTA WITH BEANS)

Stew a cup or so of cooked beans with diced fatback, onion, and some tomato puree (page 208). Cook polenta (page 119) and, about 10 minutes before it is done, stir in the beans [1]. Serve with additional beans on top [2]. This dish is a specialty of the Emilia area. You can also cut cooled cazzagai into cubes and pan-fry them.

PANISSA PIEMONTESE (PIEDMONT RICE WITH BEANS)

Toast some rice in a sauté of onion, fatback, and crumbled sausage with the casing removed. Moisten with red wine, and when most of the wine has evaporated, cook as for risotto (page 108), using broth combined with beans previously cooked with a little pork rind [1]. This dish is a specialty of the Piedmont region [2].

SOUP

Sauté a little boiled pork rind in oil with minced carrot, celery, and onion [1]. Add beans that have been previously soaked, rinsed, and drained [2]; add hot broth to cover. Simmer, covered, until the soup is very thick and the beans are tender [3]. Serve with toasted bread.

Ravioli ai cannellini

ravioli with cannellini beans

FILLING

1½ cups dried cannellini beans

3 tablespoons extra-virgin olive oil

2 cloves garlic

3 to 4 fresh sage leaves

1 sprig fresh rosemary, plus 1 teaspoon very finely minced fresh rosemary leaves

1 cup ricotta cheese

Fine sea salt to taste

Freshly ground black pepper to taste

PASTA

1½ cups unbleached all-purpose flour

2 large eggs

1 tablespoon extra-virgin olive oil

1 tablespoon minced fresh herbs, such as sage, rosemary, and wild fennel

Fine sea salt to taste

SAUCE

½ cup extra-virgin olive oil

2 cloves garlic, crushed

1 red, 1 yellow, and 1 green bell pepper, diced

Fine sea salt to taste

1 tablespoon minced flat-leaf parsley

1. To make the filling, soak the cannellini beans overnight, drain and rinse them, and place them in a pot with 1 tablespoon of the olive oil, the garlic, sage, and rosemary sprig. Add cold water to cover, bring this to a boil, then turn down the heat and simmer, covered, until the beans are tender, about 1 hour 30 minutes. (It's okay to overcook the beans a little, as they will be pureed.)

2. Drain the cooked beans, puree them in a food mill, and set them aside to cool.

3. Combine the cooled bean puree with the ricotta and the minced rosemary. Season with salt and pepper (the mixture will be fairly bland, so you'll have to add a fair amount of these) and stir in the remaining 2 tablespoons olive oil.

4. To make the pasta, prepare a dough with the flour, eggs, olive oil, and minced herbs following the instructions on page 78. Roll out the dough into thin sheets about 6 inches wide (see page 80). Arrange the filling, about 1 generous teaspoon at a time, 2½ inches apart down the long side of one strip of pasta, slightly off center.

5. Fold the empty half of the strip over to cover the filling. Press with your fingers around the filling to seal, then cut out the ravioli with a fluted pastry wheel.

6. Bring a large pot of water to a boil and salt it for cooking the ravioli. While waiting for the water to boil, make the sauce. Heat the oil with the garlic cloves. Add the diced bell pepper, cover, and cook over medium heat for 4 minutes. Season with salt.

7. Cook the ravioli in batches in the boiling water and remove them with a slotted spoon or skimmer shortly after they float to the surface. Transfer the cooked ravioli to a serving dish. Remove and discard the garlic cloves from the sauce. Pour the sauce over the cooked pasta, sprinkle minced parsley over the top, and serve immediately.

SERVES 6   COOKING TIME: 2 HOURS (PLUS SOAKING TIME FOR THE BEANS)

CHICKPEAS, CICERCHIE, LUPINI, and LENTILS

THE FIRST LEGUMES KNOWN TO HAVE BEEN EATEN IN THE MEDITERRANEAN AREA were diminutive lentils—legumes but not beans—which are actually mentioned in the Bible. Italy has several regional lentil varieties that are often more tender than run-of-the-mill brown and green lentils. The lentils from Castelluccio, in Umbria, are particularly prized. They are small in size and cook quickly (lentils do not need to be soaked), but they are also tender and slightly peppery.

Large lupini are also quite popular in Italy and are often eaten as a snack. You can find cooked lupini in brine in jars in specialty stores—they are eaten much like pumpkin or sunflower seeds, meaning that you split the outer jacket with your teeth and discard it, eating only the tender middle. Cooking your own lupini is rewarding but time-consuming; they are very bitter, and the procedure for taming that bitterness is lengthy. If you want to try your hand at cooking them, begin two weeks before you plan to serve them.

Cicerchie (also known as chickling vetch), another large, rustic Italian specialty legume, have only recently become available in the United States. Cicerchie are about the same size as chickpeas, but they have a more irregular shape. They are traditionally cooked in soup. Dried chickpeas and cicerchie need to be soaked before cooking, preferably overnight. In fact, chickpeas take so long to cook even after soaking that you may want to seek out a high-quality canned brand (or get out your pressure cooker if you have one).

Chickpeas

Castelluccio Lentils

Cicerchie

Lupini Beans

CHICKPEAS and CICERCHIE

Pick through and rinse dried chickpeas or cicerchie, then place them in a large bowl with plenty of room, add a generous amount of water to cover **[1]**, and allow them to soak for 12 to 24 hours, changing the water two or three times. When fully soaked, they will weigh twice as much and will swell to three times their original size **[2]**. Once they are ready, drain, rinse, and drain them again; transfer them to a pot; and add cold water to cover. Toss in 2 or 3 unpeeled cloves garlic and a sprig of sage leaves **[3]**. Simmer over low heat, covered, stirring occasionally with a wooden spoon until tender, 3 to 4 hours. If the pot gets dry, add cold water in small amounts.

Crespelle di ceci

chickpea flour crespelle

CRESPELLE

¾ cup unbleached all-purpose flour

½ cup chickpea flour

¾ cup whole milk, plus more if needed

2 large eggs, lightly beaten

¼ cup heavy cream

Fine sea salt to taste

Freshly ground black pepper to taste

3 tablespoons extra-virgin olive oil

FILLING AND SAUCE

¼ cup extra-virgin olive oil

3 to 4 small zucchini, sliced into thin rounds

3 tablespoons minced fresh herbs, such as thyme, parsley, and marjoram, plus more for garnish

¼ cup diced mozzarella cheese

1 cup ricotta cheese

Fine sea salt to taste

Freshly ground black pepper to taste

1½ pounds ripe tomatoes

Yellow bell pepper strips for garnish

A few leaves of butter lettuce for garnish

1. To make the crespelle, sift together the all-purpose flour and the chickpea flour into a large bowl. Whisk in the milk until smooth, then whisk in the eggs, cream, salt, and pepper. (The mixture should have a pourable consistency. If not, whisk in a little additional milk until it does.) Cover and set aside to rest for 1 hour, then whisk in the oil.

2. Heat a 10-inch nonstick pan or cast-iron skillet and coat it very lightly with oil by rubbing a dab of oil over the surface with a paper towel, wiping away any excess. Pour in a sixth of the batter, about ½ cup. Roll the pan in all directions to coat the surface, and then place it over medium heat until the batter has cooked into a thin crepe. Use a spatula to remove it from the pan and repeat the process, very lightly oiling the pan with the piece of paper towel each time. Set the crepes aside; do not stack them.

3. For the filling, heat 1 tablespoon of the olive oil and cook the zucchini until tender, then sprinkle on the minced herbs.

4. Combine the zucchini mixture with the mozzarella and ricotta, and season to taste with salt and pepper.

5. Make a tomato sauce by first peeling the tomatoes (see page 205), then seeding and pureeing them in a blender or through a food mill with the remaining 3 tablespoons oil. Season to taste with salt and pepper.

6. Distribute the cheese filling equally onto the centers of the crespelle, then roll them up jelly-roll style and cut them into 1¼-inch pinwheel slices. Serve them at room temperature with the tomato sauce and garnish them with additional minced herbs, bell pepper strips, and a few lettuce leaves.

SERVES 6   COOKING TIME: 1 HOUR

230

LUPINI

Lupini contain large amounts of a naturally bitter alkaloid that needs to be removed through a long soaking period—and that means really long, up to 2 weeks. Place them in a bowl (as for chickpeas and cicerchie, page 229), add abundant cold water, and soak them overnight. On the second day, drain the beans, place them in a pot, add cold water to cover, bring them to a simmer, and simmer until they're tender, about 1 hour [1]. (Lupini are not as soft as other beans—they should still have some resistance, but they should not be hard.) Then drain the lupini, rinse them well, and place them in a bowl or jar with water to cover and a generous amount of salt, about 1 tablespoon per quart of water. (You can also soak the lupini in unsalted water and salt them once they are edible.) Let the lupini soak in this brine, changing the brine at least once a day (doing it more frequently will speed up the process somewhat); you will notice that the water you are pouring off and replacing is very yellow at first and gradually becomes clearer. Taste a bean every couple of days, and you will notice its flavor changing. When they taste good, they are ready. To eat lupini, shuck off the outer peel [2]. They make a lively addition to a salad, but most often they are eaten out of hand as a snack.

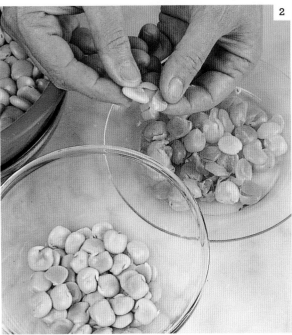

Canned legumes

Beans are delicious and nutritious, but there is no denying that preparing them from scratch can be time-consuming. Sometimes you simply don't have four hours to spend simmering your dinner. At those times, you can rely on high-quality canned beans (and lentils, though canned lentils are a little harder to find— check gourmet stores and health food stores). Just drain them, rinse them, and drain them again. (You don't want to consume any of the canning liquid.) They can be sautéed, as in the recipe for sautéed lentils (see page 235), for a quick and tasty side dish, among many other options.

CHICKPEA SOUP, PUREE, and BISCUITS

SOUP

Brown minced garlic, onion, prosciutto, and parsley in a little butter and oil. Add 1 to 2 cups soaked and drained chickpeas (see page 229), chopped escarole and celery, chopped pork ribs, 2 quarts water, and freshly ground pepper [1]. Cover the pot and cook, stirring occasionally, until the beans are tender, about 4 hours. Add 1 to 2 cups canned peeled tomatoes or fresh tomatoes that you have peeled, seeded, and chopped roughly; season with salt and simmer 20 additional minutes to combine. (These are added last because introducing acid or salt at the start will keep the beans from cooking completely.) Serve with toasted slices of rustic bread and grated aged pecorino Romano [2].

PUREE

Boil chickpeas (see page 229) and use a food mill to puree them [1]. Season with salt and a generous amount of freshly ground black pepper [2]. Whisk in a few tablespoons of extra-virgin olive oil and enough water to make a creamy puree. This is a delicious side dish for all kinds of shellfish.

BISCUITS

Beat an egg into salted chickpea puree (see above) [1]. Divide this mixture into small balls and use an offset spatula to flatten them into round cakes [2]. Dredge the cakes lightly in all-purpose flour and brown them, turning them once to cook both sides, in a little melted butter with a sprig of rosemary in it [3].

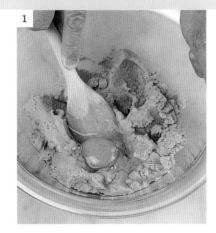

233

PANISSA LIGURE

chickpea flour cakes

Panissa—a long-cooked puree made with chickpea flour—is Liguria's answer to polenta (page 119). Sift 2½ cups chickpea flour into a pot. Whisk in 1 quart salted room-temperature water to make a smooth batter. Cook, stirring constantly, for 1 hour and 15 minutes [1]. Brush a tray or baking sheet with water and spread the cooked mixture onto the sheet in an even layer. Set it aside to cool until firm. Cut the mixture into squares, dredge them lightly in flour, and fry them in a generous amount of oil. Serve hot [2].

BRAISED LENTILS

In a pot, cook a soffritto (see page 260) of carrot, onion, and celery [1], then add 8 ounces (about 1¼ cups) lentils and toss briefly in the oil [2]. Add 2½ cups vegetable stock (page 55), bring to a simmer, cover, and cook until the lentils are tender, about 35 minutes. If the pot begins to look dry, add a couple of tablespoons of water at a time to keep the lentils from burning—the goal is for the lentils to absorb all the cooking liquid by the time the dish is done. When they are fully cooked and there is still about ¼ inch of water in the pot, add 2 teaspoons tomato paste [3]. Stir to combine and cook, covered, until all the liquid has been absorbed, 5 to 10 more minutes.

SAUTÉED LENTILS

Simmer 1 pound (about 2½ cups) lentils in water with 1 stalk celery, 1 carrot, and several sprigs of parsley until tender but not falling apart, about 35 minutes; then drain [1]. Heat a small amount of oil in a pan and brown 2½ ounces diced pancetta in it [2], then add the drained lentils (either remove the carrot, celery, and parsley or chop them and add them to the pan). Cook over medium heat, stirring frequently, for 5 minutes [3].

PASTA WITH LENTILS and RICE WITH LENTILS

PASTA WITH LENTILS

In a pot, combine 6 cups cold water and 1 cup rinsed lentils with chopped garlic, onion, and celery [1]. Cook, covered, over low heat. When the lentils are tender, about 35 minutes, add 6 ounces spaghetti, breaking the strands into 2 or 3 pieces as you drop them into the pot. Add salt and bring to a boil. Cook until the pasta is al dente (add small amounts of boiling water if the mixture is getting too thick). Drizzle on a generous amount of your best olive oil, sprinkle with a generous grinding of black pepper, and serve immediately [2].

RICE WITH LENTILS

In a pot, cook minced fatback, parsley, and garlic in ¼ cup extra-virgin olive oil. Add ½ cup tomato puree (page 208) or 4 chopped fresh tomatoes [1]. Add 5 cups water and salt to taste, bring the mixture to a boil, and stir in ½ cup short-grain Italian rice (see page 106) along with ½ cup cooked lentils (canned lentils, rinsed and drained, are fine). Cook until the rice is al dente [2].

PEAS and FAVA BEANS

THESE LEGUMES ARE OFTEN SOLD FRESH IN PODS, as well as in their dried form. Fava beans may be eaten raw—traditionally paired with salami or fresh sheep's cheese—especially when they are very young. Fresh shelled peas are usually braised or simply cooked in a little oil or butter. They may also be cooked in boiling water for 8 to 10 minutes. Fresh peas or fava beans in the pod should be kept in the refrigerator, but they are really best eaten as soon as possible after being harvested and should not be kept around for more than 24 hours after you buy them. After shelling peas and beans, you will be left with about a third of the weight that you had to start. Frozen peas are an acceptable substitute, though of course fresh are preferred. Dried peas may be either split (more common) or whole and are usually cooked into thick porridgelike soups. Fava beans are also available in a dried form suitable for making soup.

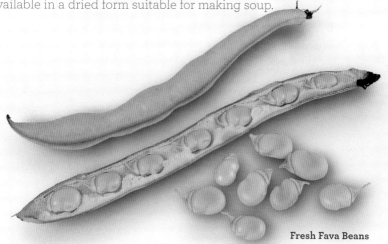

Fresh Fava Beans

Fresh Peas

SHELLING PEAS and FAVA BEANS

Open pea and fava bean pods by slitting them with a thumb along the side that has a shallow "seam" (the side where the beans or peas are attached). Knock them into a bowl and discard the shells **[1]**. Fava beans are more firmly attached than peas **[2]**. They also have a skin that needs to be removed before they can be eaten **[3]**; very young fava beans can be consumed whole, though.

BRAISED SPLIT PEAS

Cook dried split peas with oil, garlic, and aromatic herbs, then add a generous amount of hot water and simmer, covered, until the peas are falling apart. Keep the mixture thin for soup, or make a thick puree to serve as a side dish that goes particularly nicely with smoked meats.

SAUTÉED PEAS

Cook a soffritto (see page 260) of minced fresh sage and rosemary, minced garlic, and diced pancetta. Add the peas and toss over medium heat for a few minutes **[1]**. Add rice **[2]** and hot water. Simmer until the rice is cooked al dente.

FAVE ALLA BOLOGNESE
bolognese-style fava beans

Stew fresh shelled and skinned fava beans with onion, minced prosciutto fat, minced mortadella, a little classic ragù (see page 34) or other tomato sauce, and a small amount of water. Season to taste with salt and pepper. Serve with slices of rustic bread, either grilled or browned in a little olive oil or butter.

FAVA BEAN MACCO and PASTA COI BISI

MACCO (STEWED FAVA BEANS)

Soak dried, skinned fava beans overnight. (If you can't find skinned dried beans, use the unskinned type and pop them out of their skins the next day.) Drain and rinse the beans, then place them in a pot with cold water to cover [1]. Add minced onion and 2 chopped tomatoes [2]. Add 1 tablespoon sugar [3]. Simmer until the beans begin to fall apart, then add broken spaghetti [4] and cook until it is tender. Drizzle on oil, season with salt and a generous amount of freshly ground black pepper, and sprinkle grated aged sheep's cheese over the top [5].

PASTA COI BISI

Risi e bisi is a well-known Venetian dish of rice and peas, slightly soupier than a classic risotto. (*Bisi* is Venetian dialect for *piselli*, or "peas.") This dish is its pasta-based cousin and is equally delicious. Cook the peas with minced scallion, pancetta, butter, broth, salt, and pepper [1]. In a large pot of salted boiling water, cook tagliatelle (or a ridged, short dried pasta, such as rigatoni) and then toss the pasta with the vegetable mixture. Sprinkle with grated Parmigiano Reggiano and minced flat-leaf parsley and serve [2].

Passato di fave e cialde piccanti
spicy fava puree with cheese crisps

1 tablespoon minced onion

1 chile pepper

1 tablespoon extra-virgin olive oil, plus more for drizzling

14 ounces shelled and skinned fava beans (start with about 2 pounds 10 ounces in the pods), boiled until tender

2½ cups vegetable stock (page 55)

1 bunch fresh chives

Fine sea salt to taste

6 ounces (about 1½ cups) fresh firm sheep's cheese, such as pecorino Sardo, grated on the large holes of a box grater

1. Preheat the oven to 350 degrees F. For the puree, in a pot, sauté the onion and chile pepper in the olive oil. Add the beans and the stock. Mince 2 of the chives and add them to the pot.

2. Cook the mixture for 10 minutes, then add salt. Stir 1 tablespoon of the grated cheese into the mixture, then puree the mixture using a food mill.

3. To make the crisps, mince the remaining chives and mix them with about half of the remaining cheese. Line a baking sheet with parchment paper and shape the cheese mixture into 8 small disks about 2 inches in diameter. Bake them for 5 minutes, then set them aside to cool.

4. Stir the remaining grated cheese into the puree and serve it warm. Drizzle each serving with a little olive oil and top it with 2 of the crisps. You can also garnish the puree with knotted chives, whole chile peppers, or whole beans.

SERVES 4   COOKING TIME: 35 MINUTES

241

*T*UBERS AND ROOTS MAY NOT BE THE PRETTIEST VEGETABLES, BUT they are reliable and good for long storage. As such, they have sustained many civilizations over long winters. The potato is perhaps the most widely eaten food in this category. It has been cultivated in the Andes for millennia and was brought to Italy from the New World only in the late 1700s. Potatoes are now grown on a large scale in various Italian regions, especially in the Apennines and the Alps. The potato has the largest number of local varieties of perhaps any root vegetable and is most versatile, as it can be boiled or fried, roasted or braised, and it is an essential element in recipes from soufflés to gnocchi.

Turnips, carrots, and onions are also vegetables with long histories, and they have played a key role in human nourishment. Carrots are widely used in Italy, and one can scarcely imagine Italian cuisine— or any other, for that matter—existing without onions and garlic. Edible wild mushrooms, too, have been collected for thousands of years.

While these vegetables are all used throughout the book, this chapter contains recipes that highlight them as a central ingredient rather than as a flavoring.

ROOT
VEGETABLES

Potatoes, carrots, and onions: humble vegetables redolent of fall and winter. They are also very versatile and excellent on their own or incorporated into more elaborate dishes.

CARROTS and OTHER ROOT VEGETABLES

ROOT VEGETABLES ARE, LOGICALLY ENOUGH, those for which the root is the edible portion. (We often, however, eat the leaves of root vegetables as well—for example, beet greens.) Root vegetables are sturdy and reliable, available throughout the cold-weather months. Their flavor ranges from fairly bland and sweet to bitter. In general, look for roots that are firm, without soft or dark spots. The skin should be intact.

The carrot, perhaps the most popular root, originated in Afghanistan and was brought to Europe by Arabs. The original carrots were actually purple. The Dutch were the first to genetically modify carrots and make them orange, in honor of their royal family, the House of Orange-Nassau.

Carrots are a healthy addition to the diet and provide a generous amount of vitamin A. When purchasing them with their tops intact, look for fresh, fluffy green leaves. When buying carrots in bags, look for small, slender carrots (not those labeled "baby carrots," which have simply been shaved down to a smaller size), as they will have less of a woody core.

Salsify

Black Salsify

Radishes

Carrots

Red Beet

White Turnips

CUTTING and PEELING CARROTS

*C*arrots can be cut into round slices, julienne, and large and small dice and may even be grated. The cut you choose will depend on how you are going to use them—in sauces, braised, as a side dish, in salad (and look for the youngest, most tender carrots you can find if you are going to use them in salad), or in purees or soufflés. Carrots are truly a kitchen workhorse.

1] JULIENNE

The easiest way to julienne carrots is to peel them and then use a mandoline, especially if you are making very narrow matchsticks like those in the photograph. You can also grate carrots on the largest holes of a four-sided box grater. These smaller cuts are the best to select when you will be eating carrots raw, as in a salad.

2] TURNED CARROTS

Use a very sharp knife to turn carrots. When prepared this way, carrots are terrific glazed or simply boiled and dressed. If you like, you can leave a little tuft of carrot top for visual appeal.

3] DICE

Carrots cut into small dice with a chef's knife are key to soffritto (page 260) and may also be used for decoration. Larger dice is useful when preparing soups or other dishes that will ultimately be pureed.

4] ROUNDS

You can use a slicer to create ridged carrot rounds, or simply use a knife to cut carrots crosswise or at an angle into even slices.

5] PEELING CARROTS

With a paring knife, cut away any leafy tops. Peel the carrots with a vegetable peeler. About 1 pound of unpeeled, untrimmed carrots should yield about ¾ pound once this is done.

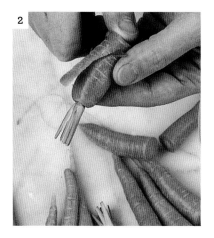

245

DECORATIVE RADISHES

Rinse the radishes, then cut off and discard the pointy tip. Cut the radishes into wedges or matchsticks, cutting almost to the bottom of the radish but not all the way through so that they remain in one piece. Soak the cut radishes in ice water until you are ready to use them.

PRESERVING RADISHES IN OIL

Trim radishes and soak them in cold water. Combine 1¼ cups water with 1¼ cups white wine vinegar, ¼ cup olive oil, ½ chile pepper, 1 tablespoon sugar, a sprig of thyme, a sprig of rosemary and a little salt in a pot. Bring the mixture to a boil and add the radishes **[1]**. Boil until they are softened but still very crisp, 5 to 7 minutes. Drain and cool the radishes, discard the herbs and chile, and transfer the radishes to a glass jar that can be hermetically sealed. Pour in olive oil to cover **[2]**. Can to preserve safely for long-term storage according to jar manufacturer's instructions.

OTHER WAYS TO CUT ROOTS

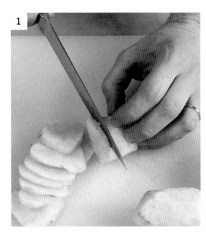

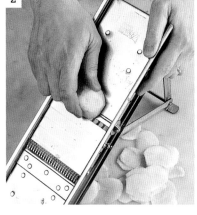

SLICES
Use a chef's knife to cut slices of varying thicknesses, depending on how they'll be cooked [1].

CHIPS
Use a mandoline to cut very thin slices of root vegetables for frying [2].

SHREDS
Use the largest holes on a box grater to grate root vegetables. Raw grated turnips and carrots make a refreshing addition to salads [3].

BALLS AND OTHER SHAPES
Use a melon baller to make equal-sized balls of root vegetable, or use a paring knife to turn them into ovals [4]. If you make the pieces all the same size they will cook evenly.

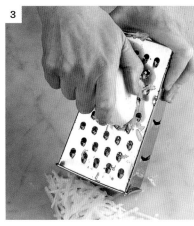

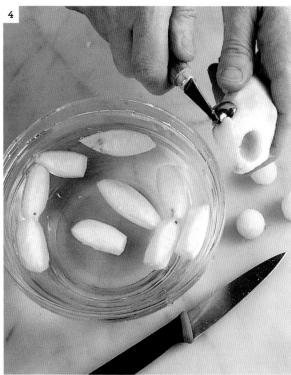

247

PEELING, CUTTING, and CLEANING SALSIFY

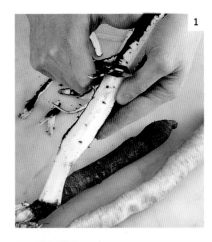

Brush off any excess soil, then trim the ends off from the salsify and peel it with a vegetable peeler **[1]**. Cut it into 2-inch pieces, rinse them, and drop them into cold water with some lemon juice in it so that the surface does not turn brown **[2]**. If the pieces of salsify are very thick, cut them into slices and discard the woody core **[3]**.

TRIMMING TURNIPS

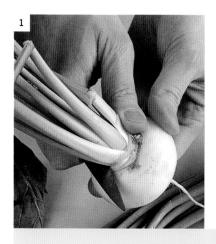

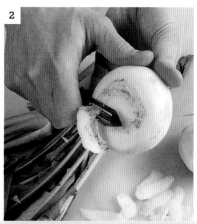

Cut off any greens from the top [1]. Peel using a vegetable peeler [2] and then cut off the pointed end and the stringy root growing there. Trimmed turnips yield about half the original weight of the vegetable.

GLAZED CARROTS

Melt butter in a skillet until foamy and add turned carrots [1] but do not brown them. Add a pinch of salt, a little sugar, and a small amount of vegetable stock (page 55) [2]. Sauté the carrots and allow the liquid to evaporate, but keep a close eye on the skillet and don't let it get too dry (add a tablespoon or two of liquid if the carrots are not cooked thoroughly and the skillet looks too dry). If it does, the sauce will separate unattractively. When the carrots are coated in a silky sauce and cooked to your liking, remove the pan from the heat.

OTHER METHODS FOR COOKING CARROTS

BUTTER-BRAISED CARROTS

Place sliced rounds of carrot in a large pot with a couple of tablespoons of butter, a pinch of salt, and a pinch of sugar [1]. Add about ½ cup water to cover. Bring the liquid to a boil, turn down the heat to maintain a simmer, and cook, covered, until the carrots are very soft, about 20 minutes [2].

CARROT PUDDING

In a food processor fitted with the metal blade, puree 1¼ pounds boiled carrots put through a potato ricer, ¾ ounce grated Parmigiano Reggiano or other aged cheese, 2 large eggs, ½ cup heavy cream, and salt to taste [3]. Distribute the mixture among buttered ramekins or other ovenproof dishes. Place the ramekins in a baking dish and add water to come up the sides of the ramekins about ½ inch. Bake at 400 degrees F for 15 minutes, then turn the oven down to 350 degrees F and cook for an additional 15 minutes. Remove the baking pan from the oven and let the puddings rest for 10 minutes, then unmold and transfer them to a serving dish. Sprinkle them with oregano before serving [4].

STEAMED CARROTS

Cut carrots into chunks or rounds. Steam them until they are tender, about 15 minutes [5].

CARROTS IN SOFFRITTO

Carrots are minced and sautéed as part of the classic soffritto (page 260) that is the base of numerous Italian dishes [6].

BOILED CARROTS

Carrots may be boiled briefly, just until tender (blanched), or cooked until they are very soft, then served as a side dish for meat or fish [7].

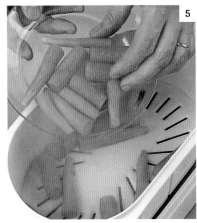

COOKING ROOT VEGETABLES

Trimmed, peeled root vegetables can be boiled whole in salted water with bay leaf and lemon until tender, about 25 minutes [1]. Sliced roots can be steamed [2]. Turned root vegetables are delicious braised with shallots, sprigs of fresh thyme, the juice of ½ lemon, some salt, and water to cover [3]. Cook the mixture in a covered pot over low heat until the vegetables are tender and most of the liquid has evaporated, 20 to 25 minutes. Thoroughly pat dry thin slices of root vegetables and fry them (do not crowd the pot) in oil heated to 350 to 375 degrees F until crisp and golden, about 8 minutes [4]. Sauté a soffritto (page 260) of onion, celery, and diced pancetta in a pan, then layer sliced root vegetables on top, overlapping them slightly, and add broth just to cover. Cook, covered, until the roots are tender, about 20 minutes [5].

ONIONS

ONIONS, WHETHER PLAIN YELLOW COOKING ONIONS OR OTHER MEMBERS OF THE onion family, such as scallions or garlic, are an important part of so many recipes. Indeed, it is the rare recipe for a savory dish that does not begin with the cooking of an onion.

You will find many varieties of onions—including yellow, white, and red—in your supermarket and at your local farmers' market. Italy's famed Tropea onions are a particularly tasty red onion. White and yellow onions are more frequently used for cooking. Flat onions are wonderful for stuffing, while the small Italian onions known as cipollini are delicious in sweet-and-sour preparations or preserved in oil or vinegar. Onions may also come in an elongated torpedo shape. Shallots are smaller onions that taste similar to garlic, while scallions, sometimes called green onions, are very young shoots that can be eaten raw or cooked. All of the white and the pale green portion of a scallion is edible, but cut away and discard the tough dark green tops.

When shopping, look for firm onions without overly developed green sprouts at the top. (If this central portion of the onion has sprouted, you'll have to cut away the core and discard it.) Onions will keep for a long time at a cool room temperature. If you have a cut onion half or quarter, you can wrap it tightly and refrigerate it for a day or two, but no more.

Onions do have one unfortunate quality—cutting them releases pungent compounds that may make your eyes water. To combat this, you can place an onion in the freezer briefly before slicing it and make sure that your knife blade is very sharp.

The ancient Egyptians, Greeks, and Romans all made use of leeks and garlic, both of which are types of onions. In spring, farmers' markets carry green garlic, which resembles scallions. As the season moves along, the garlic bulbs grow larger; the flavor of the garlic becomes sharper and the cloves are less juicy. When kept in a cool, dry place, storage garlic will last for months. If green sprouts grow out of the individual cloves, simply cut the sprouts away and discard them. A relative of both garlic and onion, leeks have a milder flavor and are used in many types of dishes from soups to stews and baked dishes. They can also be used raw and finely chopped in salads.

Cipollini

Scallions

Flat-bulb Onions

Shallots

Yellow Onions

Red Onions

White Onions

Garlic

Leeks

SELECTING, MEASURING, PURGING, and TRIMMING ONIONS

SELECTING
Recipes generally indicate small, medium, and large onions, which should weigh about 2 ounces, 4 ounces, and 8 ounces, respectively.

MEASURING
If a recipe indicates an amount of onion by weight and you don't have a scale, just keep in mind that a table-spoon of minced onion weighs about ¾ ounce and work from there.

PURGING
If you want your onions to be sweeter and dryer, because you'll either be frying them or eating them raw, slice them, separate them into rings, and sprinkle them with fine sea salt. When they give off their liquid, it will collect in the bottom of the bowl and can be discarded. Rinse off the salt and pat dry with paper towels.

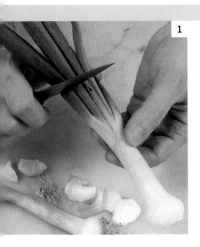

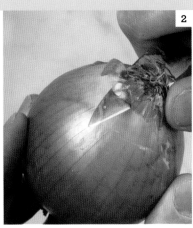

TRIMMING
Onions need to be trimmed differently for different purposes. For fresh onions, such as scallions, cut away most or all of the dark green part and peel off the external layer **[1]**. For storage onions, cut off the root end of the onion with a paring knife **[2]**. Next, trim off the other end, and peel off the external skin **[3]**.

MINCING and SEPARATING ONIONS

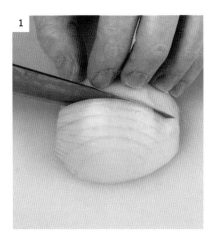

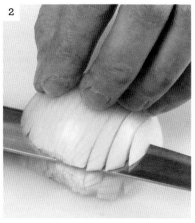

MINCING

In Italian cooking, onion appears most frequently in minced form as part of a soffritto (page 260). To mince an onion, first peel it and then cut it in half the long way. Rest the flat side of one half on the cutting board and use a sharp knife to cut vertically without cutting all the way through one end so that the onion half remains intact **[1]**. Repeat the process, cutting horizontally **[2]**. Finally, make a series of cuts perpendicular to the first **[3]**. This will produce small, evenly sized pieces of onion that quickly become translucent when cooked in oil. Never use a food processor to chop an onion—the metal blade breaks it down too much, and you'll end up with watery pulp.

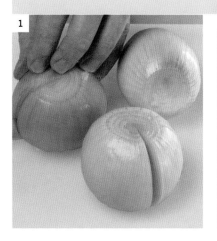

SEPARATING

Peel round white onions and trim the ends. Cut a thin wedge from top to bottom in each onion **[1]**. Blanch the onions in boiling water, then set them aside until they are cool enough to handle. Carefully separate the layers without breaking them **[2]**. Onion layers of this type may be stuffed or baked in a casserole.

Cipolle brasate allo speck

onions braised with speck

3½ ounces speck

1 tablespoon extra-virgin olive oil

1 pound small onions, peeled and left whole

¼ cup crushed tomatoes

Fine sea salt to taste

1. Dice the speck. In a pot or skillet with high sides that is large enough to hold the onions in a single layer, sauté the speck in the olive oil to render the fat. Add the onions and tomatoes. Pour in enough water to cover the onions halfway.

2. Salt lightly (remember that the speck is already salty), bring the water to a boil, then turn the heat down to maintain a simmer and braise, covered, until the onions are very tender, about 40 minutes.

3. If the pot appears to be drying out, add a tablespoon or two of water.

4. Adjust the salt to taste and serve immediately.

NOTE: *Speck is similar to prosciutto—a ham hock cured in salt and with other spices, such as bay leaves and juniper berries. Speck can be purchased at specialty food stores or online. See Sources on page 454. If you can't find speck, purchase a high-quality artisanal bacon.*

SERVES 6   COOKING TIME: 50 MINUTES

BOILING, STEWING, and HOLLOWING OUT ONIONS

BOILING
Sometimes you want milder-tasting onions. To achieve this, boil them in a mixture of water and white wine vinegar with bay leaf and peppercorns.

STEWING
In a pot, combine sliced onions with cold water to cover, a little butter, and a sprig of sage. Simmer over low heat.

HOLLOWING OUT
To hollow out an onion, cut it in half. Then scoop out the center with a melon baller.

257

ROASTED ONIONS

Wrap whole onions, with the skins left on, in aluminum foil and roast them at 400 degrees F until they are extremely soft, about 2 hours **[1]**. Remove the onions from the oven, open the foil, and allow them to cool until you can handle them. Then peel them (the peel should come away very easily) **[2]**.

Onions roasted in this manner can be pureed in a blender **[3]**. Drizzle in some extra-virgin olive oil and season with salt and pepper. Roasted onion puree is delicious with boiled meats and vegetables, or spread it on some toasted bread and serve it as an antipasto.

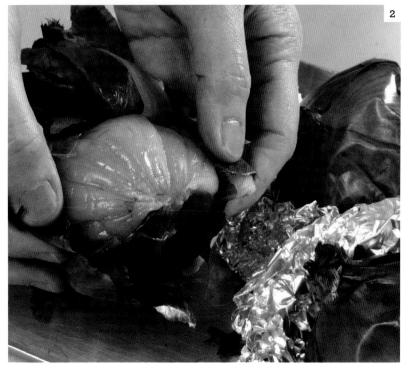

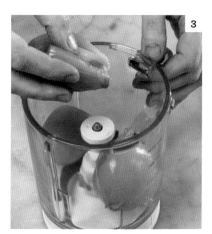

ONION MARMALADE and GLAZED CIPOLLINI ONIONS

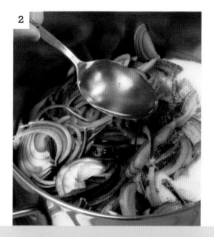

ONION MARMALADE

For the most eye appeal, use red onions. Peel and thinly slice 10 ounces onions **[1]** and place them in a pot with 1 tablespoon honey **[2]** and ¾ cup sugar. Cook, stirring occasionally, until the mixture is very thick, about 1 hour. Stir a small amount of balsamic vinegar into the cooked mixture. Onion marmalade is a wonderful accompaniment to boiled and grilled meats.

GLAZED CIPOLLINI ONIONS

Glazed whole cipollini are an excellent side dish for braised meats. Blanch 3 to 4 ounces peeled cipollini onions. Sauté them in a skillet in a small amount of butter with a bay leaf **[1]**. Sprinkle on 1 tablespoon sugar and add a handful of raisins (soaked to soften, if necessary). Add boiling broth to cover **[2]**. Simmer until the onions are golden and the liquid is reduced and syrupy.

Soffritto is a sauté of minced vegetables that is the basis for Italian dishes from tomato sauces to braises. Soffritto almost always combines some form of onion (including garlic, shallots, or leeks) with carrot and celery. Other aromatics may be included as well.

The Secrets of Soffritto

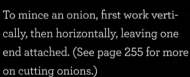

To mince an onion, first work vertically, then horizontally, leaving one end attached. (See page 255 for more on cutting onions.)

The vegetables for soffritto may be chopped, diced, minced, or cut into julienne (left to right in the above photograph). Generally, the larger chunks are used only in dishes that will be cooked for a long period and then pureed or strained.

If garlic is in the soffritto, whole cloves can be used (with the peels left on for long-cooking dishes) and then removed before you continue with the dish. If the garlic is going to remain in the finished dish, it should be peeled and cut into thin slices or minced.

An onion may also be used whole, and it may be studded with whole cloves or have bay leaves inserted into slits, as that makes the onion and seasonings easier to remove. Whole onions are most commonly used in meat dishes such as braised beef.

Cooking time and temperature will vary depending on how you have cut the vegetables and how intense you want their presence to be in the finished dish. In any case, keep a close eye on your soffritto to be sure it doesn't burn—if it does, you will have to discard it and start over. A dish with a burnt soffritto as its base will always taste bitter.

If herbs are included in the soffritto, be sure not to expose them to extreme heat. As soon as they start to sizzle, add a small amount of water to keep the temperature down.

TRIMMING and CLEANING A LEEK

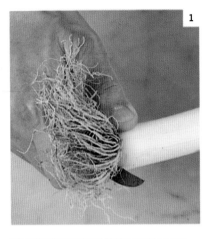

TRIMMING AND CLEANING
Cut off the base of the leek to remove the roots [1], then trim off most of the dark green top [2]. Make a shallow cut and remove and discard the two outermost layers of the leek, or more if they seem especially tough [3]. Cut the leek in half the long way [4]. Wash halved leeks in running water to remove any dirt. (Sometimes leeks have dirt all the way in the center.) In general, you'll discard more than half of a leek when trimming it.

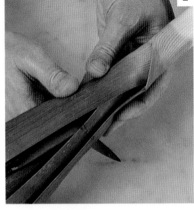

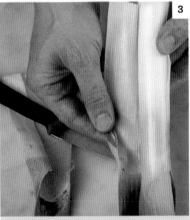

CUTTING
You can cut a trimmed leek into thin matchsticks [1] to sauté or fry.

A leek can be sliced into rounds [2] and used for soffritto, puree, soups, and sauces.

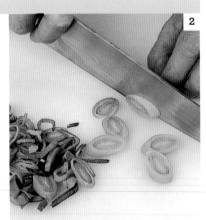

BLANCHING LEEKS

Peel apart the leaves of a leek. Cook them in boiling salted water for 2 minutes, then transfer them to a bowl of ice water to stop the cooking process and keep the leeks green **[1]**. Drain and dry on a clean dish towel **[2]**. Blanched leeks like these can be stuffed with various fillings (see page 266) or used to line a mold for a vegetable or meat timbale.

BUTTER-BRAISED LEEKS

Cut 1 bunch of leeks into thin rounds (see page opposite). In a pot, combine the leeks with a tablespoon or so of butter. Add about ¼ cup water, cover, and braise for 30 minutes. Finally, remove the cover and boil off any remaining liquid. These can be used for soups, meat dishes, and sauces.

PEELING GARLIC

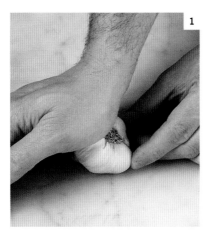
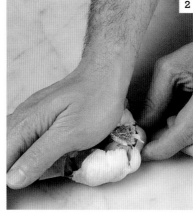
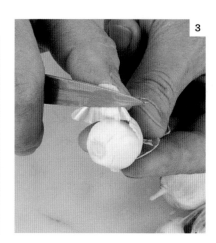

Place the palm of your hand on a head of garlic and press down **[1]** so that the peel breaks and the cloves separate **[2]**. (Or break off one or two cloves as needed.) Pull off the cloves, discarding the outer papery skin, and then use a small paring knife to peel the skin from each clove **[3]**.

The right tool

A GARLIC PRESS

A garlic press can be used to crush a whole clove of garlic, with or without its peel. Simply place the garlic in the bucket of the press and close it, pushing the two handles together firmly. The garlic flesh will be extruded through the grid of holes, and if the peel was present, it will remain in the press.

MINCING GARLIC

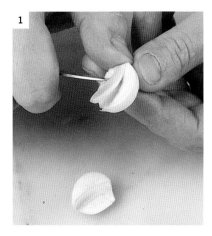

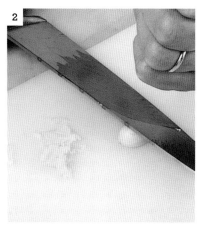

Cut a peeled garlic clove in half the long way and discard the green sprout at the center, if any, as this is bitter **[1]**. Crush the clove with the flat side of a chef's knife to release its essential oils **[2]**. Mince the garlic very finely **[3]**.

ROASTING GARLIC

Roasted garlic has a gentler flavor than the raw bulb. To roast garlic, simply wrap whole heads of garlic in aluminum foil and roast them at 250 to 265 degrees F until very soft, about 1 hour. (A toaster oven is useful for this.) You can make a sauce with roasted garlic by simply peeling the cloves and pureeing them with some extra-virgin olive oil. Roasted garlic cloves can also be spread on toasted slices of rustic bread for a terrific snack or used in place of the milk-cooked cloves to make the garlic sauce on page 63.

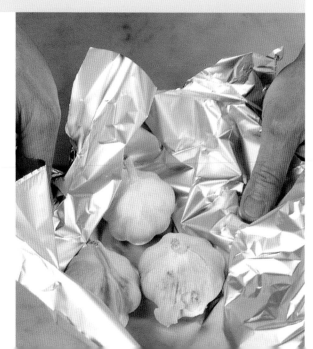

RICE WITH LEEKS, BREADED LEEKS, and STUFFED LEEKS

RICE WITH LEEKS

Cook a soffritto (page 260) consisting of leeks and any other flavorings you like in some butter. Add another 3 ounces sliced leeks and 3 ounces peeled, sliced potatoes [1]. Pour in 5 cups water and season with salt and freshly ground black pepper. Add 1 cup short-grain rice and simmer until the rice is tender, about 15 minutes. Stir in a little butter and serve [2].

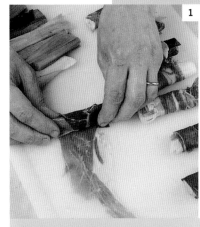

BREADED LEEKS

Cut 3 leeks into 2-inch pieces and place them in a heavily buttered baking dish. Salt and pepper the leeks and pour in enough white wine to cover them about halfway. Bake at 400 degrees F for 20 minutes. Allow the leeks to cool, and as soon as you can handle them, wrap each one in a slice of prosciutto [1]. Dredge the wrapped pieces of leek in beaten egg, then in fine bread crumbs; fry them until they are crisp and golden [2].

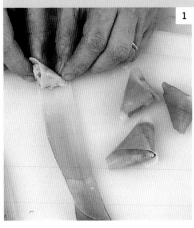

STUFFED LEEKS

Soak 3 slices of bread in ⅓ cup heavy cream until soft, then crumble them. Prepare a stuffing with this soaked bread, 3 ounces scamorza cheese, 2½ ounces minced prosciutto, and your choice of herbs or other flavorings. Place a small amount of filling at the base of a blanched leek (see page 263) and fold it up to form a triangle. Repeat with the remaining filling and more leeks [1]. In a skillet, melt butter over medium heat and brown the triangles for about 6 minutes, turning them carefully. Serve hot [2].

MUSHROOMS

THERE ARE MANY TYPES OF EDIBLE MUSHROOMS, but only a small number of those varieties are tasty enough to be worth eating. Italy's porcini and ovoli mushrooms are highly prized, and of course, aromatic truffles are treasured.

Mushrooms can be eaten raw or cooked (in Italy the latter is much more common). They can also be dried. Dried mushrooms must be rehydrated before use. The soaking liquid from dried mushrooms can be filtered through cheesecloth or a paper coffee filter and incorporated into recipes as well.

Because of their high water content—a fresh mushroom is 90 percent water—mushrooms do go bad quite quickly. Look for firm caps without holes or soft spots. The stems should look fresh and moist, but not swollen with excess water. Mushrooms should have a delicate fragrance—no moldy overtones. They can be refrigerated in a brown paper bag for 1 to 2 days at most, but don't ever put mushrooms in the crisper drawer of your refrigerator; they will turn soggy and inedible.

Cremini

Chanterelle

Honey

Oyster

Ovoli

Porcini

CLEANING and TRIMMING MUSHROOMS

 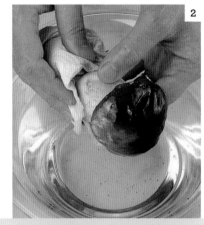

PORCINI

Cut away the soil-covered base of porcinis using a sharp knife or a vegetable peeler **[1]**. Give the mushrooms a quick rinse under running water, then use a soft brush or cloth to clean off any remaining soil **[2]**. Dry thoroughly.

BUTTON OR CREMINI

To prepare these cultivated mushrooms for cooking, cut away the base of the stem **[1]**. Then, using a sharp knife, peel any tough skin off the caps of larger mushrooms **[2]**. Finally, give them a quick rinse **[3]** and dry them.

OVOLI

Ovoli mushrooms should be peeled completely. Using a sharp paring knife, work from the base of the cap to the top. Rinse the peeled mushrooms quickly and dry them thoroughly. If you are going to preserve the mushrooms in cans or jars (see page 271), dry them extra carefully.

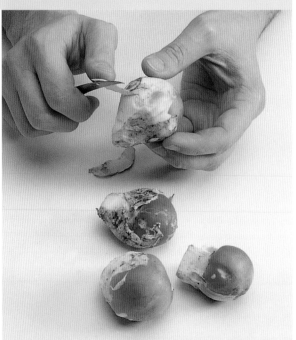

SLICING MUSHROOMS

Once they have been cleaned and trimmed, porcini mushrooms (as well as button or cremini mushrooms) can be sliced very thinly. These make a flavorful addition to salads and other dishes. Use a mandoline or a truffle shaver. Season them to taste with salt and drizzle them with extra-virgin olive oil.

The right tool

TRUFFLE SHAVER

Mushrooms can be thinly sliced with a knife or mandoline, but if you are lucky enough to have fresh truffles on hand, you will need a truffle shaver. This is a metal blade with a handle that allows you to make minutely thin slices. You can also slice mushrooms on a truffle shaver.

BLANCHING CHANTERELLES

Certain types of mushrooms, including chanterelles, develop an unpleasant viscosity when cooked. This can be avoided by blanching them for about 1 minute in boiling water, removing them with a slotted spoon or skimmer [1], and blotting them dry on paper towels [2]. Use the blanched chanterelles in sautéed mushroom dishes, risottos, or sauces.

SAUTÉED PORCINI MUSHROOMS

Trim the porcini and slice them. Heat some olive oil in a skillet, add the mushrooms, the minced leaves of 1 sprig flat-leaf parsley, and ½ clove garlic, also minced [1]. Cook over medium-high heat until softened, about 7 minutes [2].

Truffles

Truffles are mushrooms that grow underground. As with most foods, the best way to eat truffles, whether Italy's white Alba truffles or black truffles, is to purchase them fresh. Given their cost, however, you may want to look for some alternatives. A drop or two of truffle oil drizzled on a finished dish (truffle oil should never be heated) will give off the distinctive aroma of truffle. This is one of the few occasions in Italian cooking when you do not want extra-virgin olive oil. Look for truffle oil made with vegetable oil, as its lack of flavor and aroma lets the truffle shine through. Truffle paste can be purchased in tubes and stirred into pasta sauces that have finished cooking. If you are lucky enough to acquire a whole truffle, store it packed in some rice—the rice will absorb plenty of truffle flavor and make a truly spectacular risotto, with or without a few shavings of truffle topping it.

PORCINI MUSHROOMS FRIED and in TOMATO SAUCE

FRIED PORCINI

Prepare a batter of 2 eggs, 3 tablespoons unbleached all-purpose flour, salt, and enough white wine to make a mixture the consistency of sour cream or a little thinner. Dredge cleaned, trimmed, sliced porcini mushrooms in the batter, then fry them in a generous amount of boiling oil, turning them once to cook both sides [1].

PORCINI IN TOMATO SAUCE

In a skillet, heat a generous amount of extra-virgin olive oil with 1 minced clove garlic, and 1 whole clove garlic, as well as minced fresh oregano and flat-leaf parsley. Add chopped porcini mushrooms and about ¼ cup tomato puree (see page 208) [2]. Season to taste with salt and cook over low heat until the mushrooms have given up their liquid and most of it has evaporated, about 20 minutes.

PRESERVING PORCINI MUSHROOMS IN OIL

Smaller porcini mushrooms are best for eating raw (combined with a few slices of fresh truffle, if possible) and for preserving in oil. Larger porcini are best used in cooked preparations.

Bring 1¾ cups water and 2 cups white wine vinegar to a boil with 5 whole garlic cloves, bay leaves, whole peppercorns, and salt [1]. Blanch the porcini mushrooms in this mixture for 1 minute, then remove them with a skimmer or slotted spoon, and spread them on a clean dish towel to cool [2]. Transfer the mushrooms to sterilized glass jars, layering in slices of garlic, bay leaves, and whole cloves as well. Add olive oil to cover and arrange two toothpicks on top to keep the mushrooms immersed [3]. Can to preserve safely for long-term storage according to jar manufacturer's instructions.

MUSHROOM RISOTTO and LASAGNE

RISOTTO

Sauté minced onion in oil, then add 1 cup short-grain rice to the pan and toast it (see page 107). Moisten the rice with white wine and add about ½ cup sautéed porcini or other mushrooms [1]. Cook according to the instructions on page 108 using broth, stir in butter and grated Parmigiano Reggiano cheese, and serve immediately [2].

LASAGNE

In a small amount of extra-virgin olive oil, sauté a sliced onion, then add 2 peeled and seeded fresh tomatoes cut into wedges [1]. Cook for 2 to 3 minutes over medium heat, then add 1⅓ cups sliced mushrooms [2]. Cover the pan and cook until the sauce has thickened, about 15 minutes. Salt to taste. Bring a large pot of water to a boil, salt it, and cook egg lasagne noodles (page 36). Smear the bottom of an ovenproof dish with a little of the mushroom sauce and top it with a layer of cooked noodles [3]. Continue to alternate layers of sauce and noodles, sprinkling a little grated Parmigiano Reggiano cheese on top of each layer of sauce [4]. Finish with a generous layer of grated cheese. Bake at 400 degrees F for 20 minutes and serve hot.

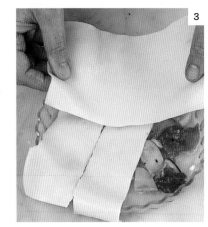

Vellutata di porcini
porcini mushroom soup

¾ pound porcini mushrooms

3 tablespoons extra-virgin olive oil

½ small onion, minced

1 clove garlic

Leaves of 1 sprig fresh sage

2 cups chicken broth (page 56)

Fine sea salt to taste

Freshly ground black pepper to taste

⅓ cup rice flour

1½ cups whole milk

1. Set aside the prettiest mushroom. Trim the rest and thinly slice them.

2. Heat the oil in a pot and sauté the onion and garlic. Add the sage and the sliced mushrooms. When the mushrooms have wilted slightly, add the broth. Season with salt and pepper and cook over medium heat for 6 minutes.

3. In a small bowl, whisk together the rice flour with the milk until smooth. Pour the milk mixture into the soup, whisking constantly. Cover the pot and cook for 15 minutes. Transfer the soup to a blender and puree until it is smooth.

4. If the soup has cooled, reheat it before serving, then ladle it into individual soup plates. Thinly slice the reserved mushroom and garnish each portion with a couple of slices. Serve hot.

SERVES 4   COOKING TIME: 1 HOUR

273

POTATOES

ORIGINALLY FROM PERU, THE POTATO WAS IMPORTED TO EUROPE BY THE SPANISH in the late 1500s, but in many places, including Italy, it was seen as a botanical curiosity rather than a food. Potatoes caught on in Italy only in the 1800s.

Today, the potato is one of the most popular and versatile vegetables in Italy and a cornerstone of the Italian diet. Potatoes feature in side dishes, but they are also used as ingredients in other dishes, most notably gnocchi.

There are numerous varieties of potatoes available, and they are usually broken down by color, skin thickness, and whether their flesh is waxy or starchy. New potatoes are not a particular variety of potato, but simply potatoes that are harvested young. They are small in size with thin skin and are not yet very starchy; they are best roasted.

New Potatoes

Ratte Potato

Bintje Potato

Asterix Potato

Liseta Potato

Désirée Potatoes

SELECTING and PEELING POTATOES

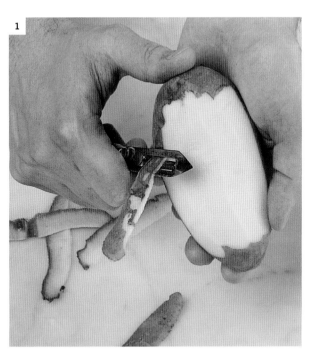

Potatoes should be firm, unwrinkled, and free of soft spots and green sprouts. Store potatoes in a dark, cool place in order to keep them from sprouting. The green sprouts are not only bitter, but they are toxic.

A vegetable peeler is very useful for peeling raw potatoes, as it removes only a thin layer of peel [1]. Peeled potatoes will turn an unattractive brown if exposed to air, so drop them into a bowl of cold water if you're not using them right away [2].

Potato peels

It's always best to cook potatoes with their peels on, whether you're boiling or steaming them, even if you plan to peel them afterward. This keeps them from losing vitamins and minerals and helps them hold together while cooking. The peels should slip right off when the potatoes have cooled enough for you to handle them but are still warm.

Before roasting or frying potatoes, you may want to blanch them briefly. This helps guard against their absorbing too much oil.

CUTTING POTATOES

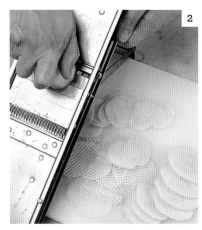

1] DICE To cut potatoes into cubes, first cut them lengthwise into slices. Cut the slices into long sticks, then cut several sticks at a time to any size dice that you like.

2] SLICES OR CHIPS A mandoline is best for cutting very thin slices of potato for layering as a crust or making potato chips. You can even cut waffle chips easily with a mandoline, using a special blade.

3] BALLS Use a melon baller to make small, uniform balls of potato. These can be cooked any way you like.

4] STICKS AND JULIENNE Use a sharp chef's knife or mandoline to cut potatoes into sticks of various sizes. These are usually either fried or roasted.

The right tool

FRENCH FRY CUTTER

A French fry cutter is a grid of blades that makes short work of cutting a peeled potato (or unpeeled, if that's your preference) into strips. Simply trim the ends of the potato to make them flat, stand the potato on one end with the cutter resting on the other, and press down, using both hands.

FRIED and BOILED POTATOES

FRIED

For French fries that are soft on the inside and crispy on the outside, rinse the potatoes after you cut them, then dry them well. Heat a generous amount of oil to 285 to 300 degrees F and fry the potatoes for 7 to 8 minutes [1]. Drain them, raise the heat of the oil to 350 degrees F, and then fry the potatoes for an additional 3 minutes [2]. Serve immediately.

BOILED

Remove the dirt from the potatoes with a soft brush, leaving the skin on, then boil them in salted water [1] until they can easily be pierced with a paring knife, 25 to 45 minutes, depending on size. If you are going to peel the potatoes, do it as soon as they are cool enough to handle [2].

CROQUETTES and MASHED POTATOES

CROQUETTES

To make breaded potato croquettes, mash boiled potatoes with egg and flour to make a dough. (You should be able to grasp a bit in the palm of your hand and make a compact ball by closing your fist.) Form this potato dough into small cylinders. Dredge the cylinders in egg **[1]** and then in bread crumbs **[2]** and fry them. These are terrific appetizers to serve with cocktails.

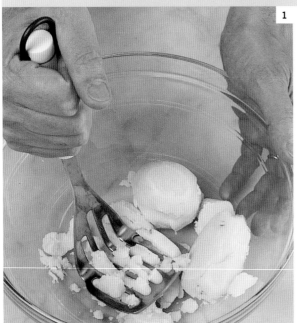

MASHED

Boil potatoes (page 277) and as soon as they are still cool enough to handle, peel them and mash them with a potato masher **[1]**. In a pot over low heat, combine the mashed potatoes with salt, butter, and enough milk to make a smooth puree **[2]**.

MACARIO POTATOES and POTATO CAKE

MACARIO POTATOES

Mash peeled boiled potatoes (see page 277) with minced parsley and season with salt and pepper **[1]**. Spread them in a baking dish and top them with grated Parmigiano Reggiano cheese and bread crumbs. Dot the surface with butter and bake until it is golden and crisp **[2]**.

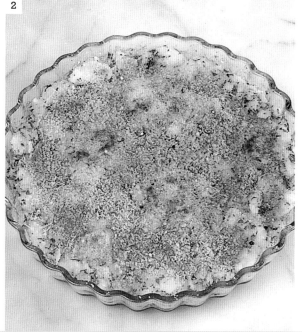

POTATO CAKE

Puree boiled potatoes (page 277) through a food mill (not a food processor—it will make them gluey). Add an egg, some grated cheese, a grating or two of nutmeg, and salt to taste. Spread a little over half of the mixture into a baking dish so that it covers the bottom and sides. Fill the center with prosciutto cotto **[1]**, then top it with the remaining potato mixture. Bake until golden **[2]**.

Perfect roasted potatoes have a crisp golden crust enclosing tender potato flesh. Here are a few tips for making perfect roasted potatoes every time. Pair them with any type of roasted meat for a classic combination.

Roasted Potatoes

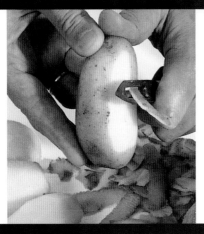  

Use yellow potatoes such as Yukon golds, rather than white varieties, and choose the dense type of potato, not the starchy type. Rinse off all dirt, then peel the potatoes, making sure to remove any eyes or dark spots with the tip of a paring knife or the tip of the peeler.

Cut the potatoes into equal-sized pieces, ¾ inch or 1 inch. This produces the best ratio of crispy exterior and soft interior.

To keep the potatoes from falling apart in the oven, blanch them first. Bring lightly salted water to a boil and acidulate it by adding 3 tablespoons white wine vinegar for every 4 cups water. When the water returns to a boil, toss in the potatoes, cook them for 2 minutes, drain them, and allow them to rest until they have cooled.

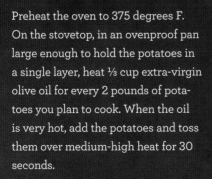

Preheat the oven to 375 degrees F. On the stovetop, in an ovenproof pan large enough to hold the potatoes in a single layer, heat ⅓ cup extra-virgin olive oil for every 2 pounds of potatoes you plan to cook. When the oil is very hot, add the potatoes and toss them over medium-high heat for 30 seconds.

Without adding salt, transfer the pan to the preheated oven. Roast until the potatoes have formed a golden crust and are easily pierced with a paring knife, about 35 minutes. Halfway through cooking, turn the potatoes once. Otherwise, leave them undisturbed. While the potatoes are roasting, mince any fresh herbs you'd like to use to season them: Rosemary, sage, marjoram, and thyme are all good choices.

When the potatoes are cooked, remove them from the oven and toss them gently with salt and the minced herbs, using a spatula to detach them from the pan if necessary. Roasted potatoes are best served warm, but not extremely hot, so let them rest for 10 minutes or so if possible.

*I*F YOU HAVE BEEN TO TUSCANY, you may have had the pleasure of feasting on Chianina beef, almost always served in the form of a bistecca Fiorentina, a thick slab of meat simply grilled with rosemary and sea salt. Chianina is a short-horned breed of cow that traces its ancestors back to the days of the Etruscans and ancient Romans, who used the animals in processions and sacrificed them to the gods. Chianina are the largest cows in the world. Piedmont has its own breed, known as Piemontese, which also yields excellent beef and has been around for 30,000 years.

Beef is highly valued in Italy, but in a country that was largely populated by farmers for many years, cows were valuable for plowing fields and for milk, and so beef was a rare treat, generally reserved for Sundays and holidays. True to their farming roots, today's Italians still eat relatively few meals with beef at the center of the plate. One way they extend beef is to grind it and use it to make meatballs, meatloaf, and of course meat sauce to be served over pasta.

BEEF & VEAL

Protein-rich and deeply satisfying, beef is not only a favorite around the world, but one of the most emblematic foods of two Italian regions in particular: Piedmont and Tuscany.

OSSOBUCO

ossobuco

Ossobuco (literally "bone hole") is a cut of meat and also refers to dishes made by cooking that cut of meat until it is extremely tender. A good butcher will be able to prepare ossobuco for you by sawing crosswise through veal shanks so that each slice includes a piece of marrow bone. The membrane surrounding the shank holds the meat on the bone, which you want, but it also contracts during the long cooking process and can make the cut curl up unattractively. To remedy this without detaching the meat from the bone, use the tip of a sharp knife to cut 3 to 4 slits around the perimeter of each ossobuco before cooking.

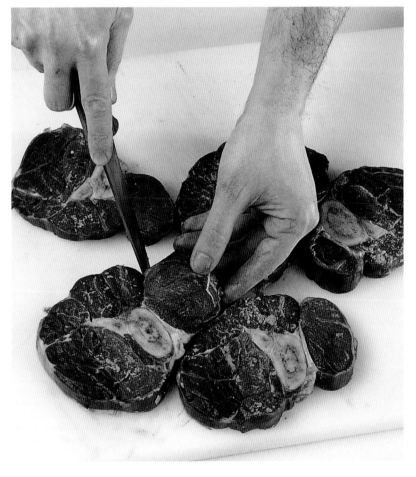

OSSOBUCO ALLA MILANESE

In a Dutch oven large enough to hold your ossobuco cuts in a single layer, heat extra-virgin olive oil and brown the meat on both sides. Remove and set them aside, then cook a soffritto (page 260) of minced carrot, celery, and onion in the Dutch oven until soft. Return the meat to the pot and pour in about ¼ cup white wine, ½ cup peeled, roughly chopped tomatoes and their juices, and enough beef broth (page 56) to cover the meat. Cover and simmer over low heat until the meat is very tender (you should be able to shred it with a fork) and the sauce has thickened, about 2 hours. Every 30 minutes or so, turn the meat and baste it with a little of the cooking liquid (add a small amount of water if it looks as if the pot is drying out). Taste and season with salt and pepper. Make a gremolade by mincing together the zest of 1 lemon, the leaves of 3 sprigs flat-leaf parsley, and 1 clove garlic. Spoon the sauce on top of the meat just before serving.

OSSOBUCO ALLA ROMAGNOLA

This is a less well-known but equally tasty ossobuco preparation from the Romagna region. In a Dutch oven large enough to hold your ossobuco cuts in a single layer, melt butter and cook a soffritto (page 260) of minced carrot, celery, and onion until soft. Dredge the meat in flour and brown it in the Dutch oven. Add 3 to 4 fresh sage leaves and 1 cup or so white wine, and season to taste with salt and pepper. Cook until the wine has evaporated, then add enough beef broth (page 56) to cover the meat. Turn the temperature down to maintain a simmer, place the lid on the pot, and cook until the meat is very tender and the sauce is thick, about 2 hours, turning the meat and basting it with the cooking liquid every 30 minutes or so. If the pot appears to be drying out, add more broth in small amounts. Adjust the salt and pepper to taste and serve.

SHANKS

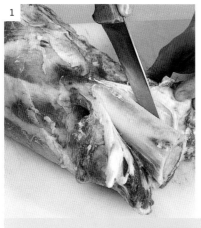

The shank is the shin of a cow. It is a cut rich in connective tissue that melts during long cooking, leaving the meat caramelized and crisp. The best way to cook whole shanks is to braise them until they are very tender. The finished shanks will look prettier if you use a sharp knife to cut the meat, then peel it back to expose a couple of inches of bone [1]. Wrap aluminum foil around the bone during cooking so that it doesn't burn [2].

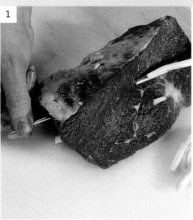

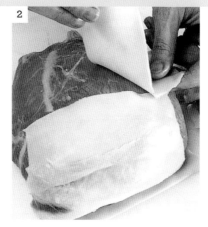

LARDING and TYING A ROAST

LARDING BY THREADING

To keep meat tender and moist when it is roasted, cut strips of fatback or pancetta and insert them, using a larding needle [1] and working in the direction of the grain of the meat.

LARDING BY WRAPPING

Alternatively, wrap the piece of meat in thin slices of fatback, overlapping them slightly [2].

TYING

Use kitchen twine to tie a roast so that it doesn't lose its shape. Wrap the string around at even intervals, and then tie it in a knot [3]. For further information on tying see page 306.

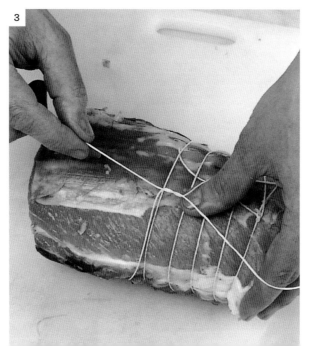

SCALOPPINE and SPIEDINI

SCALOPPINE
A veal scallop, a cut usually taken from the rump of the animal, must be very thin (about ¼ inch thick) to cook properly. Fold in any corners so that the finished scallop will have a regular thickness and a rounded shape [1], then pound it with a meat pounder [2].

SPIEDINI
Slice sirloin or another tender, lean cut of meat into long strips and then cut the strips crosswise into cubes [1]. Thread the cubes onto skewers, alternating them with sage leaves and pieces of fatback [2], and either grill them or cook them in a large skillet.

SPEZZATINO DI MANZO
beef stew

Cut 2 pounds of boned shank into chunks **[1]**. In a Dutch oven or heavy pot, heat extra-virgin olive oil, then dredge the chunks of meat in flour and brown them. Remove the meat and set it aside; add a soffritto (page 260) of chopped celery, carrot, and onion to the pot. Cook until the onion is translucent and return the meat to the pot **[2]**. Pour in 1¾ cups red wine **[3]**. Cover and simmer until the meat is tender and the sauce is thick, about 1 hour and 30 minutes. Pair the stew with boiled or mashed potatoes or polenta (pages 277, 278, or 119, respectively).

287

MARINATING IN WINE and HERBS

MARINATING IN WINE
Place cubes of meat in a bowl with sage leaves, bay leaves, rosemary, chopped celery, chopped carrots, chopped onion, and garlic cloves. Add red or white wine, cover the bowl with plastic wrap, and marinate in the refrigerator for 3 to 6 hours.

MARINATING WITH HERBS
Toss cubes of meat in a bowl with sage, rosemary, bay leaves, and crushed garlic cloves with the peels still on. Marinate in the refrigerator for 30 to 60 minutes. Spices such as lightly crushed black peppercorns, lightly crushed juniper berries, and cinnamon sticks can also be used. Before cooking, lift the meat out of the marinade and remove any large pieces of herb or spice still clinging to the meat.

Brasato al Barolo

beef braised in barolo wine

8 whole cloves

2 medium-sized yellow onions

1 stalk celery

2 carrots, halved

2 cloves garlic, peels left on, crushed

1 bouquet (see page 141) of parsley, sage, bay leaf, and rosemary

6 whole black peppercorns

Pinch fine sea salt

Pinch ground cinnamon

Pinch freshly grated nutmeg

1 boneless beef chuck roast, about 2 pounds

1 (750-ml) bottle Barolo wine

1 tablespoon unsalted butter

1 cup brandy

1. Stick 4 cloves into each of the onions and place the onions in a large nonreactive bowl with the celery, carrots, garlic, bouquet, peppercorns, salt, cinnamon, and nutmeg. Place the meat in the bowl and pour the wine over it. Cover the bowl with plastic wrap and refrigerate it for at least 6 hours, preferably overnight.

2. When you are ready to cook the meat, in a Dutch oven or heavy pot with a tight-fitting lid, melt the butter. Remove the meat from the marinade, reserving the marinade; pat the meat dry, and brown it on all sides in the butter. Pour the brandy over the meat, then flambé the brandy.

3. As soon as the alcohol has burned off, strain the marinade and add the liquid and the onions, carrots, celery, garlic, and bouquet to the pot with the meat. Cover and cook over very low heat until the meat is tender, about 4 hours. Remove and discard the cloves from the onions, and the bouquet. Puree the remaining sauce along with the onions, garlic, carrots, celery, and cooking juices and return this to the pot with the meat.

4. Braise the meat for an additional 10 minutes, then carve and serve it hot with the sauce. Pair it with mashed potatoes or polenta (page 278 or 119).

SERVES 6   COOKING TIME: 5 HOURS

HERBS and SPICES FOR MEAT

1] ROSEMARY
Rosemary goes well with beef, pork, poultry, or lamb, and it is a key ingredient in the roasted potatoes (see page 280) that are a classic accompaniment to all of these. Fresh rosemary flowers are edible and can be incorporated into salads.

2] ALLSPICE
This berry has notes of cinnamon, cloves, and nutmeg. It is used in braised meats and also in sauces.

3] BAY LEAF
The slightly bitter flavor of fresh bay leaves disappears if the leaves are left to dry at room temperature for a few days. Bay leaves add subtle flavor to red meat, pork, and beef broths and stocks.

SALT-CURING MEAT

Rub a single fillet with a mixture of coarse salt, dried thyme, crushed black peppercorns, and rosemary leaves [1]. Wrap it tightly in plastic and refrigerate for 2 to 3 hours, then wipe off the salt mixture [2]. The meat can be roasted whole at 425 degrees F for 15 minutes.

GROUND BEEF

POLPETTINE (MEATBALLS)

Soak 1 to 2 slices of stale bread in milk until soft. Crumble the bread and combine it with about 1 pound ground lean beef, 1 small minced onion, a couple of tablespoons minced flat-leaf parsley, ¼ cup grated Parmigiano Reggiano cheese, and salt and pepper to taste. Mix by hand, then add 1 lightly beaten egg and stir until very thoroughly combined. Shape the mixture into balls 1 inch in diameter. Heat a few tablespoons of extra-virgin olive oil in a large skillet and cook the meatballs (working in batches to avoid crowding the pan) until they are browned on all sides, turning them occasionally, about 6 minutes. If you want to serve the meatballs in tomato sauce, remove all but about 1 tablespoon of fat from the skillet. Add a cup or two of chopped peeled tomatoes and their juices and return the meatballs to the pan. Simmer, turning the meatballs occasionally, until the tomatoes have thickened into a sauce, about 20 minutes. For a more unusual preparation, rather than adding chopped peeled tomatoes to the pan, add a chopped red bell pepper and some pitted black olives and cook until soft, about 5 minutes. Return the browned meatballs to the pan until heated through, then serve.

POLPETTONE (MEAT LOAF)

Combine 1 pound ground lean beef, ⅓ cup grated Parmigiano Reggiano cheese, a couple of tablespoons minced flat-leaf parsley, a couple of tablespoons of minced prosciutto, 1 minced clove garlic, and salt and pepper to taste. Add 2 lightly beaten eggs and use your hands to combine. On a work surface, form the mixture into a large loaf shaped like a flattened cylinder about 2½ inches in diameter. Dredge the meat loaf in bread crumbs. In a skillet large enough to hold the meat loaf, heat ¼ cup extra-virgin olive oil. Stick 1 or 2 cloves in a whole peeled onion and place the onion in the skillet. When the oil is hot, add the meat loaf and brown it on both sides, turning it very carefully with 2 spatulas. When the meat loaf is browned, pour in about ½ cup white wine. Cook until the wine has evaporated, then add 1¼ cups beef broth (page 56). Turn down the heat until the broth is just simmering, cover the pot, and cook, turning the meat loaf once, until cooked through, about 1 hour. Remove the meat loaf to a cutting board and let it rest for at least 15 minutes before serving. Cut it into slices and serve warm or at room temperature.

POLPETTONE RIPIENO (STUFFED MEAT LOAF)

Preheat the oven to 350 degrees F and line a baking sheet with parchment paper. Combine 2 pounds ground lean beef with 2 pieces of stale bread moistened in milk and crumbled; season with salt and pepper to taste. Mix in 2 lightly beaten eggs using your hands. Transfer the meat mixture to the parchment on the baking sheet. Wet your hands and press the meat into a 12-by-14-inch rectangle of even thickness. On top, layer some or all of the following (in this order): 2 to 3 slices prosciutto (these should cover the surface but leave a 1½-inch border), a few matchsticks of firm cheese such as fresh pecorino Romano or Taleggio, about ½ cup cooked spinach shaped into a log, 5 to 6 cooked green beans, 2 to 3 hard-boiled eggs laid end to end. Roll up the meat around the filling, using the parchment paper. Pinch the ends and seams of the loaf together to be sure the stuffing is completely enclosed. Twist the ends of the parchment paper to make the meat loaf look like a large candy in a wrapper and tie the ends with kitchen twine. Bake for 1 hour. Allow the meat loaf to rest for at least 15 minutes before cutting it into slices to reveal the stuffing.

BOLLITO

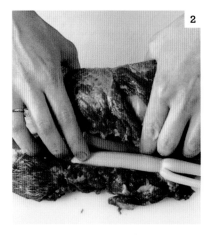

BOILED BEEF

When cooking boiled beef, bollito, you can flavor the water with celery, onion, carrot, and bay leaf, but if you'd like the dish to be more strongly flavored with those elements, you can also use them to stuff the meat itself. Spread out the beef brisket and beef shoulder and place peeled carrots and celery stalks on the surface **[1]**. Roll up the meat **[2]** and make sure all the vegetables are tightly enclosed **[3]**. Tie the rolled meat with kitchen twine **[4]**. For further information on tying see page 306. You may want to cut the meat into 2 pieces in order for it to fit better in the pot **[5]**.

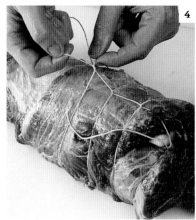

Bollito con Salsa di Rafano

boiled beef with horseradish sauce

2 pounds beef brisket

1 large onion, peeled

4 large carrots, peeled

2 stalks celery

1 tablespoon black peppercorns

2 bay leaves

2 pounds boneless beef shoulder

1 pound turnips, peeled

1½ pounds potatoes, peeled

4 slices day-old bread

½ cup white wine vinegar

2 cloves garlic

Leaves of 1 bunch flat-leaf parsley

Grated fresh horseradish to taste

3 tablespoons extra-virgin olive oil

Fine sea salt to taste

Freshly ground black pepper to taste

1. Place the brisket and the onion, 2 of the carrots, and the celery in a large pot and add cold water to cover. Add the peppercorns and bay leaves. Bring the water to a boil over high heat and simmer the broth for 30 minutes. Add the beef shoulder and cook for an additional 1 hour and 40 minutes.

2. Meanwhile, cut the 2 remaining carrots, the turnips, and the potatoes into equal-sized pieces.

3. Remove the solids from the pot. Degrease the broth. Return the meat to the pot, discarding the whole carrots, celery, and onion. Add the uncooked vegetables to the broth, bring it to a simmer, and cook for an additional 20 minutes. Slice the meat and transfer it to a platter along with the vegetables.

4. For the sauce, soak the bread in the vinegar until soft. Squeeze out the excess liquid and transfer the bread to a blender, along with the garlic, parsley, and horseradish. (Horseradish begins to lose potency almost immediately, so don't make the sauce far in advance.) Puree the mixture while pouring in the oil. Season with salt and pepper. Serve the sauce alongside the hot meat and vegetables.

SERVES 8   COOKING TIME: 3 HOURS

295

The drippings that collect in a pan when meat is cooking can be made into gravy for the resulting roasted meat.

Sauce from a Roast

Before cooking, place the meat and any scraps trimmed from the meat in the pan and add aromatic herbs and minced onion, celery, and carrot. Roast the meat as usual, basting it occasionally with a little white wine.

When the meat is cooked, remove it and keep it warm. Place the pan on the stovetop and boil off as much water as possible. The sauce is properly reduced when the fat rises to the top and bits of meat begin to stick to the bottom of the pan and caramelize.

Spoon off the fat and add 1 to 2 teaspoons unbleached all-purpose flour. Stir to combine. Deglaze the pan with ½ cup white wine and 1 to 2 cups water, using a spatula to scrape the bottom of the pan and loosen any bits that have stuck. Add a sprig of any aromatic herb you like and boil the sauce for a few minutes, then season it with salt and pepper.

Use a spatula to scrape the bottom of the pan and loosen any bits that have stuck. Add a sprig of any aromatic herb you like and boil the sauce for a few minutes, then season with salt and pepper.

Strain out the solids. Carve the roasted meat and spoon the sauce over the meat.

Alternatively, transfer the sauce to a container or containers, seal tightly, and store in the refrigerator or freezer.

297

Spinacino con verdure

veal breast stuffed with vegetables

1 boned veal breast with a pocket cut into it, about 1¾ pounds (see note)

2 large potatoes

6 ounces sausage, casings removed

Fine sea salt to taste

Freshly ground black pepper to taste

Pinch ground cinnamon

Pinch freshly grated nutmeg

2 tablespoons unsalted butter

1 shallot, minced

Leaves of 1 sprig fresh rosemary, minced

1 large egg, lightly beaten

1 tablespoon grated Parmigiano Reggiano cheese

1 pound celery root, peeled and diced

6 carrots, peeled and diced

3 bay leaves

1 onion, chopped

1 slice pancetta, chopped

2 tablespoons extra-virgin olive oil

1 cup dry white wine

1 tablespoon minced fresh sage

1. Preheat the oven to 400 degrees F. If your butcher has not cut the veal breast for you, use a very sharp knife to cut a deep slit and make a pocket.

2. Place 1 of the potatoes, with its peel still on, in a pot with water to cover, bring it to a boil, and cook until the potato is tender, about 20 minutes. Peel and dice the remaining raw potato.

3. As soon as the cooked potato is cool enough to handle, peel it and pass it through a potato ricer into a bowl with the sausage; season with salt, pepper, cinnamon, and nutmeg.

4. In a skillet, melt the butter and brown the diced potato with the shallot and rosemary. In a medium bowl, combine the riced potato and the sausage. Add the egg, Parmigiano Reggiano, salt and pepper to taste, and the cooked potato, and combine thoroughly.

5. Stuff the sausage mixture into the pocket in the veal. Sew the veal closed with kitchen twine and season the exterior of the meat with salt and pepper.

6. Toss the celery root, carrots, bay leaves, onion, pancetta, olive oil, and salt and pepper to taste in a Dutch oven to combine. Place the veal on top of the vegetables. Cover and cook in the preheated oven for 40 minutes. Add the wine and continue cooking the veal, covered, until a thermometer inserted into the thickest part of the meat reads 170 degrees F, about 40 additional minutes. Sprinkle on the minced sage and serve the veal hot, carved into thick slices, with the vegetables.

NOTE: *A spinacino of veal is a triangular section of leg round sold by Italian butchers and that is perfect for stuffing as this recipe describes. Butchering varies widely from country to country, however, and this cut of veal simply doesn't exist in the United States. A boned breast of veal makes a good substitute, and a reputable butcher will be happy to bone it and cut it to create the pocket for you.*

SERVES 8　　COOKING TIME: 2 HOURS

INVOLTINI

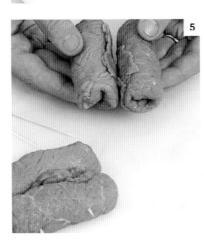

Involtini are thin slices of meat, usually veal, filled with various stuffings and rolled up. To pound slices of veal very thin and break up the fibers and muscles without tearing the meat, either moisten your meat pounder or place the veal between two layers of plastic wrap when pounding it [1]. Cut the pounded slices into the size you prefer. Place a small amount of filling in the center of each piece of veal [2]. (Shown here is a filling made of equal parts scamorza cheese and prosciutto cotto ground together, but almost any filling you like will work. Just don't overstuff the roll.) Fold the long sides of a piece of meat into the center, then roll up the veal from the short end [3]. Repeat for each roll. Place 2 rolls next to each other, with the seam sides pressed together, and thread the pair onto 2 toothpicks [4]. Alternatively, you can use long wooden skewers and thread more than 2 rolls, but always do them in pairs and keep the seam sides facing each other to prevent them from curling up or unfurling when cooking [5]. Place the involtini in a skillet with a little oil and melted butter. Place aromatic herbs above and/or below the rolls. Cover and cook the rolls for 4 minutes over medium heat. Turn the rolls, add white wine or broth, and simmer them, uncovered, until fully cooked [6]. Season to taste with salt and pepper, and sprinkle with a little minced parsley, if you like. While it's traditional to cook involtini on the stovetop, if you are making a lot at one time, you may find it easier to roast them in the oven.

BUTTERFLYING MEAT FOR STUFFING

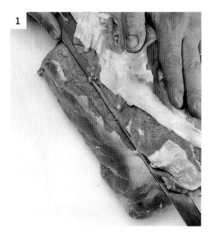

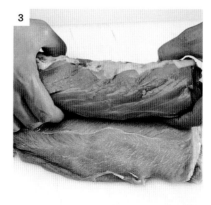

Ask your butcher for a large slice of loin, boned and cleaned of any connective tissue. Lay it flat on your work surface and, using a long, sharp knife held parallel to the surface of the meat, cut horizontally about a third of the way through the thickness **[1]**. Stop an inch or two before you reach the end and open up the meat like a book **[2]**. Repeat the same cut in the other direction, starting at the base of the first cut, to create a second "page." The piece should now lie flat and be of equal thickness. It is ready to be stuffed, rolled up **[3]**, and roasted.

TENERONI and BAULETTI

TENERONI are spirals of veal or other meat that make good use of the fatty shoulder blade steak or other cuts that require long cooking. Cut the meat into long strips. Roll into spirals and tie tightly with kitchen twine **[1]**. Dredge the spirals in flour and brown them in a combination of extra-virgin olive oil and butter over high heat, then braise them, covered, in broth or other liquid until tender, about 2 hours.

BAULETTI are veal packets. Make a filling of ground meat, stale bread moistened with milk and then crumbled, grated Parmigiano Reggiano, an egg, and seasonings. Pound veal slices thin and lightly flour one side only, shaking off any excess. Place the slices floured side up on your work surface and arrange a small amount of filling at the center of each one. Fold each in half to enclose the filling, then pound around the edges, first with the blade of your knife and then with the blunt side, to seal **[2]**. Brown the bauletti in melted butter, then deglaze the pan with white wine, simmer them in the wine for a few more minutes, and serve hot.

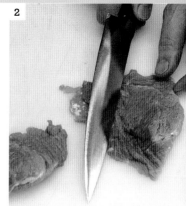

ONE OF THE OPERATING PRINCIPLES OF THE ITALIAN KITCHEN is "throw away nothing," and perhaps no food source lends itself better to that philosophy than the pig. Italians use the flesh, fat, organs, blood, and skin of the animal, as they have for generations. The tradition of breeding pigs in the North dates back to the Gauls, who arrived in the Italian Alpine region in the second century B.C. The densely wooded areas in northern Italy were perfect for raising swine, and even the ancient Romans were heavy pork consumers. Written sources testify to their tradition of smoking and salting every part of the pig, much as modern Italians do today.

In the Middle Ages, a culture of self-sufficiency developed that led families to raise pigs in their homes. That was also when the tradition of the *norcino*, a dedicated pig butcher, began to develop. As Christmas approached, the *norcino* would travel from house to house, butchering pigs for families. Today, pig butchering remains a major activity on many farms. After the pigs are butchered, they are divided into parts and used to make prosciutto, fatback, guanciale (preserved pig jowl), and other items. The various regions have developed their own pork specialties, such as Rome's porchetta and Sardinia's porceddu, both roast suckling pig dishes. In Calabria, pig's blood is even used to make a dessert—the rich and funky-tasting sanguinaccio, which includes chocolate, sugar, spices, candied fruit peel, almonds, milk, and bitter cocoa.

PORK &
PORK PRODUCTS

Flavorful pork is also versatile–and
Italians use every part of the pig.

Filetto di Maiale alla Boscaiola

roast pork loin with mushrooms

1 boneless pork loin roast, 1½ to 2 pounds

Fine sea salt to taste

Freshly ground black pepper to taste

5 tablespoons extra-virgin olive oil

½ cup dry white wine

7 ounces porcini mushrooms

7 ounces chanterelle mushrooms

1 tablespoon unsalted butter

1 shallot, minced

1 tablespoon minced red bell pepper

1 tablespoon minced flat-leaf parsley leaves

2 fresh sage leaves, minced

1 tablespoon snipped chives

1 tablespoon minced fresh mint leaves

½ cup vegetable stock (page 55)

1. Preheat the oven to 350 degrees F. Place the pork loin in a baking dish that can be used on the stovetop and season it with salt and pepper. Drizzle on 2 tablespoons of the olive oil and roast the meat for 40 minutes, basting it occasionally with the wine.

2. Meanwhile, trim the porcini mushrooms and slice them. Trim the chanterelles and blanch them for 1 minute and 30 seconds; after draining the chanterelles, chop any that are very large. (For more on preparing mushrooms, see page 268.)

3. Melt the butter in a skillet, add the remaining 3 tablespoons olive oil, and cook the shallot and minced bell pepper until the shallot is transparent. Add the chanterelles and cook for 3 minutes, then add the porcini mushrooms and cook for an additional 3 minutes. Sprinkle on the parsley, sage, chives, and mint; season with salt and pepper, and remove from the heat.

4. Transfer the loin to a serving dish and deglaze the baking dish on the stovetop with the stock, whisking energetically to scrape any browned bits off the bottom. Add this liquid to the skillet with the mushrooms and simmer for 1 minute. Transfer the mushrooms to the serving dish with the pork. Carve the pork into slices at the table and serve each slice with some of the mushrooms.

SERVES 6   COOKING TIME: 50 MINUTES

PORK LOIN BRAISED IN MILK

*I*n Bologna, pork loin is commonly braised in milk, which makes it very tender. Be sure to use whole milk for this preparation, as skim and low-fat won't yield a creamy sauce.

First, tie a boneless pork loin roast (1½ to 2 pounds) with kitchen twine. To do this, place the loin on the work surface, perpendicular to you. Slide a length of kitchen twine (leave it attached to the ball so you don't have to estimate how much you'll need) under one short end. Pull the twine taut around the meat and knot it firmly, but not so tightly that the twine is squeezing the flesh and making an indentation. Pull the twine perpendicular to this first loop and place your finger on it about an inch from the knot. Wrap the twine around the short way again, passing it through the point where you are holding the string so that you form a second loop parallel to the first one. Continue in this way, making a row of loops about 1 inch apart. When you get to the end, knot the twine and cut it. Season the loin with fine sea salt and freshly ground black pepper. Tuck some sage leaves and/or bay leaves under the string. In a pot just large enough to hold the loin (an oval Dutch oven is ideal), heat 3 tablespoons extra-virgin olive oil.

Add the meat, fat side down, and cook until it is browned on all sides. Slowly add enough whole milk to come about two-thirds of the way up the sides of the pork. Bring the milk to a boil, then turn the heat down to maintain a simmer. Cover with a lid set slightly askew and simmer until the meat is tender, 1½ to 2 hours, basting the meat occasionally. Don't worry if the milk appears to be curdling—you want it to coagulate. Remove the cooked meat to a cutting board and let it rest for a few minutes. If the sauce in the pot is not dark brown, turn up the heat under the pot and reduce it until it is. Spoon off and discard any liquid fat that floats to the top (but try not to disturb the milk clusters—you want these). Taste and adjust the seasoning. Cut off the twine, remove and discard the leaves, slice the pork, and serve the slices with some of the pan juices.

HOMEMADE SAUSAGE

The meat you use to make sausage must be very fresh. Choose cuts from the thigh, shoulder, and belly. For 2 pounds sausage, you'll need 1¾ pounds lean shoulder and thigh meat and 7 ounces pork belly **[1]**. Cut the meat into a dice, trimming off and discarding any connective tissue **[2]**. Grind the meat a little at a time, alternating lean and fattier cuts. If you prefer larger chunks of meat in your sausage, grind the meat only once, but if you prefer a finer grind, put the mixture through the grinder twice. Spread the meat on a work surface, and for every 2 pounds of meat, sprinkle on 1 heaping tablespoon of fine sea salt and a generous amount of freshly ground black pepper **[3]**. Work the seasonings in by kneading the meat. If you like, you can also knead in other flavorings, such as crushed red pepper, fennel seed, and minced garlic. Prepare the sausage casings for stuffing. Casings preserved in salt must be rinsed in a mix of water and white wine vinegar, but even if you have fresh casings, it's not a bad idea to rinse them before using them **[4]**. To stuff the casings, use your hands to hold the open end of a casing against the end of the stuffing tube **[5]**. You can leave the sausage in one long piece or tie it off into lengths **[6]**. Fresh sausage will keep in the refrigerator for 3 to 4 days.

COTECHINO SAUSAGE

Cotechino is a very flavorful pork and fatback sausage from Modena that is traditionally served with lentils and mashed potatoes. It is available in gourmet specialty stores either fresh or cooked. To prepare cotechino, tie the sausage with twine. Poke it with a toothpick at regular intervals and then insert the toothpick into the cotechino. Pricking prevents the skin from bursting and allows excess fat to escape [1]. To protect the sausage while it is cooking, wrap it in cheese-cloth and secure the cloth with more twine [2]. To cook fresh cotechino, place it in a large pot, add cold water to cover, and bring it to a boil; turn down the heat to maintain a simmer and cook for 3 hours. For aged cotechino, boil the sausage for 30 minutes, then transfer it to a fresh pot of cold water, and boil it for 2½ hours [3]. When the cotechino is cooked, remove the cheesecloth, twine, and toothpick; peel off the casing; and cut the sausage into slices. Serve very hot [4].

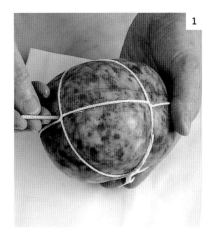

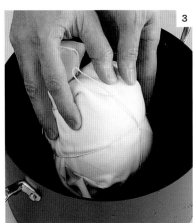

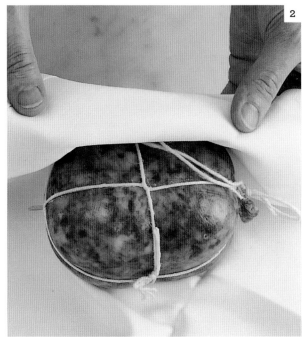

LARDO

fatback spread

Mince slices of fatback with the leaves of a sprig of fresh rosemary **[1]**, flat-leaf parsley, and garlic until the mixture is smooth and creamy. Serve the lardo with tigelle (page 13) **[2]** or spread it on toasted bread.

Arrosto Farcito con Cotechino

veal roast stuffed with cotechino

1 fresh cotechino sausage, about 1½ pounds

1 boneless veal rump, about 1¼ pounds

2 tablespoons unsalted butter

1 small onion, minced

¾ pound chestnuts, boiled and peeled

Fine sea salt to taste

Freshly ground black pepper to taste

6 ounces pancetta slices

¼ cup dry white wine

1 stalk celery, minced

2 carrots, minced

1 sprig rosemary

1 bay leaf

6 ounces jarred Cremona mostarda, plus a little more for serving

1. Cook the cotechino, following the instructions on page 308. Remove the cheesecloth, then let the sausage cool. (Cotechino can be prepared up to 1 day in advance and refrigerated.)

2. Preheat the oven to 400 degrees F. Place the veal rump on a work surface, cover it with a piece of plastic wrap, and use a meat mallet to pound it into a very thin, regular shape.

3. In a skillet, melt the butter and sauté the onion until it is soft. Add the chestnuts and sauté for 5 minutes. Season the mixture with salt and pepper, mash the chestnuts with a wooden spoon, and set the pan aside until the mixture is cool enough to handle.

4. Spread the cooled chestnut mixture over the surface of the meat. Place the whole cotechino on top.

5. Roll up the meat so that it encloses the chestnut mixture and cotechino. Use your hands to shape it into an even cylinder.

6. Lard the cylinder with the slices of pancetta. Tie the roast with kitchen twine (see page 306 for instructions), set it in a baking pan, and bake it for 30 minutes. Then, baste the roast with the white wine and add the celery, carrots, rosemary, and bay leaf to the pan. Cook for an additional 20 minutes. Remove the roast and set it aside to cool slightly. Remove and discard the bay leaf and rosemary sprig. Use a food mill to puree the roasted vegetables, pan juices, and mostarda. Cut the twine from the roast and transfer the roast to a serving platter. Transfer the pureed sauce to the serving platter as well. Carve the roast into slices and serve them with some of the sauce and additional mostarda alongside.

SERVES 12 ॐ COOKING TIME: 1 HOUR (PLUS TIME TO MAKE THE COTECHINO)

A GUIDE TO ITALIAN PORK PRODUCTS

GUANCIALE is pig jowl that has been salted and seasoned with black pepper (or sometimes chile pepper) and cured for 3 months. It is used frequently in dishes from the Lazio region, including bucatini all'amatriciana (page 48).

LARDO, confusingly, is not lard (*strutto* in Italian), but fatback. To make it, the layer of fat right under the pork rind is salted and cured (sometimes with the addition of herbs and spices). It has a creamy, unctuous texture and is spreadable.

MORTADELLA is what Americans call bologna (logically enough, as it is native to the city of Bologna), but it is far superior to the presliced, packaged bologna you ate as a child. Mortadella is 60 percent lean meat and 40 percent fat. The thin slices are studded with white chunks of fat and sometimes whole black peppercorns. Imported Italian mortadella has only recently become available here.

PANCETTA is salt-cured pork belly. It is the closest thing Italy has to American bacon, though bacon is smoked and pancetta is not. Artisanal American bacon makes an acceptable substitute. When a recipe calls for diced pancetta, purchase a thick slice rather than several thin slices.

PROSCIUTTO COTTO is cooked pork leg, similar to the baked ham available in the United States. It is rosy pink in color and generally lower in salt than its American counterpart.

PROSCIUTTO CRUDO, probably Italy's most famous and beloved pork product, is the salt-cured and air-dried haunch of a pig. Prosciutto is cured for at least 11 months and has an unusual flavor with a mix of sweet and salty undertones. Italian prosciutto is available in the United States and is generally regarded as being far superior to American products. Prosciutto di Parma is pink and sweet; prosciutto di San Daniele, from the Friuli region, is darker in color and has a slightly tangier flavor. Prosciutto is almost always sold thinly sliced (it may also be cut by hand into thicker, chewier slices). These days, it is available in general grocery stores, but it is best to purchase it from an Italian or gourmet specialty store, where the meat is likely to be stored and handled properly.

SALAMI of various types is made and cured all over Italy, but as of the writing of this book, Italian salami is not imported to the United States because of government restrictions. Several reputable salami makers here offer a close facsimile of Italian salamis, however. Look for finocchiona, Tuscan fennel seed salami; soppressata, a mix of lean and fatty meat that may also be spicy; and culatello, made from the haunch.

SPECK hails from northern Italy, in the Trentino–Alto Adige area. It is the boneless haunch of a pig that is smoked and then cured. Speck is strongly flavored—a little goes a long way—and high-quality bacon makes an able substitute for it.

*A*T ONE TIME, it was the rare house in Italy that didn't have at least a few chickens running around the yard. These birds were kept mainly as laying hens, and eating chicken as meat was a luxury few could afford. Today, in Italy as elsewhere, chicken is a low-cost and widely available choice. As a result, however, most chickens are raised in less-than-ideal conditions. Perhaps with no other food product is there such a gap between industrially produced items and those from smaller farms. A chicken purchased at a farmers' market will no doubt be substantially more expensive than the factory-raised bird you buy at a mainstream grocery store; it will also be far superior in flavor and texture. Indeed, it will taste like chicken. If you want to enjoy chicken as it is eaten in Italy, the investment is worthwhile.

As is true of Americans, Italians go far beyond chicken in the poultry category, enjoying turkey, goose, duck, pheasant, and squab. Larger birds are often the centerpiece of Christmas dinner in Italy, especially in the Lombardy and Veneto regions.

POULTRY

The rich and varied category of poultry has versatile chicken at its center but also includes squab, game birds, turkey, and more.

ROASTED CHICKEN

There are few simple pleasures in life as gratifying as a properly roasted chicken. The most important ingredient, unsurprisingly, is the chicken itself—purchase a small bird that was raised locally.

Preheat the oven to 400 degrees F. Season the chicken liberally with salt (even better, do this a couple of hours in advance) and freshly ground black pepper. Place sprigs of rosemary or sage leaves and a couple of peeled cloves of garlic in the cavity. Place the chicken breast side up in a roasting pan just large enough to hold it. Roast for 20 minutes. Turn the bird breast side down and roast for 20 minutes. Turn the bird right side up again and roast it until the skin is extremely crispy, 20 to 30 additional minutes. Let the chicken rest for at least 15 minutes before carving. For a one-dish meal, place diced potatoes and carrots tossed with a little extra-virgin olive oil in the base of the pan and each time you turn the chicken, toss the vegetables with the fat rendered from the chicken, using the spatula to scrape up any bits from the bottom of the pan as you go.

FLAVORING POULTRY

It can be very effective to place flavorful items between the skin and the flesh of the poultry before cooking it. Use your index and middle finger to loosen the skin without detaching it completely [1]. Slip herbs and other seasonings (shown here are sprigs of rosemary and slices of truffle being used as flavorings) and position them at regular intervals all over [2]. Return the skin to its original position. It will hold the flavorings in place.

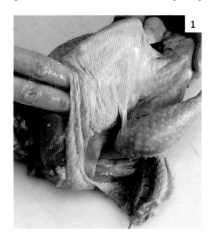

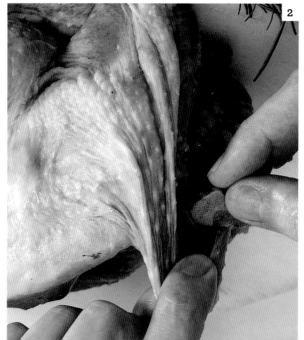

Faraona farcita

stuffed pheasant

10 ounces boneless, skinless chicken breast

1 egg white

¼ cup milk

Fine sea salt to taste

¼ cup shelled boiled peas (see page 238)

¼ cup shelled boiled fava beans (see page 238)

½ cup cooked sliced asparagus (see page 155)

1 pheasant, about 2½ pounds, breastbone removed, legs and wings trimmed but bones left intact

2 tablespoons extra-virgin olive oil

½ cup dry white wine

1 small onion, chopped

1. Preheat the oven to 350 degrees F. In a food processor fitted with the metal blade, grind together the chicken breast with the egg white, milk, and a pinch of salt. Transfer the mixture to a bowl and combine it with the peas, fava beans, and asparagus.

2. Season the pheasant with salt, fill the center with the stuffing, sew the cavity closed with kitchen twine, truss the pheasant, and place in a baking dish. Rub the outside of the bird with the olive oil and roast for 20 minutes. Pour the white wine over the pheasant. Scatter the chopped onion in the baking dish and cook until the skin of the pheasant is browned and the juices run clear, about 30 additional minutes.

3. To be sure the stuffing has cooked long enough to be safe to eat, an instant-read thermometer inserted into the center of the stuffing should read 165 degrees F. The thickest part of the pheasant breast should be 160 degrees F.

4. Let the pheasant rest for at least 15 minutes. Carve and serve it hot or cold with a green salad with raspberries dressed in a vinaigrette made with the highest quality extra-virgin olive oil and balsamic vinegar.

SERVES 4 COOKING TIME: 1 HOUR

Polletti alla diavola

spicy cornish hens under a "brick"

4 Cornish game hens, about 10 ounces each

¼ cup extra-virgin olive oil

Fine sea salt to taste

Freshly ground black pepper to taste

1 tablespoon spicy mustard

½ cup bread crumbs

1. Preheat the oven to 500 degrees F. Place the chickens on a work surface, breast side up. Insert a long chef's knife into the cavity of one chicken and work it all the way through until it emerges from the neck end. Cut down, all the way through the backbone.

2. Turn the chicken over and cut into the breastbone with the knife, but do not cut all the way through. Open the chicken so that it lies flat and place it, skin side up, on the work area.

3. Make two small slits in the skin at the belly end and tuck the legs into those slits. Tuck the wings under.

4. Flatten the chicken as much as possible with a meat pounder. Repeat with the remaining chickens.

5. Heat a cast-iron grill pan until it is very hot. Brush the chickens with 2 tablespoons of the oil and season them with salt and pepper. Place as many chickens as will fit on the prepared grill pan. Place weights on top and press down periodically as they cook. Cook the chickens until they are nicely browned on the outside, 7 minutes per side. Repeat with the remaining chickens, transferring each bird to a baking sheet or pan as it is browned.

6. Brush a little of the mustard on each chicken, then sprinkle each with the bread crumbs, drizzle on the remaining oil, and bake the chickens for an additional 10 minutes. Finally, broil them for 1 to 2 minutes to brown the bread crumbs. Serve immediately.

SERVES 4 COOKING TIME: 30 MINUTES

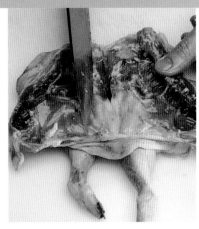
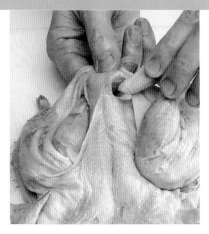

$\mathcal{R}$OASTED LAMB IS ALWAYS AT THE CENTER of the Easter table in Italy. The lamb is a potently symbolic figure in Christianity, and if you peer closely at many of Italy's most famous Renaissance paintings, you're almost certain to see a placid lamb, in the foreground or background. Milk-fed baby lamb, Rome's famous abbacchio, is particularly tender and mild in flavor. This is sometimes sold as hothouse lamb in the United States.

The farming of sheep is more common in Italy, with its mountainous terrain, than cattle ranching. Regions with high numbers of sheep, such as Abruzzo and Lazio, logically enough often feature lamb on the menu, as well as a variety of sheep's milk cheeses.

Game is eaten frequently in Italy, especially in the wooded regions where hunting hare, deer, and boar, as well as game birds, remains a popular sport. Game can taste, well, gamy, so it is often cooked with spices to mellow its flavor a little bit. Venison—the game meat most widely available in the United States—is low in fat, so it needs to be treated in ways that help it retain moisture and should not be overcooked, as it can dry out easily.

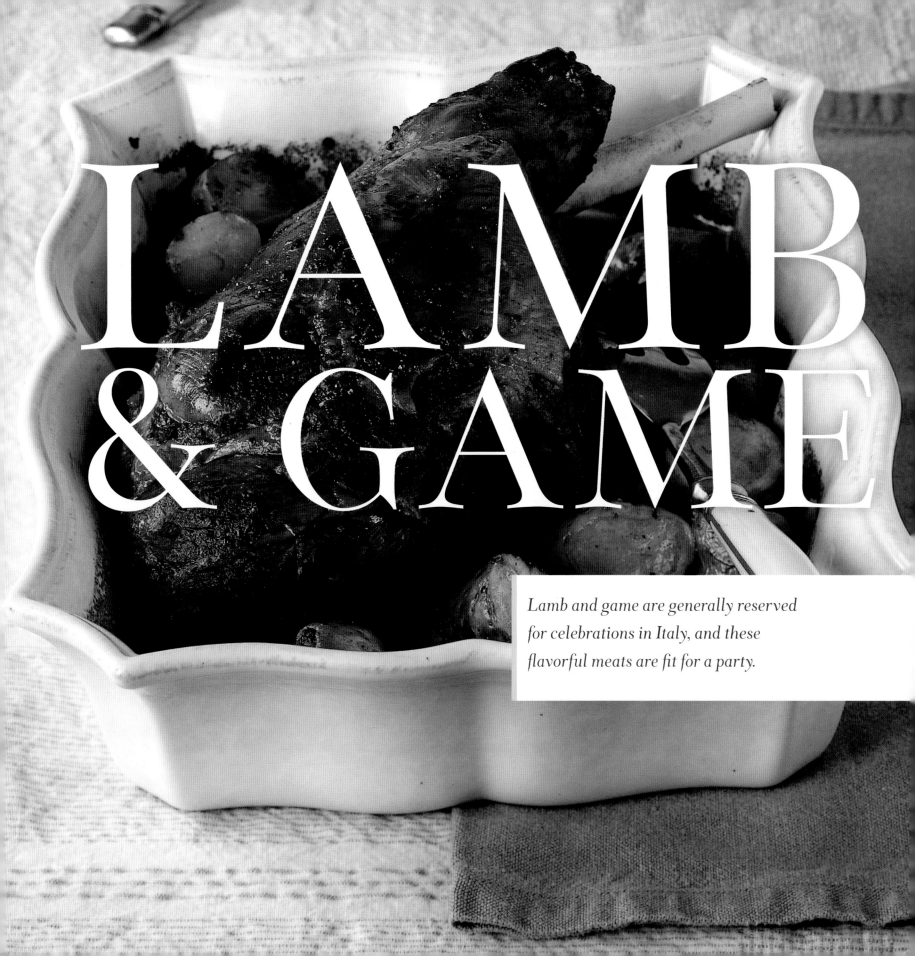

LAMB & GAME

Lamb and game are generally reserved for celebrations in Italy, and these flavorful meats are fit for a party.

Carré panato alle erbe

herb-crusted rack of lamb

2 slices day-old bread

1 clove garlic

Leaves of 1 sprig flat-leaf parsley

6 fresh mint leaves

Leaves of 1 sprig fresh thyme

7 tablespoons unsalted butter, softened

Fine sea salt to taste

Freshly ground black pepper to taste

2 frenched racks of lamb

1. Preheat the oven to 375 degrees F.

2. In a food processor fitted with the metal blade, grind together the bread, garlic, parsley, mint, thyme, and butter. Season with salt and pepper.

3. Coat the lamb with this mixture, patting it on to make it stick. Transfer the lamb to a baking pan and cook in the preheated oven for 20 minutes, then tent the meat loosely with foil and roast until a thermometer inserted into the thickest part of the meat reads 135 degrees F for medium-rare (recommended), about 10 additional minutes.

4. Transfer the meat to a carving board and let it rest for 10 minutes. Carve it into chops and serve.

SERVES 4 COOKING TIME: 40 MINUTES

SCOTTADITO
lamb chops

The word *scottadito* means "finger burning," because these smell so delicious as they cook that diners can never resist grabbing them while they're still piping hot.

Make a marinade by whisking together olive oil and white wine and flavoring it with any or all of the following: bay leaves, juniper berries, rosemary sprigs, thyme sprigs, whole black peppercorns, peeled garlic cloves, and lemon wedges. Marinate baby lamb chops in this mixture in the refrigerator overnight (12 hours), turning the meat occasionally. When you're ready to cook, heat a grill (or grill pan, but be sure you have a very efficient fan in your kitchen) until it is very hot. Remove the chops from the marinade, pat them dry, and grill them, basting them once or twice with the marinade. Serve the chops very hot with a sauté of bell peppers and scallions.

ABBACCHIO ALLA ROMANA
roman-style milk-fed lamb

Using paper towels, dry chunks of the shoulder and leg meat of a milk-fed lamb (a hothouse lamb or baby lamb) as thoroughly as possible. Dredge the meat in flour and season it with salt and pepper. Heat about ¼ cup olive oil or lard with a couple of whole garlic cloves, a couple of fresh sage leaves, and a sprig of rosemary in a large skillet and brown the lamb pieces well on all sides. Add about

½ cup white wine vinegar and boil until it evaporates. Add ⅓ cup water, turn the heat down to maintain a simmer, and cook, covered, until the lamb is very tender, turning the meat occasionally. This will take 30 to 60 minutes, depending on the age of the lamb. If the pan begins to look dry, add a tablespoon or two of water. When the lamb is cooked, remove it

from the pan. Make a sauce with a few tablespoons of the pan juices ground in a mortar with a pestle with 2 rinsed and drained anchovy fillets. Whisk this sauce back into the pan, then return the lamb to the sauce and mix until the lamb is coated, 1 minute at most. Serve immediately. Artichokes are a delicious and traditional accompaniment.

SPICES FOR MEAT

1] PEPPER Pepper should always be freshly ground and is usually added at the end of the cooking process; sometimes whole peppercorns are used and then discarded before serving. Black peppercorns have a stronger taste, while white peppercorns are more delicate, but the biggest difference between the two is visual—most recipes for white or light-colored sauces call for using white pepper so that the flecks aren't visible. Green peppercorns are simply peppercorns picked before they are fully ripe. They, too, are used with both meat and fish.

2] CLOVES Cloves are the dried buds of a plant in the myrtle family. They have a strong flavor and can either be used whole and removed before serving or be incorporated in ground form. Cloves are used for braises, boiled meats, and cooking game, as well as in sweet dishes such as poached fruit and bakery items. Because cloves are shaped like small nails, they are often inserted into a whole onion, making them easy to retrieve when the cooking process is complete.

3] JUNIPER BERRIES These are the slightly bitter berries of an evergreen plant, and they do smell faintly of a resinous pine tree. Juniper berries should be crushed lightly before they are used in marinades for meat and game. They may also be used in braising liquid.

SPICE SACHET

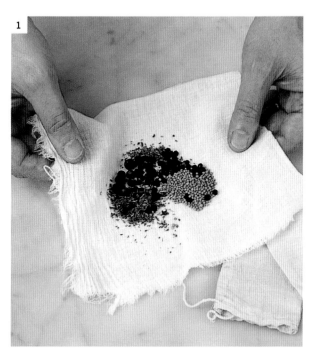

Place a selection of spices (a combination of juniper berries, peppercorns, mustard seeds, and dried herbs is shown here) in the center of a small square of cheesecloth [1]. Gather up the sides of the cloth and tie the bundle closed with a piece of kitchen twine [2].

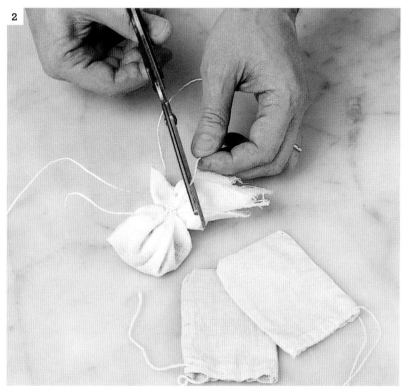

Cervo con crema di porro

venison with leek puree

½ (750-ml) bottle red wine

3 to 4 sage leaves, fresh or dried

1 sprig rosemary

1 large onion, roughly chopped

1 teaspoon whole cloves

1 tablespoon whole black
peppercorns

2 bay leaves

1 venison roast, about 1¾ pounds

5 tablespoons extra-virgin olive oil

¼ cup dry white wine

3 large leeks

1 tablespoon unsalted butter

Fine sea salt to taste

1 head roasted garlic (see page 265)

3 russet potatoes

3 tablespoons milk

1 teaspoon cornstarch dissolved in
2 tablespoons cold water

1 tablespoon brown stock (page 55)

1. In a large nonreactive bowl, combine the red wine, sage, rosemary, onion, cloves, pepper-corns, and 1 of the bay leaves. Place the venison roast in this marinade, cover the bowl, and refrigerate it overnight, turning the meat once or twice. When you are ready to cook the venison, remove it from the marinade. Strain the marinade, discarding the liquid and reserving the herbs and spices.

2. Preheat the oven to 400 degrees F. Pat the meat thoroughly dry with paper towels. Place ¼ cup of the oil in a Dutch oven or other heavy pot that can go from stovetop to oven and place it over medium-high heat. Sear the venison roast on all sides. Scatter the reserved herbs and spices from the marinade over the venison and roast the venison for 20 minutes. Add the white wine to the pot and continue roasting until a thermometer inserted into the thickest part of the meat reads 140 degrees F, about 45 minutes total.

3. While the meat is roasting, clean and roughly chop the leeks (see page 262) and cook them briefly in the butter in a small saucepan; add salt and water to cover, and braise until the leeks are tender. Peel the roasted garlic and puree it along with the cooked leeks in a food processor. Place the potatoes in a pot with cold water to cover and the remaining bay leaf. Bring the water to a boil, then simmer until the potatoes can easily be pierced with a paring knife. Drain, peel, and cut them into thick slices.

4. When the meat is ready, let it cool for a few minutes, sitting in the juices. Meanwhile, thin the leek puree with the milk and whisk until the mixture is smooth. Reheat the puree if necessary, drizzle in the remaining 1 tablespoon olive oil, and season with salt. Remove the venison to a cutting board, carve it, and arrange several slices with potatoes and some of the leek puree on each plate. Strain the cooking juices from the baking pan into a small saucepan, place it over low heat, and bring it to a simmer. Stir in the dissolved cornstarch and the stock and cook, whisking constantly, until thickened, about 1 minute. Pour the gravy over the meat and potatoes and serve.

SERVES 6 COOKING TIME: 1 HOUR

The word marinate *actually derives from the same root as* marine, *because the original marinades were brines or seawater. Today, marinating generally calls for letting meat or fish sit in any of several liquids (including oil, vinegar, wine, or lemon juice) flavored with aromatic herbs. Sometimes the chemical interaction between a marinade with high acid content and the meat or fish serves to "cook" the item; other times, a marinade is simply intended to flavor the meat or fish and make it more tender after it has been cooked.*

Classic Marinade

Herbs and vegetables, spices, salt, sugar, lemon juice, vinegar, and wine are the ingredients that most commonly appear in marinades for meat and fish.

Red meat and game are usually marinated in red wine (which makes them more tender) and flavored with vegetables, herbs, and spices. The marinating time required will depend on the size of the piece of meat.

If you want to cut down on the waiting time, bring the marinade to a boil, cool it slightly, and then pour it over the meat. Let it sit for 1 to 2 hours. Large cuts of pork or beef can also be dry-rubbed with a mixture of coarse salt and spices and allowed to rest overnight before cooking.

For a quick application of seasoning that works well with meat or fish that is to be grilled, simply sprinkle on herbs and spices and drizzle with extra-virgin olive oil.

Very fresh fish fillets can be cured in a marinade of 2 parts coarse salt, 1 part sugar, and herbs. After 6 to 10 hours, scrape off the salt.

All over the Mediterranean, very fresh fish is "cooked" by being marinated in lemon juice, in the refrigerator, until its flesh is white and firm. Remove the fillets from the marinade and season them with extra-virgin olive oil and fresh herbs.

THE MEDITERRANEAN DIET HAS INCLUDED FISH since the time when the equipment for catching it was at its most rudimentary—meaning man had to wade into the water and grab it with his hands. Ancient Greeks and Romans quickly realized that the long shoreline in their region was a terrific source of nutrition, and ancient Romans cooked both saltwater and freshwater fish.

The categorization of fish by origin into freshwater, or lake and river fish, and saltwater, or ocean fish, is common. In Italy, however, fish are usually categorized as flat, round, or "blue." Flat fish, such as sole, have a very delicate flavor. Round fish—which include the most common types in the Mediterranean, such as bass and dorade—are stronger in flavor, and the most strongly flavored of all are oily fish, termed *pesce azzurro,* or "blue fish" (not to be confused with the bluefish, which is a particular species). These are also abundant in Italian waters and include anchovies, sardines, and mackerel. Fish offers excellent nutrition. It contains plenty of protein and vitamins and minerals, and many varieties are rich in valuable omega-3 fatty acids.

Fish can be cooked in many different ways—grilled, steamed, stewed, fried, or roasted—or not cooked at all and served in the form of crudo. All along the extensive coast of the Italian peninsula, it appears in antipasto, pasta, and rice dishes and as a second course.

FISH

Fish is a diet staple, or at least it should be–it's tasty, versatile, and healthful. Simple fish fillets have the added advantage of cooking relatively quickly, though whole fish and other seafood preparations make use of classic slow techniques as well.

BUYING FISH

ITALIANS TEND TO COOK AND EAT WHOLE FISH MORE FREQUENTLY THAN AMERICANS, and you would do well to imitate them in this respect—fish cooked on the bone remains moist and tender, and filleting a whole cooked fish is really not terribly complicated. A good fishmonger will usually gut and scale a whole fish for you when you purchase it.

When shopping for fish, whether whole, fillets, or steaks (available for meaty fish such as swordfish and tuna), look for firm, shiny skin. Fresh fish will smell, logically enough, fresh. An unpleasant odor is a sure indicator that fish is past its prime. If the fish is filleted, the flesh should look moist, not dry. Seek out a market with good turnover, as fish does not have a long shelf life. Cook it within a day of purchase, or two days at the most.

Ruffe

Sea Bass

Tuna

Turbot

Mullet

Hake

Sea Bream

Dorade

Sardine

Anchovy

Needlefish

Spiedini di pesce con scalogno e timo

fish skewers with shallot and thyme

10 ounces hake fillet, skinned
(see note)

10 ounces dogfish fillet, skinned
(see note)

10 ounces swordfish steak, skinned

7 ounces (about ½ pint) cherry
tomatoes

2 medium zucchini

2 tablespoons extra-virgin olive oil

1 shallot, minced

Leaves of 2 sprigs fresh thyme,
minced

Fine sea salt to taste

1. If using wooden skewers, soak them in water. Heat a grill. Meanwhile, cut the hake, dogfish, and swordfish into cubes. Halve the cherry tomatoes.

2. Slice the zucchini into rounds about ¼ inch thick.

3. Assemble the skewers. Each one should have a tomato half at each end. In between, alternate cubes of fish with slices of zucchini.

4. Grill the skewers, turning them so they cook on all sides, about 6 minutes total.

5. Heat the olive oil in a small pan and briefly cook the shallot and minced thyme leaves until the shallot is transparent.

6. Brush the hot skewers with the shallot and thyme sauce, sprinkle them with salt, and serve immediately.

NOTE: *Hake and dogfish are fairly thick white fillets. Cod and halibut are both appropriate substitutes.*

SERVES 4   COOKING TIME: 20 MINUTES

BUTTERFLIED and PANFRIED FRESH SARDINES

To butterfly the fish, with your fingers or a knife, remove the head at the level of the gills. The guts will come away with the head. Run one finger down the back to remove the dorsal fin, then down the stomach, which should open the fish up without breaking it in half. Take care to remove any remaining guts, then rinse the fish [1]. Lift off the central spine (it should detach easily), leaving the two halves of the fish attached [2].

Mince together parsley, garlic, and rinsed and drained capers [1]. Transfer this mixture to a bowl and combine it with bread crumbs. Stir in enough extra-virgin olive oil to moisten it [2]. Dredge the sardines in this mixture and press to make the crumb coating stick to both sides [3]. In a skillet, heat a little extra-virgin olive oil. Cook the fish, turning them once, until they are browned and crisp on both sides. Serve hot [4].

FISH MARINATED IN LEMON JUICE

Gut, butterfly, and bone fresh anchovies (see page opposite). Place them in a nonreactive bowl or pan in a single layer, then pour the juice of 1 lemon and an equal amount of white wine vinegar over them. Cover the fish with plastic wrap and marinate them in the refrigerator for 6 to 12 hours. The anchovies are ready to eat as they are, without further cooking.

HERBS and SPICES FOR FISH

1] TARRAGON Used sparingly, this herb lends a delicate sweet-and-sour flavor and the faint taste of licorice to fish.

2] PINK PEPPERCORNS With a more delicate flavor than black peppercorns, this spice is perfect for fish. Pink peppercorns, actually berries from a type of rose plant, are often paired with white wine.

3] CHERVIL Similar to parsley but with a less obtrusive flavor, chervil can be minced raw and sprinkled over cooked fish.

335

SALTED ANCHOVIES and CAPERS

SALTED ANCHOVIES

If you have used only the purplish-gray anchovy fillets that come tightly packed in oil, whole salted anchovies will be a revelation. These are layered horizontally with coarse salt and are available in Italian specialty shops. They have a delicious briny flavor and a meatier texture than the fillets packed in oil. To use whole salted anchovies, rinse them briefly under running water, rubbing off any scales. Pinch off the tail and fins. Divide the anchovy in half (you can probably pull it apart with your hands, but if not, slit it with a paring knife down the belly), open it up, and simply lift out the skeleton. Roughly chopped anchovies virtually dissolve when sautéed.

SALTED CAPERS

As with anchovies, salted capers are also preferable to the most common version sold in the United States: capers packed in vinegar. Look for capers imported from the Italian island of Pantelleria, which are extra large and meaty. Salted capers should be soaked in water for 10 minutes or so before use. Lift them out of the water, leaving the salt at the bottom of the bowl—in other words, don't pour out the water along with the capers—and use them as desired. You may want to chop them roughly if they are especially large.

SALT-CURING FISH

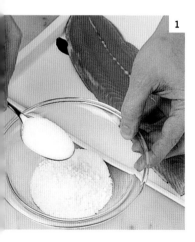  

Prepare a combination of 2 parts coarse salt and 1 part sugar **[1]**. Place a skinned fillet of fresh salmon or other fish on a plate or tray. Spread about half of the salt mixture on top of the fillet and press with your hands to make it stick to the fish **[2]**. Add fresh dill or other herbs **[3]** and a little more of the salt mixture. Repeat on the other side of the fish and wrap the whole thing tightly in plastic. Refrigerate for 4 to 8 hours, depending on how cured you would like the results to be. Slice the fish thinly and serve it with toasted bread.

BACCALÀ

Baccalà (salt cod) and its cousin, stoccafisso (dried cod or stockfish, cod that has been dried without salt), were lifesavers for generations of Italian sailors, as they could be stored almost indefinitely. Dried cod was also considered a handy food for the poor, as it was inexpensive and enabled them to eat fish on Fridays. (Confusingly, in Venice, where baccalà mantecato is quite commonly served, what is used to make the dish is actually stockfish. Fortunately, the two fish are more or less interchangeable, so you can make the recipe below with either and it will taste delicious.)

PREPARING THE FISH

Dried cod needs to be rehydrated before it is used and will have a chewier texture than fresh cod. You can purchase chunks of baccalà and stoccafisso at gourmet stores. To rehydrate them, simply rinse and then place them in a bowl with cold water to cover by 2 inches. Cover the bowl with a plate and store it in the refrigerator, changing the water three times a day until the fish is pliable and, in the case of baccalà, a small piece tastes pleasantly but not overwhelmingly salty, 1 to 3 days. When the fish has softened, tweeze out any bones and remove and discard any skin.

BACCALÀ MANTECATO (WHIPPED BACCALÀ)

This Venetian dish is labor-intensive, but in no way difficult. Place a soaked, skinned, and boned piece of dried cod in a pot and add cold water to cover. Bring it to a boil and simmer for 20 minutes, skimming off any foam. Drain the fish and transfer it to a large bowl. (You may want to run your hands over it to be sure it doesn't have any pesky bones remaining.) Add a clove of minced garlic. Mash the fish against the sides of the bowl with a wooden spoon to break it up, then beat the fish vigorously while slowly adding olive oil until it takes on a fluffy, mousselike consistency. It may take as long as 30 minutes to achieve the proper consistency doing this by hand. Although it's not traditional, you can use an immersion blender or a food processor fitted with the metal blade if you prefer. When the mixture is light and fluffy, taste it and add salt, if needed, and freshly ground black pepper. You can serve the whipped baccalà in a bowl with toast on the side, or spread it on toast or on thin triangles or rectangles of cooked polenta that you have quickly browned or grilled until crisp (see page 119). Either way, sprinkle it with a little minced flat-leaf parsley before serving.

LIVORNO-STYLE BACCALÀ

Peel, seed, and chop 1 pound fresh tomatoes. Heat a couple of tablespoons of extra-virgin olive oil in a skillet. Mince an onion and a garlic clove and cook them until transparent. Add the tomatoes and simmer until they break down, about 20 minutes. Meanwhile, cut a soaked, skinned, and boned piece of dried cod into chunks. Squeeze out as much liquid as possible and pat the fish dry with paper towels or a clean dish towel. Dredge the chunks of baccalà in flour and, in a separate skillet, cook them in about 1 inch of extra-virgin olive oil, turning the pieces with tongs, until they are browned on both sides. Blot excess oil from the fish with paper towels and add it to the pan with the tomatoes. Simmer for 5 additional minutes. Sprinkle the fish with minced parsley and serve it hot or at room temperature.

This technique is an ancient one. When a whole fish is cooked in salt, no additional fat is called for; the salt keeps the fish flesh moist and flavorful. Although the technique is most commonly used with fish, it will also yield excellent results with some cuts of beef and poultry, as well as pork (see note). Mix aromatic herbs with the salt for added flavor.

Cooking in Salt

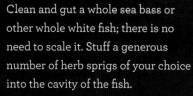

Clean and gut a whole sea bass or other whole white fish; there is no need to scale it. Stuff a generous number of herb sprigs of your choice into the cavity of the fish.

Place about 1 inch of coarse salt in a baking dish, set the fish on top of it, then add enough additional coarse salt to cover it completely. Roast the fish at 375 degrees F until it is cooked through, about 45 minutes for a 2-pound fish. When it is done, the skin will peel off easily.

338

Smaller fish can be dredged in salt with a finer crystal and then roasted on a parchment-lined baking sheet. A 10-ounce fish will be ready in about 18 minutes.

To create a salt crust, which seals in juices even more effectively than loose salt, make a paste of 1 pound coarse salt, 4 cups flour, and a little water. Roll this paste out like a dough and wrap it around a whole fish (you can also cook a chicken this way). Roast the fish at 375 degrees F for 45 minutes (a chicken will take about an hour). The salt paste will harden into a crust as it cooks. To open the crust, hit it with a cleaver and then cut it open with a serrated knife and lift off the top.

NOTE: *The salt-baking technique also works well with pork shanks. Create a bed of coarse salt in a Dutch oven or other heavy pot with a tight-fitting lid. Place pork shanks, whole unpeeled potatoes, and herbs on the salt and cover them with additional coarse salt. Put the lid on the pot and bake at 375 degrees F for about 45 minutes.*

WHOLE FISH IN ACQUA PAZZA

*A*cqua pazza literally means "crazy water." Fish is cooked this way in the Campania region, and it results in a two-course meal—pasta prepared and sauced with the cooking juices, followed by the fish as an entrée. Use a delicately flavored medium-thick fish—sea bream is perfect.

Place a couple of tablespoons of oil in a skillet large enough to hold the fish, add peeled and crushed garlic cloves, and turn on the heat to medium. Sauté until the garlic is browned, then remove and discard it. Add minced onion and cook just until it is transparent. Add a pint or two of grape or cherry tomatoes (as many as will fit in a single layer in your skillet) and season with salt and pepper. Cook until the tomatoes have softened and the skins on about half of them have burst. Add equal amounts of white wine and water, just enough to submerge the tomatoes, and bring the mixture to a simmer.

Place one or two scaled, cleaned whole fish on top of the tomatoes, cover the pan (aluminum foil is fine, but tent it so that it doesn't touch the fish), and simmer until the fish are cooked through, 15 to 20 minutes, depending on their size. Jiggle the pan occasionally to keep the fish and tomatoes from sticking. Add a few tablespoons of water if the pan looks dry before the fish are done. When they are ready, moisten the tops with a little liquid from the pan and transfer the fish to a serving platter.

Meanwhile, cook spaghetti in boiling salted water until softened but not yet al dente (it should still be crunchy at the center). Drain the spaghetti, add it to the pan with the tomato mixture, and cook over medium-low heat, tossing constantly with a large fork and spoon, until the pasta is al dente. Serve it as a first course. For the second course, fillet the fish. Sprinkle the fillets with a little minced parsley and serve them with lemon wedges, if desired.

WHOLE ROASTED FISH

Place one or more scaled and gutted whole fish in a baking dish. Drizzle them with a little extra-virgin olive oil and rub the oil to coat both the outsides and cavities of the fish. Season to taste with salt and pepper, and stuff the cavity with a few lemon slices and some herbs, if desired. Roast the fish at 400 degrees F until it is cooked through, 15 to 25 minutes, depending on the size. To judge doneness, pierce the fish at its thickest point with the tip of a small paring knife—the flesh should be opaque near the bone. Whole fish can also be grilled or broiled, turning them once, until the skin is charred and the flesh is cooked.

TUNA PRESERVED IN OIL

*I*talians make wonderful use of canned tuna, which is more frequently sold in glass jars in Italy. No matter how it's packaged, preserved tuna is one of the world's great convenience foods. When buying it, look for tuna imported from Italy and preserved in olive oil. Ventresca is tuna belly and is particularly good. You can also make your own tuna in oil, as described below.

HOMEMADE TUNA IN OIL

Place a stalk of celery, a carrot, an onion, and 2 garlic cloves with peel left on in a pot of water and boil them for 15 minutes. Add a 2-inch-thick piece of fresh tuna, with or without skin, and simmer it for 40 minutes. Turn off the heat and let the tuna cool completely in the cooking liquid. Next, drain it, discard the skin if you left it on, and cut the tuna into large chunks. Pat the chunks dry with a dish towel or paper towels and place them in glass jars. Add extra-virgin olive oil to cover, seal the jars, and refrigerate them. Let the tuna rest for at least 24 hours before using it. Tuna prepared this way can be stored in the refrigerator for up to 5 days.

PASTA WITH WHITE TUNA SAUCE

Drain the tuna from a can or jar of imported Italian tuna, 6 to 8 ounces. Mince an onion and a chile pepper and cook them in a small amount of olive oil. Flake in the drained tuna and cook for a couple of minutes to heat through. Add a handful of rinsed and drained capers. Cook pasta and add it to the pan. Toss over heat to combine. Sprinkle with toasted bread crumbs and serve immediately.

PASTA WITH RED TUNA SAUCE

Set a pot of water on the stove to boil, salt it, and cook the pasta of your choice. Meanwhile, drain the tuna from a can or jar of imported Italian tuna. Cook some chopped garlic in a small amount of olive oil for about 1 minute; do not let it brown. Add tomato puree and cook until it thickens, about 10 minutes. Flake in the drained tuna and cook for a couple of minutes to heat the sauce through. When the pasta is ready, add it to the pan and toss over heat to combine. Sprinkle the pasta with minced flat-leaf parsley and serve.

TUNA AND BEAN SALAD

Flake the drained tuna from a can or jar of imported Italian tuna and combine it with cannellini beans cooked soft (see page 224). Add some thinly sliced scallion and minced flat-leaf parsley, whisk together extra-virgin olive oil and lemon juice, and dress the salad. Season to taste with salt and a generous amount of freshly ground black pepper. Serve at room temperature.

TOMATOES STUFFED WITH TUNA

Slice the tops off of large beefsteak tomatoes and seed the tomatoes with a spoon, leaving them whole. Flake drained tuna from a can or jar of imported Italian tuna and mix it with rinsed and drained capers and minced hard-boiled egg (page 366). Drizzle on a little extra-virgin olive oil and salt and pepper to taste. Stuff the tuna mixture into the hollowed-out tomatoes. You can decorate the top of each with a pitted olive or an anchovy fillet if you like.

TUNA SAUCE AND VITELLO TONNATO

Drain the tuna from a can or jar of imported Italian tuna. In a food processor fitted with the metal blade, process the tuna, 4 to 5 rinsed and drained anchovy fillets, the juice of ½ lemon, and a few tablespoons of rinsed and drained capers until very creamy and smooth. Fold this mixture in to 1 to 2 cups mayonnaise. Taste and add salt if necessary. This sauce is delicious spread on toasted bread for bruschetta (see page 6). To use it to make vitello tonnato, poach a veal roast, let it cool completely, and spread slices of the veal with the sauce. Serve at room temperature, garnished, if desired, with lemon slices, whole capers, pitted olives, and flat-leaf parsley leaves.

Involtini di pesce spada

swordfish rolls

1 cup fresh shelled peas (see page 238)

1 red bell pepper

1¾ pounds tomatoes

3 tablespoons extra-virgin olive oil

1 clove garlic, sliced

4 anchovy fillets, rinsed, drained, and chopped

5 to 6 slices bread, crusts removed

1 tablespoon minced flat-leaf parsley

1 tablespoon minced fresh rosemary

Fine sea salt to taste

Freshly ground black pepper to taste

3 tablespoons grated pecorino Romano cheese

12 thin slices swordfish, about 1¾ pounds

1. Preheat the oven to 200 degrees F. Boil the peas until they are just cooked through, 3 to 5 minutes. Roast the bell pepper following the instructions on page 200. Peel the tomatoes (see page 205), cut them into wedges, and seed them.

2. Place the tomato wedges on a baking sheet lined with parchment paper and roast them for 40 minutes. When they are cool enough to handle, chop them. Peel the bell pepper and chop it. Turn the oven up to 450 degrees F.

3. In a skillet, heat 1 tablespoon of the olive oil and cook the garlic and anchovy fillets and the chunks of roasted pepper for 4 minutes. Discard the garlic and transfer the rest of the contents of the skillet to a food processor fitted with the metal blade or blender. Puree until creamy while slowly adding water; it will take about ⅓ cup total.

4. To make the filling, in a food processor fitted with the metal blade or in a blender, combine the bread, parsley, and rosemary. Add 1 tablespoon of the olive oil and season with salt and pepper. In a medium bowl, combine the bread mixture with 2 tablespoons of the grated cheese and the chopped roasted tomatoes. Taste and adjust the seasoning if necessary.

5. Spread a slice of fish on the work surface. Place a heaping tablespoon of filling on top and roll it up jelly-roll style.

6. Transfer the bell pepper puree to a baking dish. Scatter in the cooked peas, then place the swordfish rolls on top in a single layer. Drizzle them with the remaining 1 tablespoon of oil, sprinkle on the remaining 1 tablespoon of cheese, and bake until the fish is cooked through, 18 to 20 minutes. Place 2 rolls on each plate and serve hot.

SERVES 6 COOKING TIME: 1 HOUR 35 MINUTES

343

There are an unlimited number of variations on fish soup cooked all along Italy's coastline. Each region has its own, from the cacciucco of Livorno to the buridda of Liguria. Brodetto hails from the northern and central Adriatic coast. All these fish soups share one thing in common—they use strictly local ingredients. Since some varieties of fish are simply not available in the United States, substitutions are indicated where they may be necessary, but the best way to pay homage to a truly Italian fish soup is to choose the varieties that are freshest and best in your area rather than to follow a recipe strictly.

Brodetto

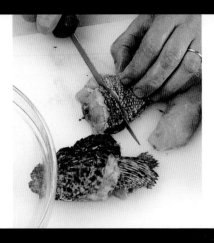
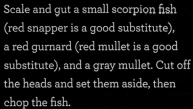

Scale and gut a small scorpion fish (red snapper is a good substitute), a red gurnard (red mullet is a good substitute), and a gray mullet. Cut off the heads and set them aside, then chop the fish.

Gut a mackerel, cut off and reserve its head, and chop the fish. Gut 4 hake, again reserving the heads when you cut them off. Skin and gut 4 small sole; scale and gut a few striped mullet.

Heat a small amount of extra-virgin olive oil in a pot and cook 1 minced onion until it is transparent. Add the minced leaves of 1 sprig flat-leaf parsley and 1 or 2 cloves garlic, sliced. Add the reserved heads, the contents of a 14½-ounce can peeled tomatoes and their juices or tomato puree, and 2 cups water. Boil for 30 minutes.

Pass the cooked mixture through a food mill and discard the solids. Transfer the resulting thick, brothy mixture to a pot and bring it to a boil.

Add 3 cleaned cuttlefish to the pot; cook for 10 minutes. Add 8 mantis shrimp (or crayfish) and 4 jumbo shrimp; after 5 additional minutes, add the gray mullet and the mackerel, and after another 2 minutes, add the sole and the red mullet. Cook for 5 minutes, then add the scorpion fish, gurnard, hake, and 7 ounces dogfish. Cover and return to a boil.

When the soup returns to a boil, stir in ¼ cup white wine vinegar. Transfer the soup to a serving vessel and serve it at the table, placing a slice or two of toasted bread in the bottom of each soup bowl and then ladling both broth and fish over it.

*I*TALIANS HAVE ALWAYS MADE WONDERFUL USE of the mollusks from the surrounding seas, such as cuttlefish, octopus, mussels, and scallops. Venice is well known for its use of cuttlefish—similar to squid—and their ink, which is used to make "black" pasta and risotto. Cuttlefish stewed with peas is a popular dish along the Adriatic coastline, while the residents of Liguria stew their cuttlefish with herbs. In general, squid, cuttlefish, and the like should either be cooked very, very quickly or stewed for a long time. Mussels and clams must be cleaned carefully to be sure that they don't contain any sand, but once the cleaning process is complete, cooking is fairly swift.

Crustaceans such as crabs and lobster, with their starkly white flesh, are also quite popular in Italy, especially along the coastline. Even in the days of ancient Rome, lobster was a symbol of wealth and privilege. Most crustaceans cook quickly and are featured in dishes that highlight their delicate flavor, such as pasta and risotto. They may also be boiled and served with sauce.

SHELLFISH & OTHER SEAFOOD

Cuttlefish, calamari, clams, mussels, crabs, and lobster, among others, are all in this wide-ranging category. They're united by how tasty they are, and they're beloved in Italy.

MOLLUSKS

MOLLUSKS ARE SEA CREATURES THAT DO NOT HAVE BONES. They fall into three groups: cephalopods, lamellibranchs, and gastropods.

CEPHALOPODS These creatures have legs attached directly to their heads (octopuses are an example) and sacs containing ink that they can release into the water to help them hide from predators. When you buy cephalopods, they should be shiny and bright looking. They can also be purchased frozen, though they will be softer, with less resistance. Baby octopus can be stewed or grilled. Calamari and cuttlefish are excellent stuffed but can also be stewed or cooked in sauce for pasta. Of course, when cut into rings, calamari are delicious fried.

There is a basic rule about both calamari and cuttlefish: They should either be cooked very briefly (grilled or sautéed for a couple of minutes) or cooked for long periods of time (stewed, simmered, or baked for at least 45 minutes). Either of these approaches will yield tender results, but to cook them for some intermediate time—20 or 30 minutes, say—will leave them tough.

LAMELLIBRANCHS Members of the Lamellibranchia class have hinged two-part shells and include oysters, mussels, clams, and scallops. Except for scallops, which are usually purchased shelled, these must be alive when you purchase them. Their shells should be tightly closed, and once they are opened, you should see that their bodies are still attached to the shell. They should smell pleasantly of the sea.

GASTROPODS Shellfish that have a single-part shell only, the gastropods include sea snails, not easy to purchase in the United States and not of great culinary value.

Baby Octopus

Cuttlefish

Baby Musky Octopus

Squid

Clams

Oyster

Scallop

Mussels

CLEANING CLAMS

To clean clams, soak them in salt water **[1]** in the refrigerator for a long time, up to 12 hours, changing the water occasionally. Then use your hands to lift them out of the soaking water, leaving the sand in the bowl **[2]**.

STEAMING CLAMS and MUSSELS

To steam open clams and mussels, clean them (see pages 349 and opposite) and place them in a pot with some oil and garlic. Place the pot over heat, and when it begins to sizzle, add a splash of water or dry white wine **[1]**. Cover the pot and cook for 3 to 10 minutes, depending on the size of the shellfish **[2]**. The shells will open over the heat. Remove the shellfish one by one as soon as this happens to avoid overcooking them. Discard any that do not open. Serve steamed clams or mussels in the shell with toasted bread **[3]**. Alternatively, remove the shells **[4]** and use the clams or mussels in dishes such as pasta. Shelled steamed clams can also be dredged in a flour-and-water batter and fried. Reserve the cooking liquid and filter it through cheesecloth **[5]** or a paper coffee filter, then incorporate it into the finished dish. Shelled steamed clams and mussels can be stored, immersed in their filtered cooking liquid **[6]**, in the refrigerator for 4 days.

CLEANING and SHUCKING MUSSELS

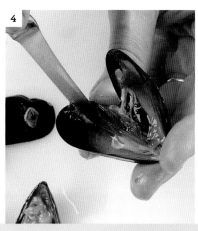

CLEANING

Soak the mussels in water and rub them against each other. If they are stuck together, gently detach them. Mussels grow united by a kind of web, so they often have strings stuck to their shells. Remove all of these [1]. Remove the beard from each mussel by tugging on it and pulling it through the opening of the shell [2]. Scrape the remaining beard from the shell with a paring knife [3]. Use a plastic pot scrubber to clean any lingering bits of beard, sand, or buildup from the exterior of the mussel shells. Place the mussels in a bowl in the sink and run a trickle of cold water over them until the water in the bowl is clear, at least 30 minutes.

SHUCKING

To shuck raw mussels, use the tip of a curved paring knife to pry the shell open. Then use the knife to cut the muscle that attaches the meat to the shell and discard the shell [4].

SAUTÉED SHELLFISH

Mince 1 zucchini, 1 carrot, and 1 leek and set them aside. Clean 1½ pounds clams and mussels; steam them open over high heat with just a splash of water (see page opposite). Transfer the shellfish, using a slotted spoon, to a bowl. Strain the cooking liquid through a coffee filter or cheesecloth if it has even a speck of sand or grit in it and then return it to the pot. Put the minced vegetables into the pot and cook them for 3 minutes. Crumble in a pinch of saffron, return the cooked shellfish to the pot, stir to combine, and serve.

Cozze con pescatrice

mussels with monkfish

1⅓ pounds monkfish

2 pounds mussels

4 thick slices rustic bread, crusts removed

Leaves of 2 sprigs basil

Leaves of 2 sprigs marjoram

Leaves of 1 sprig flat-leaf parsley

Leaves of 1 sprig thyme

5 cloves garlic

Fine sea salt to taste

Freshly ground black pepper to taste

1 pint cherry tomatoes, halved

6 tablespoons extra-virgin olive oil

1. Bone the monkfish, remove any membrane, and cut it into 2 fillets. Chop the fillets into 32 cubes about 1 inch on the sides.

2. Clean the mussels and open 32 of them (page 351) but leave them attached to their shells. Place the opened mussels in a sieve set over a bowl to collect their liquid.

3. Mince together the bread with the leaves of 1 sprig of the basil, 1 sprig of the marjoram, and the parsley and thyme leaves. Peel 1 of the cloves of garlic and mince it with the other ingredients. Season with salt and pepper and stir to combine the ingredients. Transfer the bread crumb mixture to a bowl and toss the monkfish pieces in the mixture to coat them. Press the bread crumb mixture against the fish with your hands to make it stick.

4. Place 1 coated piece of monkfish inside each of the open mussels. (Reserve the mussel liquid.)

5. Tie each of the stuffed mussels closed with a piece of kitchen twine. This isn't difficult, but it is a bit time-consuming. The fastest way to do it is to work assembly-line style: Cut 32 pieces of twine about 10 inches long. Wrap each piece of twine around a mussel twice, then knot it.

6. Place the remaining 4 cloves of garlic, with the peels still on, in a pot. Add the remaining basil and marjoram leaves, the tomatoes, and the unopened mussels. Set the stuffed mussels on top. Drizzle on the liquid collected from the mussels and the olive oil. Cover the pot and cook the mussels over medium heat for 25 minutes. Transfer the stuffed and unstuffed mussels and the tomatoes to a serving platter (open some of the stuffed mussels, if desired) and drizzle the cooking liquid from the pot over them before serving.

SERVES 4 COOKING TIME: 1 HOUR 30 MINUTES

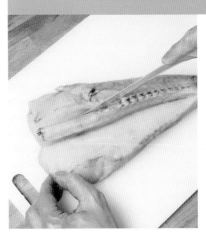

353

CUTTLEFISH IN INK

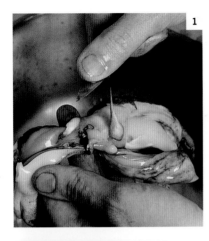

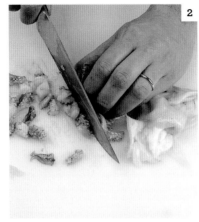

Clean a 1-pound cuttlefish, reserving its ink sac (located inside the body, possibly behind the eggs) **[1]**. Alternatively (and more likely to be necessary in the United States), purchase cleaned cuttlefish and ink separately. Cut the cuttlefish body into strips and chop the tentacles **[2]**. Heat ¼ cup extra-virgin olive oil and cook 1 minced small onion and 1 minced clove of garlic until transparent, then add the cuttlefish **[3]**. Add dry white wine, cover the pot, and cook for 6 minutes. Squeeze the cuttlefish ink out of the sac into the pot or add 2 to 3 tablespoons cuttlefish ink if purchased separately **[4]**. Stir to combine and cook for a few additional minutes **[5]**. This is an excellent sauce for about 1 pound spaghetti or other dried pasta.

Ink

CUTTLEFISH INK AND SQUID INK

Cuttlefish ink and squid ink (which are more or less interchangeable) add a unique flavor and color to risotto, pasta, and other dishes. Cuttlefish and squid use this dark substance for defense—when threatened, they squirt a cloud of it into the water to hide them from predators. Almost all cuttlefish and squid sold in the United States are already cleaned, and their messy ink sacs have been removed. This is good news and bad news. On the one hand, it saves you time; on the other hand, if you want the ink to use in a dish, you'll have to purchase it separately. It is sold in glass jars and can be purchased in gourmet specialty stores. See Sources (page 454) for some suggestions.

STEWED OCTOPUS

Clean 2 octopuses weighing about 2 pounds each. In a pot, combine them with 6 cloves garlic with the peels still on, ½ cup extra-virgin olive oil, 1 pint cherry tomatoes, and freshly ground black pepper or crushed red pepper [1]. Bring the mixture to a boil, turn the heat down to maintain a simmer, cover the pot, and cook for about 45 minutes. The tomatoes should break down and provide enough liquid for a simmer, but if the pot looks dry, add a small amount of water. When the octopus is almost done, add a generous amount of chopped flat-leaf parsley and basil leaves [2]. Serve the octopus with toasted bread, or chop it and serve it in the sauce over pasta.

Seppie ripiene al forno
baked stuffed cuttlefish

1 large egg

Fine sea salt to taste

Freshly ground black pepper to taste

1¼ cups bread crumbs

¾ cup grated fresh sheep's cheese

¼ cup minced flat-leaf parsley

1 clove garlic, minced

4 cuttlefish, about 2 pounds each, cleaned and tentacles removed from bodies (see note)

1 pound potatoes

¾ cup extra-virgin olive oil

1. Preheat the oven to 375 degrees F. Beat the egg with a little salt and pepper, then combine it with the bread crumbs. Using a fork, mix until all the bread crumbs are moistened.

2. Add the sheep's cheese to the bread crumb mixture, along with the parsley and garlic. Mix to combine.

3. Reserve about 2 tablespoons of the bread crumb mixture. Stuff each cuttlefish body with about a quarter of the remaining mixture, pressing to pack it in firmly. Close each cuttlefish with 3 to 4 toothpicks.

4. Roughly chop the cuttlefish tentacles.

5. Peel the potatoes and thinly slice them. Arrange about half of the potatoes in a single layer on the bottom of a baking dish. Sprinkle the chopped tentacles over them.

6. Arrange the stuffed cuttlefish on top of the tentacles. Cover with the remaining potato slices. Drizzle on the olive oil, season with salt, and add ½ cup water; cover the dish and bake for 30 minutes. Sprinkle on the reserved bread crumb mixture and continue to bake, uncovered, until the cuttlefish are very tender, an additional 15 to 20 minutes.

NOTE: *This same stuffing and method will work very well using calamari in place of cuttlefish, though calamari are much smaller. If the bodies of the calamari are whole, you won't need to close them with toothpicks. Just use your fingers to stuff a small amount of the bread crumb mixture into the center of each. Stuffed calamari are also delicious grilled.*

SERVES 4 COOKING TIME: 1 HOUR 30 MINUTES

CRUSTACEANS

CRUSTACEANS ARE ANIMALS THAT LIVE ALONG THE SHORELINE among the rocks and sand. With the exception of crabs, which are basically round, crustaceans are long, narrow animals with shells covering their back ends and legs extending outward from the middle of their bodies. These legs have pincers that they use both to pick up items and to defend themselves. What we call the "tail" of a lobster and other crustaceans is actually the abdomen—the real tail is the fanlike structure at its far end.

LOBSTERS AND CRABS Lobsters and crabs must be alive when purchased and cooked immediately—most commonly they are simply boiled.

SHRIMP Perhaps the most popular and widely available crustaceans, shrimp come in a wide variety of colors, though once cooked they all turn pink. Most shrimp for sale in the United States are frozen. Shrimp should be deveined (the vein is actually the animal's intestinal tract), and their shells can be used to create a versatile stock. (You can collect shrimp shells in a plastic bag in your freezer until you have enough to make stock.) Shrimp cook extremely quickly—they are ready after just a minute or two in a hot pan or on a grill.

Spider Crab

Spiny Lobster

Lobster

Mediterranean Shrimp

Large Red Shrimp

Langoustine

CLEANING CRUSTACEANS

Crustaceans do not require a lot of cleaning. Most simply need to be rinsed. If you will be using crab shells for serving, scrub them briskly with a brush.

 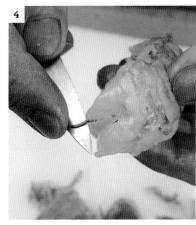

SHELLING and CLEANING SHRIMP

To clean a shrimp, hold the body with one hand and use the other to pull off the head [1]. (In the United States, many shrimp are sold in the shells but with the heads already detached, so this may be unnecessary.) Use kitchen shears to cut down the shell the long way, or pull the two sides apart using your hands [2]. Gently pull to remove the flesh in one piece [3]. To remove the unpleasant black "vein" that runs the long way down each shrimp, use the flat side of a knife to pull it out in one piece [4]. Alternatively, make a shallow cut and either pull it out or pat the cut shrimp with a paper towel—it will stick to the towel and come away easily.

359

SHELLING LOBSTER

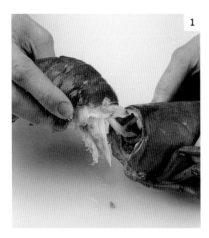

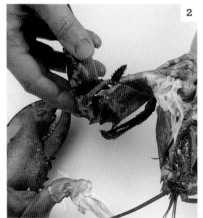

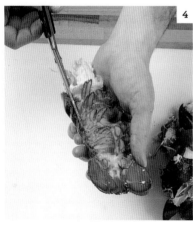

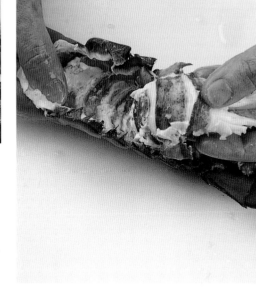

Lobster is almost always cooked before it is shelled. Cook the lobster, covered, in boiling salted water for at least 10 minutes (for a 1-pound lobster; add 3 minutes per additional pound). Let it cool to room temperature in its cooking liquid, but do not let it get completely cold. Pull off the hard shell from the tail [1]. Snap off the legs. These contain small amounts of flesh that can be extracted using a skewer [2]. Use a nutcracker to crack the claws and pull out the flesh in a single piece [3]. Turn the tail over and use kitchen shears to cut it the long way on both sides [4]. Lift off the middle section of shell and extract the tail meat in one piece [5].

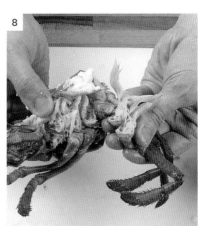

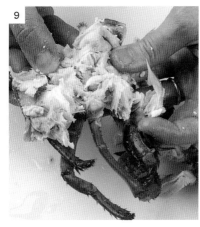

Locate the greenish liver; discard any other entrails **[6]**.
Use a spoon to scoop out the liver (it can be eaten, though
this isn't recommended in American lobsters) and any
pink eggs (which are found only in female lobsters) **[7]**.
These can be used to flavor sauces or included in a seafood
salad. Press gently on the abdomen of the lobster with
your thumbs and pull the shell apart, breaking it in half **[8]**.
This will expose the flesh **[9]**, which you can now remove
in pieces with your fingers **[10]**.

361

SHRIMP and LOBSTER

*S*hrimp and lobster have a delicate flavor that shines in simple preparations. A simply boiled lobster is a summertime treat along the shore, and shrimp, shelled or in their shells, are delicious when simply sautéed in a hot pan with a little olive oil. Turn them with tongs, and take them out as soon as they turn pink. That said, you may sometimes want to get a little fancier with shrimp and lobster. Try one of these slightly more complex preparations.

SHRIMP SKEWERS
Toss shelled or unshelled shrimp with a mixture of bread crumbs, minced parsley, and minced garlic, moistened with a little extra-virgin olive oil. Thread them onto skewers and grill.

TAGLIATELLE WITH SHRIMP AND ZUCCHINI
Shell the shrimp, chop them if they're large, and sauté them with diced zucchini. Serve them over tagliatelle pasta.

PROSCIUTTO-WRAPPED SHRIMP
Shell the shrimp and wrap them in thin slices of prosciutto crudo. Heat extra-virgin olive oil in a pan until it is very hot and briefly sauté the shrimp, about 1 minute per side.

ROCK SHRIMP TRAMEZZINI
Poach small rock shrimp until they are pink, about 1 minute. Drain and chop them, and mix them with extra-virgin olive oil and lemon juice. Fold in minced flat-leaf parsley. When the shrimp mixture is cool, spread it on sandwich bread. Trim off the crusts and cut the sandwiches into triangles.

LOBSTER AND FENNEL SALAD
Make a salad of chopped cooked lobster and thinly sliced raw fennel. Dress it with extra-virgin olive oil and orange juice. Sprinkle the salad with sliced almonds just before serving.

SPAGHETTI WITH SPICY LOBSTER
Toss chopped cooked lobster meat with a spicy tomato sauce. Use this to dress spaghetti or other long pasta.

$\mathcal{E}$GGS ARE INDISPENSABLE. Without them there would be no egg tagliatelle, no spaghetti alla carbonara, no frittatas. Not to mention the cakes and cookies that rely upon them as less high-profile ingredients. Eggs are important nutritionally, too. The yolk and white inside that fragile shell are low-cost sources of protein. The egg is also a key symbol in Italian art and culture. A physical representation of birth and rebirth, the egg is particularly closely associated with Easter.

The humble egg is used throughout this book, but the recipes in this chapter feature the egg front and center. They are also some of the most versatile dishes in the Italian repertoire. Eggs can be enhanced with numerous fillings and served either plain, with a simple butter sauce, baked, or in broth.

EGGS

Eggs appear in every course on the Italian table, from antipasto to dessert.

BASIC EGG COOKING METHODS

*A*lmost all egg-centered dishes are variations on one of the following basic egg-cooking methods. Eggs may be cooked in water or broth or milk, in butter or oil or in a bain-marie.

SOFT-BOILED

Place an egg in a small pot. Add water to cover. Bring the water to a boil and, once it reaches this point, cook for 30 seconds to 1 minute for a barely firm white and a very soft yolk **[1]**.

HARD-BOILED

Place an egg in a small pot. Add water to cover. Bring the water to a boil, immediately turn down the heat to maintain a simmer, and cook the egg for 10 minutes longer. Hard-boiled eggs, with their firm whites and hard yolks **[2]**, can be eaten out of hand, stuffed, chopped, and sprinkled over salads or used in many other preparations.

POACHED

Eggs for poaching should be very fresh. Break the egg into a small cup or bowl and slide it into simmering water acidulated with lemon juice or vinegar. Simmer for 2 to 3 minutes and serve with buttered toast **[3]**.

FRIED

Heat some extra-virgin olive oil or melt 1 tablespoon or so of butter in a pan. Crack an egg into a small bowl. Slide the egg into the pan and cook it, basting it occasionally with the oil or butter, until the white is firm and browned around the edges **[4]** and the yolk is done to your preference.

SCRAMBLED

Crack eggs into a bowl, add some milk or cream, season the mixture with salt, and whisk. Cook the eggs in a pan over low heat with a little extra-virgin olive oil or butter, stirring continuously to create creamy, soft scrambled eggs **[5]**.

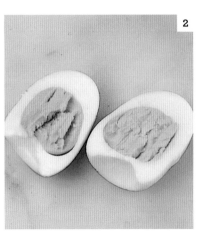

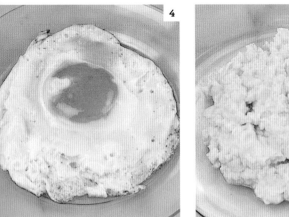

BOILED EGGS

Gently place eggs in a pot **[1]**. Add enough cold water to cover. Place over medium heat and bring to a boil. For very soft-cooked eggs, simmer the eggs for 30 seconds to 1 minute after the water comes to a boil. For slightly firmer soft-cooked eggs with a creamy yolk, simmer them for 3½ minutes. For firm soft-cooked eggs, cook them for 4 to 5 minutes, and for hard-cooked eggs, simmer them for 10 minutes. Remove the eggs from the pot **[2]** and transfer them to an ice-water bath for 2 minutes to stop the cooking process.

367

FRITTATAS

*f*rittatas can combine any number of ingredients with eggs in a nicely browned, savory cake. They make an easy and tasty meal.

SIMPLE FRITTATA

Use an oven-safe skillet if you plan to finish the frittata under the broiler. A cast-iron pan is best. In a large bowl, beat 2 eggs per person (4 eggs minimum) with a pinch of salt and freshly ground black pepper. Heat extra-virgin olive oil in the skillet over medium-low heat. Pour in the eggs. Every few seconds, tilt the pan and push the more solid eggs from the edge into the center so that the uncooked egg fills in the space. When the bottom of the frittata is firm but the top is still soft, cook it undisturbed for 2 to 3 minutes until the bottom is browned and the top has a narrow margin of cooked egg around the perimeter. To finish the top of the frittata, choose one of these approaches:

- Slide the frittata onto a plate, invert the skillet over the plate, and flip both plate and skillet together to return the frittata to the pan; cook for 2 to 3 minutes longer to brown the bottom.
- Heat the broiler and place the pan under it for 1 to 2 minutes.

FRITTATA ADDITIONS

A frittata is an excellent catchall for leftover vegetables and bits of cheese. To use raw vegetables, heat extra-virgin olive oil and cook them in the pan you plan to use for the frittata; then stir the cooked vegetables into the beaten eggs, pour the mixture into the pan, and proceed as for a simple frittata. Leftover cooked vegetables can simply be added to the beaten eggs or scattered on top once you've poured the eggs into the pan. Here are some suggested of frittata additions:

- browned sliced yellow onion or grilled red onion
- sautéed or grilled zucchini
- grated Parmigiano Reggiano or other aged cheese, stirred into the eggs
- cooked greens, squeezed dry and minced
- shavings of fresh pecorino Romano cheese, scattered on top
- sautéed sliced mushrooms
- diced mozzarella or other cubes of cheese dotted on top before finishing the frittata under the broiler

EGG BATTER

To make an egg batter for fried foods, separate 3 eggs and set aside the whites. Whisk the yolks together with 3 tablespoons unbleached all-purpose flour and ¼ cup white wine. You can also substitute milk or beer for the wine—the results will be less crispy. Add minced herbs if desired [1]. Whip the 3 egg whites with a pinch of salt, then fold them into the yolk mixture [2]. Whisk gently to combine [3]. If you prefer a very light batter, incorporate more whipped egg whites.

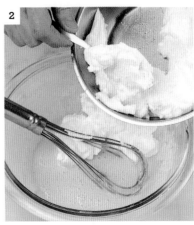

The right tool

A FLAT WHISK

A flexible flat whisk is perfect for mixing yolks, whites, salt, and herbs, as well as incorporating just the right amount of air into light and fluffy egg dishes.

CRESPELLE

savory crepes

For about 20 crespelle to serve 10 people, place 2¾ cups unbleached all-purpose flour in a bowl. Make a well and add 6 eggs **[1]**. Begin to incorporate the eggs with a whisk. When the mixture is fairly smooth, whisk in about 1 cup of milk **[2]**. Whisk vigorously to eliminate any lumps, then add 2 more cups of milk and whisk until the batter is smooth. Whisk in a pinch of salt and 3 tablespoons melted butter **[3]**.

To cook the crespelle, heat a 9-inch nonstick skillet. Ladle in enough batter to cover the surface of the skillet very thinly **[4]**. When the edges of the crepe begin to pull away from the pan and brown, slide a wooden or silicone spatula underneath and quickly flip it **[5]**. Cook for 30 additional seconds, then slide the crepe onto a tray **[6]**. Crespelle can be used immediately or set aside at room temperature and filled just before serving. Traditional fillings include ricotta and spinach (page 101). Crespelle—either empty or filled—may also be served in broth.

Ravioloni all'uovo e spinaci

giant ravioli with eggs and spinach

PASTA

2 cups unbleached all-purpose flour

½ cup semolina flour

3 large eggs

1 egg yolk

Fine sea salt to taste

FILLING

9 egg yolks

1 tablespoon extra-virgin olive oil

½ cup sliced almonds

1 clove garlic, minced

10 ounces fresh spinach, rinsed and left wet, chopped

¼ cup grated Parmigiano Reggiano cheese

Fine sea salt to taste

Freshly ground black pepper to taste

8 ounces ricotta cheese

SAUCE

2 teaspoons cornstarch

2 cups whole milk, cold

1 cinnamon stick

5 ounces Castelmagno cheese, diced (see note)

¼ cup grated Parmigiano Reggiano cheese, plus more for passing at the table

1. To make the pasta, follow the instructions for making egg pasta dough on page 78, using the flours, eggs and egg yolk, and salt. Wrap the dough in plastic and set it aside to rest for 30 minutes.

2. For the filling, line 8 cups in a muffin tin with plastic wrap. Place a yolk in each of the lined indentations. Place the tin in the freezer.

3. In a large skillet, heat the olive oil and cook the almonds with the garlic until they are browned and fragrant. Add the spinach and cook until it is wilted and there is no liquid in the skillet. Transfer the mixture to a bowl and stir in the Parmigiano Reggiano. Season it with salt and pepper and set it aside to cool.

4. When the spinach mixture is cool, mix in the ricotta.

5. Roll out the pasta (page 80) into 2 thin, wide strips of equal size. Lightly beat the remaining egg yolk and brush the top of each strip of pasta with it. Divide the spinach and ricotta mixture into 8 equal portions and place them down the center of 1 strip of pasta on the yolk-brushed side, leaving about 6 inches between them. Place a frozen egg yolk on top of each mound of filling. Cover with the second strip of pasta, yolk-brushed side down. Press between the mounds of filling very gently, being careful not to break the yolks. Cut out the ravioloni with a 5-inch round cookie cutter or by tracing around the filling with a ravioli cutter.

6. Bring a large pot of water to a boil and salt it. Cook the ravioloni in the water for 5 minutes.

7. Meanwhile, to make the cheese sauce, dissolve the cornstarch in about 1 tablespoon of the milk. Place the remaining milk in a saucepan and bring it to a boil. Turn down the heat to maintain a simmer, whisk in the cornstarch mixture, and add the cinnamon stick and Castelmagno cheese. Whisk continuously until the sauce thickens. Whisk in the Parmigiano Reggiano. Discard the cinnamon stick and place some of this cheese sauce on each serving plate. As the ravioloni are cooked, use a skimmer to transfer them from the boiling water to the prepared serving plates. Serve them immediately, with additional grated cheese on the side. The egg yolks will break when the ravioloni are cut.

NOTE: *Castelmagno is a semifirm cheese from the Piedmont region. When aged, it develops veins and turns into a blue cheese, but at the Castelmagno stage, it is mildly flavored and a little crumbly. If you can't find it, choose any other semifirm cheese that will melt smoothly and won't overpower the delicate taste of the pasta. If you are a fan of blue cheese, you could seek out a mild one and use that.*

SERVES 8 COOKING TIME: 2 HOURS

THE WORLD OF CHEESE IS VARIED AND FASCINATING. Cheese can be fresh,

semiaged, or aged for many years. It can be made with sheep's milk, cow's milk, goat's milk, or a combination of any or all of those. It can be wrapped in leaves, grape skins, or ash before aging, and in Italy many traditional cheeses are aged in caves, pits in the ground, or by other unusual methods.

The tasty results of acidulating cheese were probably discovered accidentally very early on; curd cheese was already known as long ago as 2300 B.C. in Egypt. The ancient Romans had their own cheese, called *moritum,* flavored with garlic and herbs and spices.

Today, Italy counts more than 450 types of cheese. Many of these are covered by DOP (Denominazione d'Origine Protetta) certification, meaning they can be made only in certain regions and using certain methods. These include Roman ricotta, Sardinian sheep's cheese, Castelmagno and Gorgonzola from the North and, of course, Parmigiano Reggiano from Emilia-Romagna, perhaps Italy's most famous dairy product.

DAIRY

Fontina, ricotta, mozzarella, and provolone are just a few of the Italian cheeses that are now well known everywhere in the world. Italy boasts so many types of cheese, and often they are made in limited areas and are known only to a small number of locals.

Coagulating milk by adding rennet, or fermentation bacteria, results in fresh curd cheese, a kind of homemade ricotta. (True ricotta uses the whey left over after another cheese is made; this homemade ricotta simply uses milk.) This can be made using cow's milk, sheep's milk, or goat's milk. Cheese is usually made with raw milk, but you can use pasteurized milk if you prefer it or if raw milk isn't available in your area; it will work just as well. Rennet is sold in liquid and tablet form. Eat this simple ricotta mixed with honey or herbs, or use it as a filling for ravioli or for stuffed vegetables.

Homemade Ricotta

Heat 3 quarts of whole milk (with cream or yogurt added, if you like) to 185 degrees F, then lower the temperature and bring the milk to 95 degrees F, stirring constantly. Add ¼ to ½ teaspoon liquid rennet. Cover the milk and keep the temperature at 95 degrees F for 45 minutes. Do not stir—just allow the cheese to curdle.

At the end of this time, dip a spatula all the way to the bottom of the pot and draw it through the cheese, then do the same to make a perpendicular line (in other words, make an X). Repeat this two or three times in each direction. Cover the pot and set it aside to rest for 30 to 45 minutes.

Break up the mixture into curds. Cover and set aside to rest at 95 degrees F for 30 more minutes. Transfer the cheese to a colander or sieve lined with cheesecloth and let it drain.

Lift the cheesecloth with the cheese inside and let any remaining liquid drip out.

Transfer the curds to basket-style ricotta molds, set the baskets on a tray, and refrigerate them for 1 to 6 hours.

Set the baskets in a cool place and allow them to rest for an additional 12 hours.

FRESH CHEESE and AGED CHEESE

IN ITALY, cheese is classified largely by its degree of aging. The freshest cheeses, such as ricotta and mozzarella, are soft, while most semifirm cheeses have aged for a short time. Harder cheeses suitable for grating have aged for the longest periods.

FRESH CHEESE With its high water content, fresh cheese is, ounce for ounce, lower in fat. It should be used within a few days of purchase. Fresh cheese can simply be drizzled with a little olive oil, sprinkled with black pepper or minced herbs, and spread on slices of bread. A few slices of toast with stracchino, ricotta, or primosale can stand as a light supper when paired with a salad. Mozzarella, of course, is an ingredient in pizza and melts beautifully, but high-quality buffalo mozzarella can also be sliced and paired with tomatoes, a handful of basil leaves, and a little extra-virgin olive oil and salt for a refreshing summer salad.

Goat Cheese

Mozzarella

Primosale

Quartirolo

Robiola

AGED CHEESE During aging, cheese is allowed to ripen for a set period of time and under specific conditions with regard to humidity and temperature to encourage certain qualities in the cheese. Aged cheese is more digestible for those who are lactose intolerant, but it is also higher in fat, as aging gives the water in the milk a chance to evaporate.

Semiaged cheeses have ripened from 1 to 6 months. They are hard enough to cut into slices, but the texture remains soft. These include Taleggio and fontina. Aged cheeses have ripened from 6 to 24 months or even longer. These include various types of toma and sheep's cheese, or pecorino (*pecora* is the Italian word for "sheep"). For its part, Parmigiano Reggiano is aged from 1 to 3 years.

Italians group Parmigiano Reggiano and other cheeses aged until they are crumbly and suitable for grating together under the category of *grana*. Parmigiano Reggiano is by far the most widely available, but grana Padano also falls into this category and is often priced a little lower than true Parmigiano Reggiano. Grana cheeses can also be eaten out of hand—they go especially well with pears. There is a special spade-shaped knife used to break the hard cheese into chunks.

Fontina

Toma

Sheep's Cheese

Gorgonzola

Taleggio

Parmigiano Reggiano

Mozzarella in carozza ai carciofi

fried mozzarella stuffed with artichokes

3 balls fresh mozzarella, about 7 ounces each

4 artichokes

6 tablespoons extra-virgin olive oil

½ cup dry white wine

2 cloves garlic, peeled

3 shallots, minced

1 sprig flat-leaf parsley

Fine sea salt to taste

Freshly ground black pepper to taste

2 cups unbleached all-purpose flour

2 large eggs, lightly beaten

2 cups fine dry bread crumbs

4 anchovy fillets, rinsed

Juice of ½ lemon

Extra-virgin olive oil for frying

1. Cut 16 equal slices out of the mozzarella balls and reserve the scraps for another use. Spread the slices in a single layer on a plate and set them aside so that the cheese can give off some of its liquid. Meanwhile, trim the artichokes (page 149) and cut them into thin wedges. Place a pot over medium heat and add the olive oil, white wine, garlic, shallots, parsley, artichokes, salt, and pepper. Cook over medium heat until the liquid has evaporated and the artichokes are beginning to brown. Remove all but 4 of the artichoke wedges and remove the parsley sprig; leave everything else in the pot.

2. Pat the mozzarella slices dry (reserve the liquid they have given off) and dredge both sides in the flour. Sandwich 2 slices of the cheese around about 1 tablespoon of the cooked artichokes removed from the pot.

3. Once you have prepared all 8 of these "sandwiches," press around their edges with floured hands to seal them. Return any leftover artichoke filling to the cooking pot.

4. Dredge the sealed sandwiches in the beaten eggs, then in the bread crumbs, then again in the eggs, and, finally, in the bread crumbs for a second time. They should be thoroughly coated.

5. Return the pot with the artichokes in it to medium heat; add the anchovy fillets, lemon juice, and ½ cup water. Boil for 3 minutes, then transfer the mixture to a blender and puree it, incorporating the liquid given off by the mozzarella.

6. Fry the mozzarella sandwiches in a generous amount of hot oil, then serve them with the artichoke and anchovy puree.

SERVES 4   COOKING TIME: 40 MINUTES

SALAD with CHEESE SHAVINGS

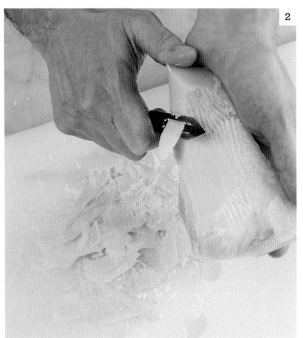

Use a truffle shaver (see page 269), mandoline, the slats on a four-sided box grater, or a vegetable peeler to cut thin shavings of an aged cheese such as Parmigiano Reggiano [1, 2]. Toss the cheese with a green salad and dress it with a vinaigrette made of extra-virgin olive oil and balsamic vinegar. (See page 139 for more on dressing a salad.) [3] These cheese shavings are especially good for salads that incorporate peppery greens like watercress and arugula.

SHEEP'S CHEESE and FAVA BEAN BALLS

Place 7 ounces fresh shelled fava beans (page 238) and 4 ounces semi-aged sheep's cheese with the rind removed in a food processor fitted with the metal blade. Process until the mixture is finely ground, but not completely smooth [1]. Use your hands to roll the mixture into small balls. Serve these with cold cuts, such as prosciutto crudo or a selection of various types of salami [2].

383

Ravioli al mais con pecorino

corn flour ravioli with sheep's cheese filling

PASTA

2¼ cups semolina flour

1 cup corn flour (see note)

Pinch fine sea salt

2 large eggs

FILLING

8 ounces ricotta cheese

8 ounces semiaged sheep's cheese, grated on the largest holes of a box grater

1 egg yolk

1 teaspoon minced fresh marjoram leaves

Fine sea salt to taste

Freshly ground black pepper to taste

SAUCE AND FINISHING

14 ounces shelled fresh fava beans (page 238)

1 tablespoon extra-virgin olive oil, plus more for drizzling

1 cup minced carrot

6 scallions, including pale green portions, chopped

Fine sea salt to taste

Freshly ground black pepper to taste

1½ cups vegetable stock (page 55)

2 tablespoons minced flat-leaf parsley

Grated Parmigiano Reggiano cheese for serving

1. In a bowl, combine the two types of flour and the salt, form a well, and add the eggs and ⅓ cup room-temperature water. Make the pasta dough, following the instructions on page 78. Form the dough into a ball, wrap it in plastic, and set it aside to rest for 30 minutes.

2. For the filling, whisk the ricotta until smooth, then combine it with the sheep's cheese, egg yolk, and marjoram. Season with salt and pepper.

3. Roll the pasta dough into strips (see page 80) and use a 3-inch cookie cutter to cut 64 disks of dough. Place a scant teaspoon of the filling in the center of each disk.

4. Fold each disk handkerchief style as shown in the photograph opposite. Pinch the seams to seal them tightly.

5. For the sauce, chop the fava beans in a food processor fitted with the metal blade until they are chunky—you do not want a smooth paste.

6. Heat the olive oil in a skillet and sauté the minced carrot and the fava bean mixture for 1 minute. Add the chopped scallions and sauté for 1 additional minute, then season with salt and pepper, add the vegetable stock, cover the pot, and simmer for 10 minutes. The result should be a fairly soupy sauce. Sprinkle on the parsley.

7. Bring a large pot of water to a boil and salt it. Cook the ravioli in the boiling water (in batches, if necessary) for about 1 minute after they rise to the surface, then remove them with a slotted spoon or skimmer. Place some of the sauce in the bottom of each individual serving bowl and top it with 8 ravioli. Drizzle on a little extra-virgin olive oil and serve immediately, passing grated Parmigiano Reggiano on the side.

NOTE: *Corn flour is a silky, finely ground flour, not to be confused with cornmeal (which is coarser and grittier) or cornstarch (which, confusingly, is labeled cornflour in the United Kingdom).*

SERVES 8 COOKING TIME: 2 HOURS

PASTA AI QUATTRO FORMAGGI

pasta with four cheeses

Sauté a little minced shallot in a tablespoon of butter and sprinkle on 1 tablespoon plus 1 teaspoon of unbleached all-purpose flour. Scatter in ½ cup cubed Taleggio, ½ cup crumbled Gorgonzola, and ¾ cup cubed fontina. Pour in 1 cup whole milk **[1]** and whisk until creamy. Cook penne until it is al dente, drain it, and add it to the pan with the cheeses. Sprinkle on ¼ cup grated Parmigiano Reggiano cheese **[2]**. Transfer the mixture to a baking dish. Dot the surface with butter and sprinkle on additional grated Parmigiano Reggiano. Broil, watching carefully, until the top of the pasta is golden and crisp **[3]**.

TOMINI ALLA PIASTRA

Place tomini or any other small individual cheese rounds with their rind in a warm pan and cook them, turning once, until they are very soft **[1]**. Remove the top rind while the cheese is still warm (it should peel off in one piece); the remaining rind will act as a bowl to hold the warm cheese **[2]**. Serve the cheese with boiled potatoes or raw carrot, celery, and fennel sticks for dipping.

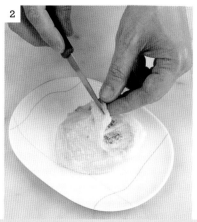

CREAM

CREAM'S FAT CONTENT ALLOWS IT TO REMAIN STABLE even at high heat and when whipped. Heavy cream and heavy whipping cream are used interchangeably in the United States for both cooking and whipping. Light cream can be used in its liquid form but should never be heated or whipped.

HEAVY CREAM
Cream can be whipped by hand, using a balloon whisk **[1]**. This task is made easier with an electric mixer **[2]**. A metal container is best when making whipped cream **[3]**. Take care not to overwhip the cream, which will cause it to clot. If you will not be using whipped cream immediately, whip it only partially and finish the job right before using.

LIGHT CREAM
The cream with the lowest amount of butterfat cannot be whipped, but it plays a role in both sweet and savory dishes. Paired with other ingredients, it makes a luxurious sauce for pasta **[4]**.

Frico is a kind of cheese crisp from the Friuli region of Italy. It is traditionally prepared with Montasio, a DOP-certified cow's milk cheese from the area. There are also variations on the frico that incorporate diced cooked potatoes, speck, or onions. The method below shows how to shape a frico into a basket that can be used as an edible container for other items. You can also let the cheese cool in disks on a parchment-lined baking sheet and eat as is.

The Perfect Frico

Cut fresh or semiaged Montasio cheese into cubes, thin slices, or strips, or grate it.

Heat a skillet over low heat and add the cheese.

Let the cheese melt. It will release some of its fat.

When the edges of the cheese begin to brown, lift the cheese in one piece with a spatula and turn it over. Be gentle; the cheese is still very soft at this stage. Cook the second side for 1 minute.

Remove the frico from the pan and shape it into a basket while it is still warm. The easiest way to do this is to drape it over a small mold and place a larger mold over it. (You can also use two cups.) Lift off the top mold once the frico has cooled.

*F*RUIT IS NATURE'S SHOWPIECE, offering a wide range of flavors and forms. It is also a priceless source of vitamins and minerals and one of the keys to good health. In the north of Italy, apples and pears are grown in large numbers and varieties. The South is home to numerous citrus groves. Central Italy yields peaches, cherries, and apricots. Grapes grow almost everywhere. Fruit is used in every course of a meal, from antipasto to dessert. It is a seemingly inexhaustible source of both health and creative inspiration.

Fancy, heavy desserts are not a part of everyday life in Italy. Instead, in almost every home, both lunch and dinner end with a bowl of fruit being brought to the table and everyone peeling and eating the fruit of his or her choice. Try keeping a big bowl of apples, pears, oranges, bananas, and any other fruit you like at room temperature on your kitchen counter or table and getting into the habit of ending meals with fresh fruit or any of the slightly more elaborate fruit desserts in this chapter. This is an easy way to work more fresh fruit into your diet, and fruit is always a refreshing palate cleanser

FRESH FRUIT

Fruit has it all: good looks, great taste, and powerful nutritional value. It regularly appears on the Italian table in its natural state, but it can also be transformed as a component in both savory recipes and desserts.

CANDIED ORANGES

Slice 2 oranges. Place the slices in a skillet and add water to cover. Bring the liquid to a boil and cook for 3 minutes. Drain the water, add fresh water to cover, and boil again for 3 minutes. Repeat a third time. Return the oranges to the skillet with ¾ cup water and ¾ cup sugar and cook, stirring occasionally, to make a syrup. Let the oranges cool in this syrup, then drain them and repeat with ½ cup water and ¾ cup sugar. Drain the oranges one final time, dredge them in fresh sugar, and set them on a cooling rack to dry.

BAKED APPLES

Preheat the oven to 375 degrees F. Core the apples, leaving them whole and with the peels on. Place the apples in a baking dish and fill the centers with a mixture of raisins, soaked to soften them; pine nuts; and sugar [1]. Pour 2 cups dry white wine into the bottom of the baking dish (try to avoid wetting the apples) [2] and bake for 20 minutes, until tender.

FRUIT GRANITA

Combine equal amounts of sugar and water. Place this over medium heat and cook, whisking, until the sugar is completely dissolved. Mix this syrup with pureed berries, pureed peeled peaches, a large amount of lemon juice, or pureed seeded melon. You can also combine two or more types of fruit. Pour the mixture into a metal pan and place it in the freezer. After 30 minutes, break up the mixture with a fork, stir, and return the pan to the freezer. Repeat every 30 minutes or so until the granita is completely frozen, about 3 hours total. Scoop it out with a spoon and serve.

393

POACHED FRUIT

Cooking fruit simply in water, wine, or syrup enhances its flavor and brings out its sweetness. A single type of fruit can be poached, or you can poach several different kinds together. You can add flavorings, such as lemon zest, cinnamon sticks and other spices, or vanilla beans to the poaching liquid. You can also sprinkle sugar into the liquid. Poached fruit is delicious on its own or spooned over a little vanilla ice cream. A simple rule of thumb: Fruits from the same season almost always marry well. To poach fruit, either peel it or don't and core or pit it. Then set the fruit in a pot with liquid to cover, bring it to a boil, turn it down to a simmer, and cook until the fruit is soft enough to be pierced easily with the tip of a paring knife. Let the fruit cool in the cooking liquid and serve it with a little of the liquid drizzled over it. Here are a few classic combinations:

- pears poached in red wine with star anise

- peaches studded with 1 or 2 whole cloves and poached in white wine

- dried apricots and prunes poached in apple cider with a cinnamon stick

- mixed berries poached in vanilla syrup (page 449) or sugar syrup with a few strips of lemon zest

MACERATED BERRIES

Macerating is to fruit as marinating is to meat. In other words, the fruit is simply allowed to sit for a time, either in flavored liquid or tossed with sugar. Eventually, it gives off its own liquid, creating a delicious syrup. Italians typically macerate berries rather than eating them fresh. Rinse the berries; hull and slice strawberries if they are large. Combine one or more types of berries such as raspberries, blueberries, and strawberries in a bowl. Sprinkle on 1 to 2 tablespoons of sugar, toss gently, and refrigerate for a couple of hours. The berries will release their juices and be sweetened by the sugar. This works beautifully with stone fruits such as peaches and apricots as well.

Finally, fruit can be macerated long term in grappa or other kinds of alcohol. Drop whole or halved pitted plums, apricots, peaches, or nectarines into a clean glass mason jar. Do not pack them too tightly. Add enough grappa to fill the jar to the top, seal it with a lid, and store it in a cool, dark place (cellar shelves are ideal) for a couple of months. The fruit will be very alcoholic when you open the jars—it's a real treat to have the taste of summer fruits in the middle of winter.

MACEDONIA
fruit salad

Italians refer to fruit salad as macedonia because it mimics that country's mélange of ethnicities. A fruit salad can contain almost any type of fruit, but a classic combination is 2 apples and 2 pears, peeled, seeded, and chopped; 1 cup strawberries, sliced if large; 2 bananas, chopped; and 1 orange, separated into wedges and chopped. Toss the fruits together in a large bowl, then sprinkle on a tablespoon or two of sugar and drizzle the juice of 1 or 2 lemons over them. Toss to combine and refrigerate.

Sfogliatine con le pere

puff pastry with pears

6 Bosc pears

1 cup turbinado sugar

1 cinnamon stick

1 cup moscato d'Asti or other
sparkling white wine

2 (8-ounce) sheets puff pastry

2 teaspoons ground cinnamon

5 Savoiardi (page 435), crumbled

Splash of Grand Marnier

4 egg yolks

2 tablespoons cornstarch

Pinch fine sea salt

Confectioners' sugar for sprinkling

1. Wash the pears and peel them in vertical strips, leaving some skin on. Cut away the bases to allow them to stand flat and arrange them around the perimeter of a pot. Add ¾ cup of the sugar, the cinnamon stick, ¾ cup water, and the moscato d'Asti and cook over medium heat for 40 minutes.

2. Preheat the oven to 400 degrees F. Place 1 sheet of puff pastry on a work surface, brush it with water, and sprinkle it with half of the remaining sugar and 1 teaspoon of the ground cinnamon. Fold it into thirds and cut it into three 4-inch squares. Repeat with the other sheet of puff pastry.

3. Place the puff pastry squares on a parchment-lined baking sheet. Set a small mold or ramekin filled with water in the center of each one (this will keep that area from puffing). Bake them until the puff pastry around the ramekins is golden and crisp, about 15 minutes. Place the crumbled Savoiardi in a medium bowl and moisten them with the Grand Marnier.

4. Remove the pears from their syrup (reserving the syrup) and core them from the bottom with an apple corer, leaving the tops intact.

5. Stuff the pears with the Savoiardi mixture.

6. Measure the syrup created by cooking the pears and add enough water to make 2 cups liquid. In a metal bowl, combine the egg yolks, cornstarch, and salt, and whisk until the mixture is smooth. Whisk in the syrup, then place the bowl over a pot of boiling water or transfer the mixture to the top of a double boiler and cook, whisking constantly, until the sauce is thick.

7. To serve, place the puff pastry squares on plates or a serving platter. Sprinkle them with confectioners' sugar. Fill the indentation in each square with some of the warm sauce. Place a stuffed pear on top of each (this will cause some sauce to spill out attractively onto the plate). Serve warm.

SERVES 6 COOKING TIME: 1 HOUR

One way to highlight the appeal of fruit is to make preserves.
Cooking concentrates the fruit's flavor, and its natural sweetness
is enhanced with sugar or honey.

Fruit Preserves

 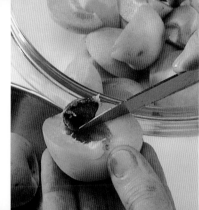 

In an environment that is at least 50 percent sugar, the growth of bacteria and mold is greatly inhibited, which is the reason preserves keep so well. During the cooking process, sugar interacts with the pectin and the cellulose naturally present in fruit to firm up the resulting mixture.

Choose perfectly ripe fruit with no soft spots (cut away and discard any blemishes). Peel, seed, and core the fruit if necessary. Chop larger items. Weigh the fruit.

Place the fruit in a pot, ideally one of lined copper (see page 115). Lined copper pots are not only excellent transmitters of heat, but they also reinforce the molecular structure of pectin.

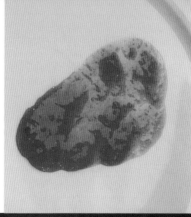

Add sugar at least equal in weight to the fruit.

Finally, add pectin, a natural substance that helps the mixture gel (check the package instructions to determine how much).

Cook until thick. Check the thickness by pouring a little onto a plate, then tilting the plate. If the mixture drips very slowly, it's ready.

*D*RIED FRUIT AND NUTS are generally winter treats in Italy, though there's no reason not to enjoy them year-round. The nuts most frequently eaten in Italy are almonds, hazelnuts, and pine nuts. While these may appear in savory preparations (such as pine nuts in pesto), they also star in numerous desserts. Sicily is famous for its treats made with almond paste, while Piedmont has gianduia, a delicious cream combining chocolate and hazelnuts. As for dried fruit, apricots, raisins, prunes, figs, and dates are the most widely used.

While nuts and dried fruits can certainly be eaten out of hand as nutritious and satisfying snacks, with a small amount of effort they can also be incorporated into other dishes or elevated by using some interesting techniques.

Store nuts in the refrigerator or the freezer. Dried fruit can sometimes grow hard as it ages. If you feel dried fruit will be challenging to chew, soften it by soaking it for 20 minutes or so in hot water, then drain.

DRIED FRUITS & NUTS

Dried fruit and nuts—including raisins, prunes, almonds, and pine nuts—are a tremendous asset in the pantry. In Italy, they are most often enjoyed in the winter, when fresh fruit is restricted largely to apples and pears.

BLANCHING ALMONDS

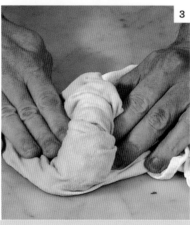

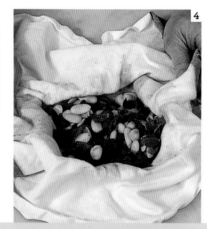

Place the almonds in a small pot [1]. Add cold water to cover and bring to a boil. Remove the pot from the heat and let the nuts sit in the water for 5 minutes. Drain and transfer them to a clean dish towel [2]. Rub the towel against the nuts and the nuts against each other for a minute or so to loosen the skins [3]. Pick through and remove any remaining skin on the almonds [4]. The same process can be used for pistachios.

REMOVING SKINS FROM WALNUTS and HAZELNUTS

WALNUTS
Boil the walnuts as for blanching almonds, above, and peel them one at a time using a paring knife (and a great deal of patience) [1].

HAZELNUTS
Spread the nuts on a baking sheet in a single layer and bake them at 200 degrees F (a toaster oven is great for this) until they are golden and aromatic, about 30 minutes. Rub the toasted hazelnuts, a few at a time, with your hands to remove any dried skin [2].

SLICING, CHOPPING, and POUNDING NUTS

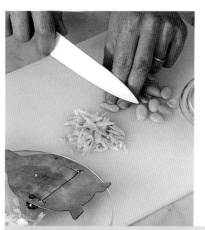

SLICING
Use a truffle slicer (page 269) or a very sharp knife to cut blanched and peeled almonds into thin slices.

CHOPPING
Chop hazelnuts, walnuts, pistachios, and almonds in a food processor fitted with the metal blade. If you will be using the nuts in a sweet preparation, include 2 teaspoons of sugar for every ¾ cup or so of nuts.

POUNDING
Place peeled nuts, such as hazelnuts, on a clean dish towel and pound them with a meat pounder, or wrap the dish towel around them and crush them with the flat side of a chef's knife.

403

USING NUTS TO CREATE A SAVORY COATING FOR MEATS

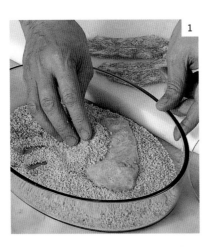

Dredge chicken breasts, fish fillets, or pork chops in flour, then beaten egg, and finally in a mixture of about 40 percent bread crumbs and 60 percent ground toasted hazelnuts (you can also use hazelnuts alone) [1]. Cook in melted butter or hot oil until the crust is golden and crisp [2].

Storing nuts

Nuts are rich with oil and therefore may go bad quickly. Buy them in small quantities from a store with good turnover. Store the nuts in a tightly sealed container (otherwise they tend to pick up the odors of the foods around them) in the refrigerator or even in the freezer. (They do not need to be thawed before using.)

SWEET and SAVORY DRIED FRUIT PREPARATIONS

CARAMELIZED DRIED APRICOTS
In a pan, combine sugar with enough water to create a "wet sand" consistency and then cook until it melts and reaches 300 degrees F. Stick skewers into dried apricots and dip them into the syrup, then place them on parchment paper to cool and harden.

SOAKED DRIED CHESTNUTS OR FRUIT
Soak dried chestnuts in water for 24 hours, changing the water three times. Dried fruit can be soaked in water or liqueur for 30 minutes to 1 hour.

RUM COMPOTE
Combine assorted dried fruits and a few blanched peeled almonds in a pot. Add 3 tablespoons butter, 2 tablespoons rum, a little sugar, the juice of ½ orange, strips of orange and lemon zest, and cinnamon sticks. Simmer, covered, for about 30 minutes. Serve with gelato.

405

SWEET and SAVORY DRIED FRUIT PREPARATIONS

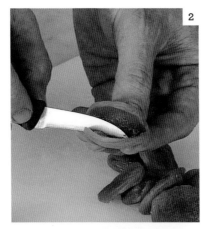

SAVORY STUFFED DRIED APRICOTS

For a sweet-and-salty appetizer, in a food processor fitted with the metal blade, grind 6 ounces chicken breast with 3 slices of day-old bread soaked in milk to soften. Add grated Parmigiano Reggiano cheese, minced parsley, and salt and pepper to taste [1]. Butterfly 12 dried apricots that you have soaked in rum and drained by cutting them open horizontally but leaving the halves attached [2]. Fill the apricots with the chicken mixture [3]. Cook them in melted butter until they are browned on all sides. Add a splash of dry white wine, cover the pan, and simmer until the chicken is cooked through, about 4 minutes [4]. Prunes can also be stuffed with this mixture.

SAVORY AND SWEET STUFFED DATES

Use a wooden spoon to whip robiola cheese with some minced chives until smooth. Butterfly the dates by cutting them open down one side but leaving the halves attached; fill them with the cheese mixture using a pastry bag fitted with a decorative tip or a plastic bag with one corner snipped off [1]. Garnish the dates with chives [2]. To make sweet stuffed dates, use mascarpone in place of the robiola, leave out the chives, top each filled date with a walnut half, and sprinkle them with cocoa powder.

RAISIN BREAD

Make a dough with 1 cup unbleached all-purpose flour and 2¼ teaspoons (1 envelope) active dry yeast dissolved in ¼ cup lukewarm water, ¼ cup lukewarm milk **[1]**, and a pinch of salt (see page 3). Shape the dough into a ball and place it in a bowl, covered with plastic wrap, to rise until it is doubled in bulk. Roll out the dough and sprinkle 1 cup soaked and drained raisins on top. Roll up the dough jelly-roll style **[2]** and set it on a parchment-lined baking sheet, loosely covered with a dish towel, to rise for 30 minutes. (If you prefer a more regularly shaped loaf, set it in a buttered loaf pan, tucking the ends under.) Meanwhile, preheat the oven to 350 degrees F. Brush the top of the bread with a little melted butter and bake until it is golden and risen, about 30 minutes. Allow it to cool completely before slicing.

GROUND ROASTED MIXED NUTS

In a skillet combine almonds, cashews, hazelnuts, and blanched pistachios (page 402). Drizzle the nuts with a little oil and season them with salt, pepper, paprika, ground cinnamon, and cayenne **[1]**. Add a little broth (page 56) to moisten them. Cook them for 30 minutes, adding more broth in very small amounts if the skillet begins to get dry **[2]**. Coarsely grind the nut mixture in a food processor fitted with the metal blade and serve it, seasoned with freshly ground black pepper, with boiled cauliflower florets, for example.

407

Children and adults alike love croccante, or almond brittle, a treat that's surprisingly easy to make at home. After long holiday meals in Italy, a few pieces of brittle are served with coffee.

Croccante *almond brittle*

Place sugar in a copper pot (or in the top of a double boiler) and place it over medium-low heat. Add raw almonds, using twice as much volume as the sugar. Add a few drops of vanilla extract as well.

Stir the mixture with a wooden spoon. The sugar will crystallize and get sticky and will begin to coat the almonds.

Continue to stir as the sugar turns into semiliquid caramel. Now the almonds will begin to stick to one another.

Pour the almonds out onto an oiled marble surface. If you like a hint of citrus in your brittle, rub the marble surface before pouring the almonds with the cut side of ½ lemon.

Let the brittle cool slightly, then begin using a large metal spatula to spread it around. Knead the mixture with the spatula while pressing it into a smooth, even rectangle about ½ inch thick.

When the brittle has cooled somewhat but is still warm, cut it into bars. (Fully cooled brittle is difficult to cut, as it shatters.) Keep the bars in a cool, ventilated place overnight. Store them in a tightly sealed container at room temperature.

409

Baci di pesca

peaches stuffed with almonds

5 ripe peaches

5 tablespoons sugar

1 tablespoon unsalted butter

1 cup mixed berries

½ cup blanched almonds, ground
(pages 402 and 403)

¼ cup cocoa powder

2 Savoiardi (page 435), crumbled

⅓ cup confectioners' sugar

Pinch fine sea salt

1 amaretto cookie, crumbled, or 1
teaspoon almond liqueur (optional)

Mint leaves for garnish

Fresh fruit cut into wedges for
garnish

1. Cut 4 of the peaches in half horizontally and remove the pits. Pit and chop the remaining peach.

2. Sprinkle 1 tablespoon of the sugar in the bottom of a heavy skillet and place it over medium heat. When the sugar begins to caramelize, place the 8 peach halves in the skillet, cut sides down. After 1 minute, turn the peaches and cook them for 1 additional minute. Remove the peach halves and sauté the chopped peach in the skillet until it is golden, about 2 minutes.

3. In another skillet, melt the butter with the remaining ¼ cup sugar. Add the berries and 3 tablespoons water and cook for 3 minutes. Crush the berries lightly with a fork.

4. Mince the caramelized chopped peach and combine it with the ground almonds in a bowl.

5. Add the cocoa powder, Savoiardi, confectioners' sugar, and salt to the almond mixture. Add the crumbled amaretto cookie or the liqueur, if you wish. Stir the mixture thoroughly.

6. Stuff 4 of the peach halves with the almond mixture and cover them with the remaining 4 halves. Serve the peaches with the caramelized berry sauce, garnished with mint leaves and fresh fruit.

SERVES 4 COOKING TIME: 30 MINUTES

HONEY WAS THE WORLD'S ORIGINAL SWEETENER, and it was featured in what was most likely Italy's first dessert, a kind of focaccia spread with honey and topped with fruit. Cane sugar was brought to Italy by Crusaders around the year 1000. This newfangled substance, which dissolved completely when melted, caused a boom in pastry making. During the mid-1700s, the process for making beet sugar evolved, and with it came modern pastry making. Italy's basic cakes and crusts—pan di spagna (sponge cake) and pasta frolla (a kind of short-crust pastry)—were invented around that period.

Pasta frolla dough is a particularly Italian invention that deserves to be more widely known. It can be used for a wide variety of tarts and pies, baked blind or with filling. It is also used for cookies and other individual pastries. It is easy to make and handle—legend has it that the sculptor Antonio Canova worked on his designs with pasta frolla dough before rendering them in marble. If you've always been afraid of pie and tart crusts, you'll be pleasantly surprised at how forgiving this dough is. And if you choose to bypass pasta frolla, you'll still find this chapter filled with easy-to-make desserts to satisfy any sweet tooth, including Italian spoon desserts like tiramisù and panna cotta.

CAKES, COOKIES, & SPOON DESSERTS

Italian bakers serve a wide variety of homemade sweets appropriate for dessert or an afternoon snack with coffee or tea.

PAN DI SPAGNA

italian sponge cake

Soft, light pan di spagna is a type of sponge cake. It is delicious on its own, but it also serves as the base for an almost unlimited number of cakes and other desserts. Pan di spagna layers can be filled and frosted with jam, whipped cream, or pastry cream (page 440), and they can be brushed with syrups, liqueurs, or coffee. They can be cut into pieces and used to make Italy's famous trifle, zuppa Inglese (page 419). Below are instructions for making pan di spagna using an electric stand mixer or hand mixer. See page 416 for instructions on making it by hand. It's the lengthy beating process that gives pan di spagna its spongy, light texture, so fold in the flour gently, then transfer the batter to pans and get it into the oven quickly, giving it as little time as possible to deflate.

Preheat the oven to 350 degrees F. Place 8 large eggs in the bowl of an electric mixer [1]. Add 1½ cups sugar, 1 teaspoon vanilla extract, and a pinch of salt [2]. Place the bowl on the mixer and whip until the mixture is very fluffy and light yellow. This step, which will take 15 to 20 minutes, is important: Incorporating plenty of air will yield a fluffy and light cake [3]. Meanwhile, brush the bottoms and sides of an 11-inch round cake pan (lined with parchment paper, if desired) with melted butter [4] and then lightly flour the pan, shaking out any excess flour [5].

When the batter is ready, it will form soft peaks (when you raise a beater, you should be able to "write" on the surface with the batter and this should remain visible, rather than sinking back in immediately) [6]. In four additions, sift 2 cups unbleached all-purpose flour over the top [7], gently folding in the flour with a wooden spoon between additions [8]. Pour the batter into the pan [9], smooth the top with a spatula, and immediately place the pan in the preheated oven. Bake until the cake is golden and springy and a tester or toothpick inserted into the center comes out clean, about 25 minutes. Unmold the cake onto a wire rack [10] and cool it completely [11].

Pan di spagna freezes well. After it has cooled completely, triple wrap it in plastic wrap, then in foil, and freeze it. It will keep for a few weeks in the freezer, and once frozen, it will be easier to handle, which is especially useful when decorating.

Beat 3 egg yolks with ½ cup sugar until light yellow and fluffy, about 5 minutes [1]. Separately, whip 3 egg whites with 6 tablespoons sugar and a pinch of salt until fairly firm [2]. Fold the whipped yolks into the whipped whites; sift 1½ cups unbleached all-purpose flour over the mixture and gently fold it in [3]. Bake as on page 414.

CUTTING PAN DI SPAGNA

LAYERS
If you want to cut a single large layer of pan di spagna (above and preceding page) into 2 or 3 layers, mark a line all the way around with a large, flat serrated knife, then cut, holding the knife blade horizontal and turning the cake [1].

SLICES
To make slices for trifles and other desserts, cut pan di spagna into ½-inch slices. If you'll be using the slices to line a round mold, cut them in half diagonally [2].

CRUMBS
Sometimes you'll want pan di spagna crumbs to decorate the frosted surface of a cake or smaller pastries. Cut slices as described above, trim away and discard the crusts, and either dice the cake into small cubes or crumble it with your hands [3].

WHIPPED CREAM CAKE

Bake a single layer of pan di spagna (page 414) **[1]**. When the cake is completely cooled, whip 1 pint heavy cream with 3 tablespoons confectioners' sugar **[2]**. Just before serving, pipe the whipped cream over the surface of the cake in a regular pattern, using a pastry tube and tip or a plastic bag with a corner snipped off **[3]**. Top the cake with thin lines of melted chocolate or other decoration **[4]**.

Variations on

PAN DI SPAGNA

Pan di spagna is extremely versatile and flexible. Once you are familiar with the technique, you will find that you can adjust the basic recipe to meet your needs. The instructions on page 414 are for a single pan di spagna layer. You can cut that cake into thinner layers, but you can also bake these layers separately. Simply divide the batter between two or three pans, 8 or 9 inches in diameter. Keep in mind that the thinner layers bake through more quickly. Start testing them after about 15 minutes to be sure they don't dry out.

You can also adjust the texture of the finished cake. If you would like a more compact and crumbly cake, add melted butter after you have folded in the flour. Using extra egg yolks will yield a cake that is less moist and finer grained; using extra egg whites will have the opposite result.

417

JELLY ROLL

Preheat the oven to 350 degrees F. Butter a baking sheet or jelly-roll pan, line it with parchment paper, then butter the parchment and flour it, shaking off any excess flour. Spread the pan di spagna batter (page 414) over the entire baking sheet about ½ inch thick. Smooth the top **[1]**. Bake the cake for 10 to 12 minutes. Remove the pan from the oven and invert onto another piece of parchment **[2]**. Leave the pan in this position until the cake is completely cooled, then remove it **[3]**. Carefully peel off the paper on top. Spread the top of the cooled cake with a mixture of equal amounts of water and liqueur or of flavored syrup in a thin layer, leaving a margin around the edges. Spread on 1½ cups preserves (page 398) and roll up the cake, using the parchment paper it is sitting on **[4]**. Wrap the jelly roll in the parchment paper and refrigerate it until firm, about 4 hours. Unwrap the jelly roll and cut it into ¾-inch slices **[5]**. This kind of cake can also be filled with flavored pastry cream (page 440).

ZUPPA INGLESE

Make a custard by scalding 3 cups whole milk with ½ vanilla bean. Remove the bean. In a bowl, beat together 4 egg yolks and ½ cup sugar. Sift in ½ cup unbleached all-purpose flour while whisking constantly, then add the hot milk in a thin stream, whisking constantly. Return the mixture to the pot and cook it, stirring constantly, over medium heat until thick, about 5 minutes. Transfer it to a bowl, cover it with a piece of plastic wrap placed directly on the surface, and refrigerate until it is completely cool. Brush slices of pan di spagna (page 414) with the liqueur of your choice. (Zuppa Inglese is traditionally made with a bright pink rosewater-flavored liqueur called alchermes that is not widely available in the United States.) In a large bowl, layer the soaked cake pieces with the custard. Refrigerate for at least 1 hour before serving.

TORTINE PARADISO

Preheat the oven to 350 degrees F. Cream 10 tablespoons (1¼ sticks) softened butter with ¾ cup confectioners' sugar and a pinch of salt [1]. Separately, whip 3 large eggs and 6 egg yolks with 1 cup sugar and a pinch of salt. Gently fold the creamed butter mixture into the whipped egg mixture [2]. Fold in 1½ cups unbleached all-purpose flour, 1 cup potato starch, 1 tablespoon baking powder, and a little grated lemon zest.

Butter and flour 16 to 20 single-serving cake baking pans (extra-large muffin pans are a good choice) and use a pastry bag to fill the individual pans or muffin cups two-thirds full of batter [3]. Bake until the cakes are golden and springy and a tester inserted into the center of one comes out clean, about 20 minutes. Unmold the cakes, allow them to cool, and sprinkle them with confectioners' sugar before serving [4].

Torta di nocciole

hazelnut–olive oil cake

½ cup extra-virgin olive oil, plus
extra for oiling pan

1¼ cups (5½ ounces) hazelnuts,
skins removed (page 402), cooled

1 cup unbleached all-purpose flour

1 tablespoon baking powder

4 large eggs

1½ cups sugar

½ cup whole milk

Finely grated zest of 1 large lemon

1. Preheat the oven to 350 degrees F. Lightly coat a 9-inch springform pan with olive oil.

2. Grind the cooled hazelnuts in a food processor fitted with the metal blade until they are finely ground but not powdery. Transfer them to a bowl. Add the flour and baking powder; whisk to combine.

3. In the bowl of an electric mixer fitted with the whisk, beat the eggs at medium-high speed until they are frothy, about 2 minutes. Gradually add the sugar, beating until the mixture is light, thick, and pale yellow, about 4 minutes. Gradually add the hazelnut-flour mixture; then add the olive oil, milk, and zest, beating 1 minute longer to combine them.

4. Transfer the batter to the prepared pan. Place it on a rimmed baking sheet, and bake until the cake is golden and a tester inserted into the center comes out clean, 35 to 40 minutes. Cool the cake completely in the pan on a wire rack, then release it from the pan and serve.

SERVES 10 COOKING TIME: 1 HOUR

BABÀ AL RUM

rum cakes

Place ¼ cup raisins in water to cover and let them soak until softened. Make a starter by combining ⅔ cup unbleached all-purpose flour and 3 tablespoons milk in a bowl. Dissolve 2¼ teaspoons (1 envelope) active dry yeast in ¼ cup warm water, let it sit until foamy, then mix it into the other ingredients. Stir until combined, then cover the bowl with plastic wrap and set it aside until the starter is doubled in volume. In the bowl of an electric mixer, combine 1¾ cups flour, 3 large eggs, the risen starter, 2 tablespoons sugar, 8 tablespoons (1 stick) softened butter, and a pinch of salt [1]. Beat until the mixture is soft and creamy. Drain the raisins and fold them in. Transfer this dough to a pastry bag and fill 18 to 20 babà molds or other small individual molds about halfway [2]. Cover the molds loosely with a clean dish towel and let the dough rise until it fills the molds to the top. Meanwhile, preheat the oven to 350 degrees F. When the dough has risen, bake the cakes until they are firm, about 15 minutes.

In a pot, combine ½ cup sugar with ¾ cup water and cook over medium heat until the sugar is dissolved. Remove the pan from the heat and add ½ cup rum. Remove the cakes from the oven and unmold them; while both cakes and syrup are still hot, dip the cakes in the syrup [3]. Place the cakes on a wire rack. Heat a small amount of apricot preserves thinned with 1 teaspoon or so of water in a small pot and brush it on the warm cakes [4]. Serve the cakes with whipped cream if desired.

PLUM CAKE

*W*hat Italians call "plum cake" (always in English) contains no plums at all! It's a mystery where the name came from—this is similar to a pound cake (with equal amounts butter, sugar, eggs, and flour by weight) and is baked in a loaf pan. It's delicious no matter what you call it, though.

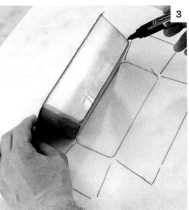

Preheat the oven to 350 degrees F. Let 8 tablespoons (1 stick) butter sit at room temperature until it is about the consistency of clay **[1]**. In a bowl, combine the butter with ½ cup sugar **[2]** and a pinch of salt and beat it, using a stand mixer or a hand mixer, until it is very fluffy and light in color, about 25 minutes. Crack 2 large eggs into separate small bowls. While the butter is being whipped, trace a loaf pan (8 by 4 by 2½ inches) on a piece of parchment paper as shown **[3]** , adding 1 inch at the top of each side. Cut out the shape. Brush the loaf pan with melted butter, line it with the cut parchment paper (turning the paper so the pencil marks are against the pan), and butter the parchment as well **[4]**.

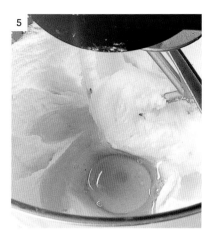

When the butter mixture is ready, add the eggs one at a time with the mixer on low speed. Beat to combine completely between additions [5]. In a bowl, combine 1 cup unbleached all-purpose flour, 1 pinch of salt, a little grated lemon zest, and 1 teaspoon vanilla extract. (If you want a less dense cake, replace ⅓ cup of the flour with an equal amount of potato starch.) [6] Sprinkle the flour mixture over the butter mixture [7] and beat it in by hand, using a wooden spoon. If you wish, you can fold some raisins, diced candied fruit, or plain dried fruit into the batter at this point. Transfer the batter to the lined pan [8]. Bake the cake until the top begins to look dry and set, about 10 minutes, then make a slash down the center of the cake. Return it to the oven and bake until it is golden brown on top and a tester inserted into the center comes out clean, about 35 minutes longer [9]. Unmold the cake and cool it on a wire rack.

Individual plum cakes

If you'd rather make individual plum cakes, generously butter ramekins, muffin tins, or other smaller pans and fill them two-thirds full of batter. Bake them at 350 degrees F until they are golden brown, 15 to 20 minutes, depending on the size of the pans. These individual cakes are great for snacks or for breakfast.

423

MAKING PASTA FROLLA DOUGH

*P*asta frolla is a crisp short crust that should be handled as little as possible. The dough will be easier to make and less likely to overheat if you start with cold tools, a cold work surface, and cold ingredients.

Measure out 4 cups of flour **[1]**. Spread 4 cups unbleached all-purpose flour on a work surface. Cut 2 sticks plus 5 tablespoons cold butter into small pieces and scatter them over the flour **[2]**. Toss the butter in the flour so that it is coated **[3]**. Rub the mixture between your palms without pressing it together **[4]** until it resembles coarse meal **[5]**.

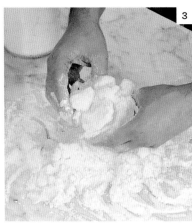

424

Sprinkle 1 cup sugar and a pinch of salt over the mixture. Mix in the ingredients without pressing them into the butter—the texture should still be powdery. Use a pastry cutter to avoid touching the butter [6]. Make a well in the center of the mixture and add 4 egg yolks [7]. Break the yolks and mix them with the other ingredients, then knead briskly with your fingertips [8]. Begin to knead with your palms, and work until the dough is compact. As soon as the ingredients are evenly distributed, stop kneading [9]. Drop the dough against the work surface a few times [10]. When the dough is smooth, form it into a loaf [11]. Wrap it in plastic [12] and refrigerate until the butter is firm again, at least 1 hour—but overnight is even better.

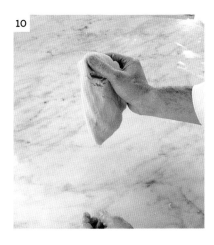

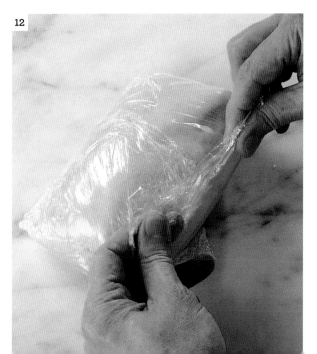

425

FREEZING PASTA FROLLA

Pasta frolla keeps quite well in the freezer—up to 2 months—and you have several options for freezing pasta frolla. You can freeze the ball of dough, wrapped in three layers of plastic and a sheet of foil. Just defrost it in the refrigerator for 24 hours before using it. You can also roll out the dough, place it in a tart pan, and freeze the unbaked crust. Alternatively, you can blind bake the dough in the pan before freezing it: Line it with foil, fill it with pie weights or dried beans, and bake it at 350 degrees F until the surface is dry, 12 to 15 minutes, then remove the foil and weights and bake until golden, about 15 additional minutes. Allow a frozen crust to defrost in the refrigerator for 24 hours before filling and baking it.

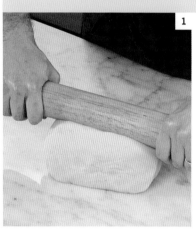

ROLLING OUT PASTA FROLLA

Place the dough on a work surface and pound it with a rolling pin to flatten and soften it **[1]**. Lightly flour the work surface and the top of the dough **[2]**. To make the rolled dough perfectly even, rest the rolling pin on two dowels of the same thickness taped down at either side of the dough **[3]**. Rotate the dough frequently, sprinkling it lightly with flour on top and bottom.

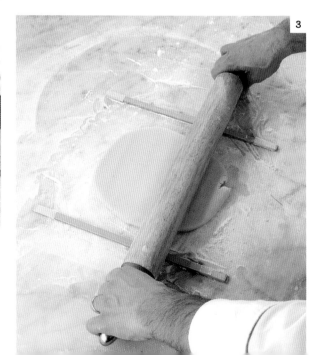

IF THE DOUGH BREAKS

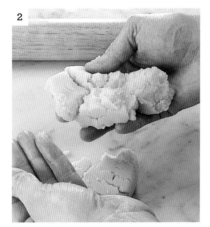

If large cracks form when you try to roll out the pasta frolla dough **[1]** or if it feels greasy and sticky and comes apart in small pieces **[2]**, the butter has overheated and is separating. This is known as "breaking." You can still bake the pastry, but it will crack in the oven. To prevent this, place the dough in a bowl and add 3 to 4 tablespoons cold water **[3]**. Knead briefly until the dough is elastic again **[4]**. Wrap and refrigerate for 1 hour.

Tartellette ripiene
stuffed tartlets

CRUST

2½ cups unbleached all-purpose flour

½ cup almond flour

⅔ cup corn flour (not cornmeal or cornstarch)

12 tablespoons (1½ sticks) unsalted butter, chilled and cut into pieces

½ cup granulated sugar

¼ teaspoon ground cinnamon

¼ teaspoon freshly grated nutmeg

Pinch fine sea salt

¼ cup whole milk

FILLING

1 small, tart apple

9 tablespoons unsalted butter, softened

¼ cup granulated sugar

½ cup rice flour

1 large egg

¾ cup confectioners' sugar, plus more for sprinkling

6 large dates, pitted and halved

2 ounces dark chocolate, chopped

1. Combine the flours in a bowl. Add the butter pieces, toss to coat them, then rub the mixture together until it resembles coarse meal. Sprinkle on the granulated sugar, cinnamon, nutmeg, and salt.

2. Make a well in the center of the mixture and pour the milk into it. Knead the dough briskly, first with your fingertips, then with your palms, until the dough is compact. As soon as the ingredients are evenly distributed, form the dough into a ball, wrap it tightly in plastic, and refrigerate it for at least 1 hour, or overnight.

3. To make the filling, preheat the oven to 475 degrees F. Peel and core the apple and cut it into thin slices. Place the slices on a parchment-lined sheet pan that has been buttered on top with 1 tablespoon of the butter. Sprinkle the apples with the granulated sugar and bake until they are golden. Set the pan with the apples on a wire rack to cool and turn the oven down to 375 degrees F.

4. Roll out the crust to ¼ inch thick. Place it on top of 12 oval tartlet pans. Press the dough into the pans and roll over it with the rolling pin so that the rims of the pans cut off any excess. (You can save the leftover dough to bake into cookies.)

5. In a bowl, whisk the rice flour with the egg, confectioners' sugar, and the remaining 8 tablespoons butter.

6. Place a couple of slices of apple in each tartlet shell, then top them with a date half and some of the chopped chocolate. Transfer the rice flour mixture to a pastry bag fitted with a smooth tip and pipe it on top of the chocolate. Bake the tartlets until the tops are golden and firm to the touch. Unmold them and sprinkle them with a little additional confectioners' sugar before serving.

SERVES 12   COOKING TIME: 1 HOUR 15 MINUTES

429

CREAM PUFF DOUGH

Cream puff dough is used to bake light, airy pastries such as profiteroles or éclairs. Their hollow insides may be filled with pastry cream (page 440) or whipped cream, and even savory mixtures. The results are impressive, and the dough is not particularly difficult to make.

In a pot, combine 1 cup cold water and 4 tablespoons (½ stick) unsalted butter [1]. Place it over medium heat and add a pinch of salt. Stir the mixture constantly with a wooden spoon [2]. The butter should melt before the water comes to a boil. As soon as the water boils, immediately add 1 cup unbleached all-purpose flour [3]. Begin mixing briskly right away. If you wait even a brief time to do this, the mixture may turn lumpy [4]. Continue stirring constantly for a few minutes. When the mixture is ready, it will begin to pull away from the sides of the pot and make a sizzling sound [5]. Turn the dough out onto a tray or a marble work surface. Spread it with a spoon [6] and let it cool. Work the dough with the spoon occasionally to be sure its surface doesn't dry out. Place the cooled dough in a bowl and use a handheld or stand mixer to incorporate 3 large eggs, adding them one at a time and beating to combine between additions [7]. Beat until the dough is smooth and creamy [8]. It will be wet but still fairly easy to work with.

NOTE: *The amounts provided above will create a dough that strikes a good balance between softness and crunch, but if you want a crisper pastry, use 1 cup water, 1½ cups flour, 7 tablespoons butter, and 3 eggs. For somewhat drier and more durable results, use 1 cup water, 2 cups flour, 2 sticks plus 2 tablespoons butter, and 6 eggs.*

FORMING, BAKING, and ASSEMBLING CREAM PUFFS

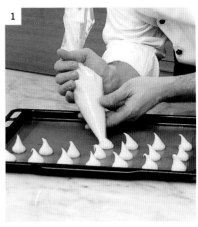

FORMING

Use a pastry bag to pipe cream puff dough (page opposite) onto baking sheets lined with parchment paper, leaving about 1 inch between the cream puffs **[1]**. You should get 40 larger cream puffs or 75 smaller ones, if you make the basic dough. Wet your index finger and use it to flatten the peaked tops **[2]**.

BAKING

Bake the cream puffs at 400 degrees F until they are golden, puffed, and dry, about 25 minutes for smaller cream puffs and 30 minutes for larger ones. Turn off the heat, open the oven door, and let the cream puffs sit undisturbed for about 10 minutes, then transfer them to wire racks to cool completely.

FILLING

When the cream puffs are cool, make a hole in the base of each one with the tip of a paring knife **[3]**. Just before serving, use a pastry bag fitted with a narrow tip to fill each cream puff with pastry cream or whipped cream **[4]**. You can top filled cream puffs with some confectioners' sugar or cocoa powder sprinkled through a sieve **[5]**, a drizzle of caramel, or a glaze (below).

GLAZING

If you'd like to glaze the cream puffs, place 1 cup confectioners' sugar in a large bowl. Add the juice of ½ lemon and whisk in enough water (about 3 tablespoons) to make a creamy mixture. Dip the top third of each cream puff into the glaze **[6]**, then set the cream puff on a wire rack over a piece of waxed paper and allow the glaze to dry completely.

431

Bignè alle pere

pear profiteroles

11 tablespoons unsalted butter, softened

Pinch fine sea salt

2½ cups unbleached all-purpose flour

4 large eggs

4 pears, about 2 pounds total, plus an additional pear for garnish (optional)

¼ cup sugar

1 vanilla bean

1¼ cups whole milk

¾ cup heavy cream

7 ounces 62% cacao dark chocolate

1 tablespoon rum or kirsch

1. Preheat the oven to 350 degrees F. Make a cream puff dough following the instructions on page 430 and using 1¼ cups water, 7 tablespoons of the butter, a pinch of salt, 1¾ cups of the flour, and the eggs.

2. Place the dough in a pastry bag with a large ridged tip and pipe 24 large cream puffs onto a parchment-lined baking sheet. Bake the cream puffs for 30 minutes.

3. Meanwhile, peel, halve, and core the 4 pears and place them in a baking pan. Sprinkle them with the sugar. Split and scrape the vanilla bean and add it to the pan. When the cream puffs are done, set the baking sheet on a rack to cool and turn the oven up to 400 degrees F.

4. Bake the pears for 40 minutes, then puree them with any liquid that has collected at the bottom of the pan (remove the vanilla bean) and set them aside.

5. Combine the milk and cream in a pot and bring the mixture to a boil. Stir in the pear puree. Combine the remaining 4 tablespoons butter and the remaining ¾ cup flour and add the mixture to the pot. Cook, stirring, for 10 minutes, then transfer the pastry cream to a bowl, cover it with plastic wrap placed directly onto the surface of the cream, and set it aside to cool.

6. When the cream puffs and the pastry cream are cool, use a pastry bag to fill the puffs. (Place the chocolate, ¼ cup water, and the rum in the top of a double boiler and cook, whisking, until the chocolate melts. Use the chocolate mixture as a glaze (see page 431 for instructions for glazing cream puffs). Serve 3 cream puffs per person, and garnish with slices of fresh pear if desired.

SERVES 8 COOKING TIME: 2 HOURS 35 MINUTES

433

CANTUCCI

*I*n Tuscany, the twice-baked cookies most commonly known as biscotti are called *cantucci*. As with biscotti, these cookies are traditionally flavored with almonds.

Preheat the oven to 350 degrees F. Spread ¾ cup blanched almonds on a baking sheet and toast until they are golden, about 7 minutes. Cool the almonds on a rack. Line a baking sheet with parchment paper. In a large bowl, whisk together the almonds, 3¾ cups unbleached all-purpose flour, 1 cup sugar, 2¼ teaspoons baking powder, and ¼ teaspoon fine sea salt. Add 4 large eggs and 7 tablespoons unsalted butter, softened. Stir with a wooden spoon to combine, then knead the mixture in the bowl until it forms a dough. Divide the dough into 5 equal pieces and shape each piece into a log about 6 inches long and 1½ inches wide. Place the logs on the baking sheet at least 2 inches apart. Press gently to flatten them slightly. Bake until they are golden and slightly firm, 25 to 30 minutes. Transfer the baking sheet to a wire rack and let the logs cool for 10 to 15 minutes. (Leave the oven on.) Use a sharp knife to cut the logs into ¾-inch slices and arrange them on the baking sheet, cut sides down, in a single layer. Return them to the oven and bake until they are golden, about 25 additional minutes, turning the cookies once. Cool them completely and store them in an airtight container for up to 2 weeks.

SAVOIARDI

crisp italian ladyfingers

You can find Savoiardi in gourmet stores, but they're not difficult to make. Using home-baked ladyfingers in place of store-bought ones will elevate any recipe in which they are a component, and a few of these crisp plain cookies make a nice accompaniment to a cup of tea or coffee.

Preheat the oven to 350 degrees F. Separate 4 large eggs. Whip the yolks with 1 cup sugar until the mixture is thick and creamy. Whip the whites, drizzling in a little lemon juice as you do, until they form stiff peaks. Gently fold the whites into the yolks, so that they deflate as little as possible. Sift 1 cup unbleached all-purpose flour into the bowl and fold until combined. Transfer the batter to a pastry bag or a plastic bag with the corner snipped off and pipe it onto parchment-lined baking sheets in strips about 3 inches long and 1 inch wide; leave 1 inch between each strip. Sift a light dusting of confectioners' sugar over the cookies. Bake until they are lightly golden, 6 to 10 minutes. Slide the cookies, still on the parchment paper, onto racks to cool. Store them in an airtight container.

TIRAMISÙ

Separate 3 large eggs. Beat the egg whites with 1 tablespoon sugar until they form soft peaks. In a separate bowl, beat the yolks with ⅓ cup sugar until the mixture is very thick and light yellow. Fold the contents of a 17.6-ounce container of mascarpone cheese into the egg yolks. Gently fold the egg whites into the egg yolk mixture, deflating the whites as little as possible. Spread 12 Savoiardi (above or store-bought) on a sheet pan or large plate and drizzle about ½ cup espresso (page 450) or strong drip coffee over them. Place 4 of the cookies in the bottom of a large baking dish or bowl. Add about a third of the mascarpone mixture and spread it smooth with a spatula. Place another 4 cookies on top. Top with another third of the mascarpone and again spread it smooth. Top with the remaining cookies and then the remaining mascarpone mixture. Decorate the tiramisù with chocolate curls or sift cocoa powder over the top. Refrigerate it for 4 hours or overnight before serving—tiramisù actually improves as it sits.

435

OVIS MOLIS

*T*hese delicious, tender cookies include a couple of unique ingredients: hard-boiled egg yolks and potato starch.

Preheat the oven to 350 degrees F. In a bowl, combine 5 hard-boiled egg yolks (see page 366), pressed through a sieve to mince, 1½ cups unbleached all-purpose flour, ½ cup potato starch, ¾ cup confectioners' sugar, and a pinch of salt **[1]**. Mix well to combine, then add 1 teaspoon vanilla extract and 1 stick plus 6 tablespoons (1¾ sticks) softened butter. Knead the flour mixture with the butter until combined **[2]**. Pound the dough against the work surface until it is compact and smooth. Form it into a loaf, wrap it in parchment paper, and refrigerate it for at least 1 hour **[3]**. Remove the dough from the refrigerator and let it rest for 15 minutes, then divide it into 5 equal logs. Cut each log into 9 equal pieces **[4]**. Working quickly so as not to overheat the dough, roll the pieces between your palms to form balls and arrange them about 1 inch apart on parchment-lined baking sheets. Use the end of a wooden spoon handle to make an indentation in the center of each cookie **[5]**. Fill the indentations with apricot or other jam. Bake them until the bottoms are lightly browned, about 15 minutes. Cool on a wire rack.

ITALIAN MERINGUE

Place 3 to 4 room-temperature egg whites in a bowl [1]. In a pot, combine 1 cup sugar and a scant ½ cup water over medium heat [2]. Add a pinch of salt to the egg whites. When the sugar syrup begins to boil, whip the egg whites [3]. Beat until the egg whites form soft peaks [4]. Measure the temperature of the syrup—it should be 226 to 230 degrees F. If it is, begin to gradually pour the syrup into the egg whites while still beating them [5]. Continue to beat the meringue until it is completely cool, has turned shiny, and has increased noticeably in volume. Stiff peaks should form when you lift the beaters out of the meringue [6]. Gradually sift in 1¼ cups confectioners' sugar [7]. Gently fold in the sugar with a spatula or a wooden spoon, pulling it from the bottom of the bowl to the top [8].

BAKING ITALIAN MERINGUES

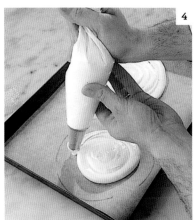

Preheat the oven to 200 degrees F. Line two baking sheets with silicone mats or parchment paper and choose in what form you'd like to bake your meringues:

- Use a tablespoon to arrange 20 large meringues on the sheets [1]. Dust them with confectioners' sugar [2].

- Transfer the meringue to a pastry bag fitted with a wide tip and pipe the meringues onto the baking sheets. Use a ridged tip and hold the bag at a 45-degree angle, lifting it as you pipe [3].

- Make disks of meringue by using a smooth tip and piping the meringue in a spiral [4].

Bake for 3 to 5 hours, depending on how dry you would like the meringues to be and how large they are [5]. Open the oven door occasionally to let humidity escape.

CUSTARD with MERINGUE

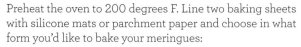

Prepare a custard by mixing 5 egg yolks with ¾ cup sugar. Stir in 2 cups whole milk and 1 teaspoon vanilla extract [1]. Cook, stirring constantly, until the mixture reaches 175 degrees F. Set the pot in a bowl of ice water and cool the custard, stirring it constantly. Beat 3 large egg whites with a pinch of salt. When the whites begin to form peaks, sprinkle in ½ cup superfine sugar [2]. Continue to beat until the egg whites are shiny and form stiff peaks. In a pot, combine equal parts milk and water and place the

mixture over medium heat. As soon as it begins to boil gently, use two tablespoons to form quenelles with the meringue mixture and drop them into the milk mixture [3]. Let them cook for 1 minute, turn them, and cook them for another minute. Remove them with a slotted spoon or skimmer [4] and transfer them to parchment-lined baking sheets [5]. Pour half of the custard into a bowl, arrange 3 to 4 Savoiardi (page 435 or use store-bought) on the surface [6], then top them with the cooked meringues [7]. Spoon the remaining custard over the meringues [8] and sprinkle a generous helping of toasted sliced almonds over all [9]. Make a caramel by melting ⅓ cup sugar with a few drops of water and cooking until the mixture reaches 330 degrees F. Drizzle the caramel over the top of the custard [10] and serve immediately [11].

439

PASTRY CREAM

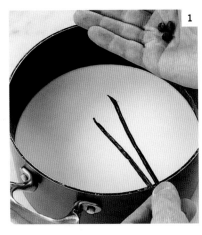

In a pot, combine 1 quart whole milk, 1 split vanilla bean, and 3 coffee beans **[1]**. Bring the mixture to a boil and immediately remove the pot from the heat. Place 8 egg yolks in a bowl **[2]**. Add 1½ cups sugar and whisk to combine without beating in any volume **[3]**. Whisk in ½ cup unbleached all-purpose flour and a pinch of salt until the mixture is completely smooth. Add another ¼ cup flour if you prefer a denser cream **[4]**. Scrape seeds from the cooled vanilla bean into the milk mixture, discard the pod, and stir **[5]**.

6

Strain the hot milk mixture into the egg yolks **[6]**. Whisk from the center out to the edge of the bowl. Transfer the mixture to a pot. Place the pot over low heat and stir with a slotted spatula, scraping the bottom to be sure the cream doesn't burn **[7]**. The cream should begin to thicken. As soon as the mixture comes to a boil, replace the spatula with a whisk and whisk until the mixture tastes cooked (the flavor of raw flour will be noticeable if it's not yet ready), 3 to 5 minutes **[8]**. Transfer the cream to a clean glass bowl, sprinkle a little sugar on the top **[9]**, and cover it with plastic wrap, placing it directly on the surface of the cream. When the cream has cooled, whisk it to smooth it out **[10]** or refrigerate it to firm it up (if you are serving it as a spoon dessert on its own). Pastry cream will keep in the refrigerator for 2 to 3 days.

The right tool

7

8

9

10

A PASTRY BAG

A pastry bag is a washable bag used to pipe pastry cream, buttercream, meringue, and other items into decorative shapes. When you buy a new bag, you'll need to snip off one corner, cutting it at an angle. Pastry bags are fitted with metal tips of various sizes and designs. Place the tip inside the bag so that the point pokes out through the hole. To fill a pastry bag, fold down the cuff about halfway. Use a spatula to scoop in the dough or cream, filling it up to the fold. Unfold the cuff and twist it gently right above the filling. Hold the bag firmly at the twist as you pipe out the shapes. If you hold the tip close to the surface you're decorating as you squeeze, you will make wider shapes, while if you hold it farther from the surface, it will make narrower shapes. As you pull the bag away and stop squeezing it, you will form small peaks.

Sfogliatelle alla crema
cream-filled pastries

PASTRY CREAM

1 cup whole milk

¾ cup heavy cream

1 vanilla bean

1 cinnamon stick

1 cup granulated sugar

8 egg yolks

⅓ cup unbleached all-purpose flour

Pinch fine sea salt

PASTRY

½ ounce lard

⅓ cup unbleached all-purpose flour

Pinch fine sea salt

6 tablespoons unsalted butter, softened

FINISHING

1 large egg, lightly beaten

Confectioners' sugar

1. To make the pastry cream, bring the milk and cream to a boil with the vanilla bean, cinnamon stick, and 3 tablespoons of the granulated sugar. Strain the mixture, discarding the vanilla bean and cinnamon stick. In a saucepan, mix the egg yolks with ¾ cup of the sugar, then sift in the flour and add the salt. Whisk in the hot milk mixture. Bring the pastry cream to a boil and cook it for 5 to 6 minutes. Transfer it to a bowl, sprinkle the surface with the remaining 1 tablespoon sugar, and cover it with plastic wrap, placing the wrap directly against the surface. Set it aside to cool.

2. To make the pastry dough, cut the lard into the flour and salt. Add ¾ cup water and knead until the mixture forms a smooth, compact dough. Divide this into 8 balls of equal size, cover them with plastic wrap, and set them aside to rest for 45 minutes.

3. Flatten the balls of dough between the rollers of a pasta machine to make long thin sheets (about 6 by 18 inches). Brush 1 sheet of dough with the softened butter. Place another sheet on top and brush that with more butter. Layer all 8 sheets like this, brushing butter in between.

4. Roll up the sheets of dough from one short end. Wrap the roll in plastic and refrigerate it for at least 2 hours and as long as 24 hours.

5. Preheat the oven to 375 degrees F. Cut the roll of stacked dough into 8 equal slices about ⅔ inch thick.

6. Place your thumbs in the center of one of the slices and use your other fingers to pull it up and out so that the layers separate slightly and the slice forms a cone.

7. Hold the cone in one hand and spoon about 1 tablespoon of the pastry cream into the center. Pinch the edges together to seal. Set the pastry on a baking sheet lined with parchment paper. Repeat with the remaining slices of dough. Brush the pastries with beaten egg. Bake them for 15 minutes, then sprinkle them with a little confectioners' sugar and continue baking until they are golden brown and crisp, about 10 additional minutes. Serve warm with additional confectioners' sugar.

SERVES 8 COOKING TIME: 2 HOURS

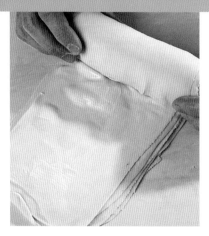

442

VANILLA GELATO

Mix 5 egg yolks with ¾ cup sugar
[1]. Scald 1½ cups whole milk with a
split and scraped out vanilla bean [2].
For a richer gelato, add ⅓ cup fresh
cream. Pour the hot milk into the
egg yolks [3] and place the mixture
over medium heat. Cook, stirring
constantly and scraping the bottom of
the pot with a slotted spatula [4], until
the temperature reaches 165 to 175
degrees F. Transfer the cooked cream
to an ice cream maker and process it
according to the instructions for the
device [5]. When the gelato is ready,
transfer it to another container [6]
and either freeze it or scoop and serve
it immediately with whipped cream
and fresh fruit [7].

PANNA COTTA

Dissolve the contents of a ¼-ounce envelope of gelatin into ⅓ cup milk. In a pot, combine 2 cups heavy cream and ⅓ cup sugar and set the mixture over medium heat. As soon as the cream comes to a boil, stir in the milk mixture and cook, stirring constantly, for 1 minute. Remove the pot from the heat, stir in 1 teaspoon vanilla extract, and pour the mixture into six ramekins or teacups. Cool the panna cotta to room temperature, then cover the ramekins with plastic wrap, placing the wrap directly on the surface. Refrigerate until the mixture is set, about 4 hours. Unmold the panna cotta onto serving plates (or serve it in the ramekins, if you prefer) and top it with fresh fruit, a drizzle of honey, or a spoonful of chocolate sauce.

CANDIED CHESTNUTS

These delicious treats are made over twelve days, but they are well worth the effort. During the last nine days, the time spent cooking is minimal. Just plan ahead.

Soak 2 pounds chestnuts in cold water overnight. Peel off the shells [1]. Blanch the chestnuts in boiling water for 2 minutes and remove them from the hot water one at a time to peel off the skins [2]. Wrap the peeled and skinned chestnuts in a piece of cheesecloth, packing them tightly so that they don't move around [3]. Place the chestnuts in a large ovenproof pot with a tightly fitting lid, add water to cover, and cook them in the oven at 200 degrees F for 2 hours—do not let the water boil. Let the chestnuts cool in the same water, then gently lift them out and let them drain overnight on a cooling rack, still wrapped in the cheesecloth. In an ovenproof pot with a lid, combine 3¾ cups sugar with enough water to cover the chestnuts (about 6 cups) [4]. Preheat the oven to 200 degrees F. Add a vanilla bean to the pot with the water and sugar, bring the mixture to a boil, and boil for 1 minute and 30 seconds. Remove it from the heat. Transfer the cheesecloth enclosing the chestnuts to the pot with the syrup [5]. Cover the pot and bake the chestnuts for 24 hours. Lift the cheesecloth-wrapped chestnuts out of the pot and set them aside on a rack to drain. Add ½ cup sugar to the syrup, boil the mixture for 2 minutes, then remove the pot from the heat. Return the chestnuts to the pot, cover them, and let them rest for 3 days. After 3 days, remove the chestnuts, add another ½ cup sugar to the pot, boil the mixture for 2 minutes, and remove it from the heat. Return the chestnuts to the pot, cover them, and let them rest for 3 days. Remove the chestnuts and repeat the process one more time, adding ½ cup sugar to the pot. In total, the chestnuts will soak in the syrup for 9 days. Drain the chestnuts and remove them from the cheesecloth [6]. Arrange them in a single layer on a rack. Make a thin sugar syrup by dissolving confectioners' sugar in a little water. Drizzle this over the chestnuts [7]. Preheat the oven to the highest heat possible (probably 500 degrees F) and bake the chestnuts, spread out on a baking sheet in a single layer, for 1 minute to dry them. Let the candied chestnuts cool completely before storing them. When they have cooled, store the candied chestnuts in a metal container with a tight-fitting lid. Line the container with waxed paper and place additional sheets of waxed paper between the layers of chestnuts. The candied chestnuts will keep for 1 to 2 weeks.

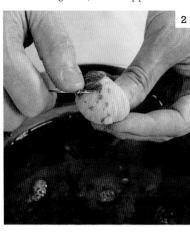

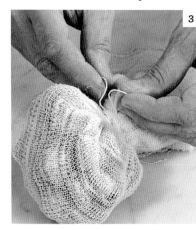

CINNAMON

*C*innamon is used largely in baked goods today, but it wasn't always so. During the Renaissance, spices, including cinnamon, were highly prized and were used to cook meat. Here are a few ways to incorporate cinnamon into your baking and cooking.

CINNAMON STICKS

When stored in a tightly sealed jar, cinnamon sticks will keep for up to 4 years. They are used in liquids and sauces and often simmered in pastry cream to infuse it with flavor. Whole cinnamon sticks [1] are always discarded after cooking—they are inedible.

CINNAMON SUGAR

Grind a cinnamon stick into very small pieces using a mortar and a pestle, or use ground cinnamon, and combine it with sugar. Store it in a tightly sealed jar and use it to sweeten tea, coffee, or milk. This cinnamon sugar [2] can also be used in desserts such as plum cake (page 422) in place of plain sugar.

CINNAMON SALT

Combine coarse salt with crushed whole black peppercorns and a few pieces of cinnamon stick and store the mixture in a tightly closed jar. The salt will absorb the flavors [3]. It can then be used to cook a whole fish or meat or poultry in salt (page 338), or it can be ground finely and used to season dishes in place of plain salt.

ROASTING WITH CINNAMON

Wrap a whole potato in foil with a few pieces of cinnamon stick [4] and roast it—the results are extraordinary. Apples and pears can also be baked in foil this way. Sprinkle them with sugar and include some diced prunes or dried apricots if you like.

VANILLA

Vanilla is a flowering plant in the orchid family. Its rough pods—called beans but actually are a fruit—are not much to look at, but they lend divine fragrance and flavor. The beans are usually split lengthwise and simmered in liquid, and then the pulp is scraped into the liquid when cooking is complete.

VANILLA BEANS
Vanilla beans should be firm and elastic, never dried out or cracked. Store them in a tightly sealed jar in a cool, dark place.

USES of VANILLA

VANILLA-FLAVORED COFFEE
Break up a vanilla bean into small pieces and mix it with ground coffee [1]. Store the coffee and brew it as usual—the resulting beverage will have a delicious undertone.

VANILLA SUGAR
Split vanilla beans lengthwise, and combine them with 2 cups sugar in a well sealed jar [2]. After a few weeks, the sugar will take on a delicate vanilla flavor. Use this in recipes in place of plain sugar. If the recipes also call for vanilla extract, you can omit it.

VANILLA-FLAVORED WHIPPED CREAM
Scald ¼ cup heavy cream with a vanilla bean split in half lengthwise. Remove the cream from the heat and allow it to cool. Scrape the seeds from the vanilla bean back into the liquid and discard the pod. Once the cream is cooled, combine it with 1 cup cold heavy cream [3]. Whip with a little sugar added.

VANILLA-FLAVORED TEA
Grind 1 or 2 vanilla beans and combine them with loose black tea. Store the mixture in a tightly sealed jar for 2 weeks, then use it to brew tea normally [4]. This tea is especially tasty with milk added.

VANILLA SYRUP
In a saucepan, combine 2 split vanilla beans, 1¼ cups sugar, and 1 cup water. Heat the mixture over low heat, stirring frequently, until the sugar is dissolved and the liquid is clear and fragrant. Remove it from the heat and let it cool. Scrape the seeds from the vanilla beans back into the syrup and discard the pods. Store the syrup in a tightly sealed jar in the refrigerator. Use it to sweeten fruit salad (page 395) and drinks and to drizzle over gelato [5].

449

ESPRESSO

*I*taly is famous for its cappuccino, latte macchiato, and espresso. There seems to be a coffee bar on every block in Italian cities, and they almost all make good coffee, but Italians also make a slightly different version of espresso at home, using a stovetop coffee maker called a moka. You can purchase these inexpensively, and it is worth having one on hand, even if you are not an espresso drinker, in order to percolate a little espresso for use in recipes.

BASIC ESPRESSO

To make coffee in a moka, fill the bottom portion with cold water; do not fill it above the little valve. Set the filter—a round strainer with holes in it—inside the basket and fill it with coffee, preferably a roast and grind specifically intended for espresso. If you like your coffee really strong, tamp it down a little; a round disk may have been provided with your moka for this purpose. Screw on the top part of the coffee maker and place the moka over low heat. (You may need a flame tamer in order to fit the coffee maker on top of your stove grid if you have a gas stove.) You will hear the coffee percolating up to the top portion of the coffee maker. When the sound turns to a sputter, remove the pot from the heat immediately. Serve the espresso hot with sugar or use it in your recipe.

USES of ESPRESSO

AFFOGATO

The word *affogato* literally means "drowned." To make affogato, simply place a scoop of vanilla gelato (page 444) in a small bowl or teacup and pour freshly made hot espresso over it.

ESPRESSO GRANITA

Dissolve ½ cup sugar (or to your taste) in 1 cup hot espresso. Pour the mixture into a metal pan and place it in the freezer. After 30 minutes, break up the mixture with a fork, stir it, and return it to the freezer. Repeat every 30 minutes or so until the granita is completely frozen, about 3 hours total. Scoop it out with a spoon and serve.

Torta glassata al caffè
chocolate espresso cake with coffee glaze

¾ cup sugar

6 tablespoons unsalted butter, softened

3 large eggs

3 tablespoons brewed espresso (page opposite)

½ cup unbleached all-purpose flour

2 tablespoons cocoa powder, plus additional for garnish

1 tablespoon finely ground espresso beans, plus additional whole beans for garnish

1 teaspoon baking powder

⅛ teaspoon fine sea salt

1 cup (8 ounces) mascarpone cheese

2 tablespoons coffee-flavored liqueur

5½ ounces semisweet chocolate, roughly chopped

½ cup heavy cream

1. Position a rack in the center of the oven and preheat the oven to 350 degrees F. Butter an 8-inch cake pan. In the bowl of an electric mixer fitted with the whisk attachment, beat the sugar and butter together at medium speed until the mixture is pale and fluffy, about 3 minutes.

2. Add the eggs and 2 tablespoons of the brewed espresso and beat for 3 minutes longer. In a bowl, whisk together the flour, cocoa, ground espresso beans, baking powder, and salt. Whisk the dry ingredients into the egg mixture. Pour the batter into the prepared pan. Bake until the edges darken and a tester inserted into the center comes out clean, about 30 minutes.

3. Cool the cake completely on a wire rack, then remove it from the pan.

4. Place the mascarpone, 1 tablespoon of the liqueur, and the remaining 1 tablespoon brewed espresso in a bowl and stir well to combine.

5. Using a serrated knife, cut the cake in half horizontally. Transfer 1 layer, cut side up, to a cake plate. Spread the mascarpone mixture over the cake. Place the other layer on top of the filling.

6. Combine the chocolate, cream, and remaining 1 tablespoon liqueur in the top of a double boiler or in a large metal bowl set over a saucepan of barely simmering water. Stir until the chocolate is melted and the mixture is smooth, about 4 minutes. Pour this glaze over the cake, using a spatula to spread it; let the cake stand until the glaze is set, about 30 minutes. Sprinkle it with cocoa powder and garnish it with whole coffee beans.

SERVES 8 COOKING TIME: 2 HOURS

Conversion Charts

All conversions are approximate

LIQUID CONVERSIONS

U.S.	METRIC
1 tsp	5 ml
1 tbs	15 ml
2 tbs	30 ml
3 tbs	45 ml
¼ cup	60 ml
⅓ cup	75 ml
⅓ cup + 1 tbs	90 ml
⅓ cup + 2 tbs	100 ml
½ cup	120 ml
⅔ cup	150 ml
¾ cup	180 ml
¾ cup + 2 tbs	200 ml
1 cup	240 ml
1 cup + 2 tbs	275 ml
1¼ cups	300 ml
1⅓ cups	325 ml
1½ cups	350 ml
1⅔ cups	375 ml
1¾ cups	400 ml
1¾ cups + 2 tbs	450 ml
2 cups (1 pint)	475 ml
2½ cups	600 ml
3 cups	720 ml
4 cups (1 quart)	945 ml (1,000 ml is 1 liter)

WEIGHT CONVERSIONS

U.S./U.K.	METRIC
½ oz	14 g
1 oz	28 g
1½ oz	43 g
2 oz	57 g
2½ oz	71 g
3 oz	85 g
3½ oz	100 g
4 oz	113 g
5 oz	142 g
6 oz	170 g
7 oz	200 g
8 oz	227 g
9 oz	255 g
10 oz	284 g
11 oz	312 g
12 oz	340 g
13 oz	368 g
14 oz	400 g
15 oz	425 g
1 lb	454 g

OVEN TEMPERATURES

°F	GAS MARK	°C
250	½	120
275	1	140
300	2	150
325	3	165
350	4	180
375	5	190
400	6	200
425	7	220
450	8	230
475	9	240
500	10	260
550	Broil	290

Sources

We live in wonderful times for curious cooks. There are few ingredients or pieces of equipment that cannot be purchased online. Below is a list of sources to get you started, but you may have your own local sources that are just as good.

ALL-CLAD

TELEPHONE: (800) 255-2523

www.all-clad.com

Good selection of all kinds of pots and pans, and copper pots.

BROADWAY PANHANDLER

65 East Eighth Street
New York, NY 10003
TELEPHONE: (866) 266-5927

www.broadwaypanhandler.com

Pizza stones, pizza peels, and mortars and pestles.

BUON ITALIA

75 Ninth Avenue
New York, NY 10011
TELEPHONE: (212) 633-9090

www.buonitalia.com

00 flour, dried pasta, polenta, mozzarella di bufala, canned Italian tuna, salted capers, salted anchovies, rice, farro, beans, lentils, prosciutto, salami, cotechino, truffles and truffle paste, Italian cheeses, baccalà, squid ink, cooked wheatberries for pastiera, and much more.

THE CHEESE STORE OF BEVERLY HILLS

419 North Beverly Drive
Beverly Hills, CA 90210
TELEPHONE: (310) 278-2855

www.cheesestorebh.com

Cheeses, salami, prosciutto, polenta, canned tuna, black truffles, and white truffles.

DI PALO

200 Grand Street
New York, NY 10013
TELEPHONE: (877) 253-1779

www.dipaloselects.com

Probably the best store in the United States for Italian cheeses, cured meats, and other specialty items. Stocks dried pasta, polenta, farro, mozzarella di bufala, squid ink, beans, rice, lentils, prosciutto, salami, canned Italian tuna, San Marzano tomatoes, and savoiardi.

FAR WEST FUNGI

1 Ferry Building, Shop 34
San Francisco, CA 94111
TELEPHONE: (415) 989-9090

www.farwestfungi.com

Truffle shavers.

FATTO IN AMERICA ARTISANAL PASTA TOOLS

TELEPHONE: (707) 939-6474

www.artisanalpastatools.com

Passatelli tools, pasta rolling pins, gnocchi boards, and other useful tools.

FOX & OBEL

401 East Illinois Street
Chicago, IL 60611
TELEPHONE: (312) 410-7301

www.fox-obel.com

Pancetta, salami, and cheeses.

GOURMET FOOD STORE

TELEPHONE: (877) 220-4181

www.gourmetfoodstore.com

Polenta, rice, beans and grains, and squid ink.

KAISER BAKEWARE

www.kaiserbakeware.com

Springform pans of various shapes and sizes, good selection of all kinds of pans and molds, and pastry bags and tips.

KING ARTHUR FLOUR

135 U.S. Route 5 South
Norwich, VT 05055
TELEPHONE: (800) 827-6836

www.kingarthurflour.com

Bread flour and 00 flour (labeled "Italian-style flour").

LUCCA DELICATESSEN

2120 Chestnut Street
San Francisco, CA 94123
TELEPHONE: (415) 921-7873

www.luccadeli.com

00 flour, cheeses, guanciale, pancetta, prosciutto, lardo, speck, San Marzano tomatoes, rice, farro, polenta, chickpea flour, salted anchovies, mostarda, olive oil, and espresso.

MARCHESE ITALIAN MARKET

1700 Pleasure House Road, Suite 106
Virginia Beach, VA 23455
TELEPHONE: (757) 460-4720

www.marchesemarket.com

Canned tuna, mozzarella di bufala and other cheeses, cured meats, cooked wheatberries for pastiera, and savoiardi.

SALUMERIA ITALIANA

151 Richmond Street
Boston, MA 02109
TELEPHONE: (800) 400-5916

www.salumeriaitaliana.com

Cheeses, salami, rice, farro, salted anchovies, olive oil, balsamic vinegar, and stovetop coffeemakers.

SUR LA TABLE

(stores around the country)
TELEPHONE: (800) 243-0852

www.surlatable.com

00 flour (labeled "Italian-style flour"), pizza stones, pizza peels, mortars and pestles, copper pots, babà molds, and pastry bags and tips.

URBANI TRUFFLES

www.urbani.com
Truffles and truffle paste.

WILLIAMS-SONOMA

(stores around the country)
TELEPHONE: (877) 812-6235

www.williams-sonoma.com

00 flour, pizza stones, pizza peels, mortars and pestles, copper pots, babà molds, and pastry bags and tips.

ZINGERMAN'S DELICATESSEN

422 Detroit Street
Ann Arbor, MI 48104
TELEPHONE: (888) 636-8162

www.zingermans.com

Cheeses, olive oil, and vinegar.

Index

467

First published in the United States of America in 2012
by Rizzoli International Publications, Inc.
300 Park Avenue South
New York, NY 10010
www.rizzoliusa.com

English translation © 2012 Rizzoli International Publications, Inc.

Originally published in the Italian language, November 2011, as *La Cucina Italiana: Enciclopedia Illustrata*.

© 2011 Editrice Quadratum S.p.A., Milan
© 2011 RCS Libri S.p.A., Milan

2012 2013 2014 2015 / 10 9 8 7 6 5 4 3 2 1

ISBN-13: 978-0-8478-3914-8

Library of Congress Catalog Control Number: 2012940386

Translator: Natalie Danford
Acquiring Editor: Christopher Steighner
Project Editor: Tricia Levi
Copyeditor: Ana Deboo
Proofreader: Deborah Weiss Geline
Indexer: Marilyn Bliss

Design: Vertigo Design NYC

Printed in China

For the original edition:
Design and pagination: Paola Polastri with Valentina Picco
Editorial coordination: Marina Mercuriali
Editing: Clara Borasio
Texts on pages 15, 41, 77, 105, 115, 129, 141, 157, 171, 253, 275, 323, 343, 375, 389, 403, 417, 445, 463, 475, 489, 513, 525, 539, 611, and indexes:
Cristina Pradella
Photography: Archivio La Cucina Italiana